CRIME AND THE
ACADÉMIE FRANÇAISE

Dispatches from Paris

PATRICK MARNHAM

VIKING

VIKING

Published by the Penguin Group
Penguin Books Ltd, 27 Wrights Lane, London w8 5tz, England
Penguin Books USA Inc., 375 Hudson Street, New York, New York 10014, USA
Penguin Books Australia Ltd, Ringwood, Victoria, Australia
Penguin Books Canada Ltd, 10 Alcorn Avenue, Toronto, Ontario, Canada m4v 3b2
Penguin Books (NZ) Ltd, 182–190 Wairau Road, Auckland 10, New Zealand

Penguin Books Ltd, Registered Offices: Harmondsworth, Middlesex, England

First published 1993
1 3 5 7 9 10 8 6 4 2
First edition

Ch. 2; Ch. 3, pp. 68-74, 78-9; Ch. 4, pp 80-84, 91-6, 108-9; Ch. 5, pp. 110- 49,
152-6, 159-61, 162-6; Ch. 6; Ch. 7, pp. 188-91; Ch. 8, pp. 194-6, 197-202;
Ch. 9; Ch. 10; Ch. 11; Ch. 12, pp. 239-40, 240-44; Ch. 13 copyright ©
Newspaper Publishing Ltd, 1986, 1987, 1988, 1989, 1990

Ch. 1; Ch. 3, pp. 75-8; Ch. 4, pp. 85-91, 96-108; Ch. 5, pp. 149-52, 156-8,
161-2; Ch. 7, pp. 191-3; Ch. 8, pp. 196-7; Ch. 12, pp. 240-41; Ch. 14
Copyright © Patrick Marnham 1991, 1992, 1993

Copyright © in this collection Patrick Marnham, 1993

The moral right of the author has been asserted

Filmset in 10/12 pt Monophoto Bembo
Typeset by Datix International Limited, Bungay, Suffolk
Printed in England by Clays Ltd, St Ives plc

A CIP catalogue record for this book is available from the British Library

ISBN 0–670–831883

To Sam White

'Et que fait un républicain s'il a le bonheur de vivre en république?'

Sartre, *Les Mots*

CONTENTS

———

ACKNOWLEDGEMENTS

From 1986 to 1990 I was Paris correspondent of the *Independent* and most of the writing in this book first appeared in the daily editions of that newspaper. I gratefully acknowledge the permission of Andreas Whittam Smith, editor of the *Independent*, to reprint it here.

The essays entitled 'His Mother was Right', 'Resistance, Terrorism and the Playground' and 'Crime and the Académie Française' are previously unpublished. A shorter version of the obituary of Miss Nesta Cox first appeared in the *Daily Telegraph*. A shorter version of the article about the sale of Picasso's 'Les Noces de Pierrette' (pp. 85–91) first appeared in The *Spectator*, entitled 'We're Talking $48m Here' and a translation of the article about Euro-Disneyland (pp. 96–100) first appeared in the French daily newspaper *Libération*. Earlier and shorter versions of 'The Man Behind the Hedge' and 'Born to Face a Firing Squad' first appeared in the *Independent Magazine*.

INTRODUCTION

———

It could be said that nothing very dramatic has occurred in Britain since the Battle of Culloden in 1746, leaving aside the Irish Question and the Blitz. In France during the same period, there have been two revolutions, two invasions, three military occupations and two civil wars. These events have left their mark. Few countries in the world can be geographically so close as England and France and yet remain so different.

This collection of essays and journalism, written over a period of nearly seven years' residence in France, is not intended to give a general picture but simply represents a selection of the topics which seemed interesting at the time. It covers the period of early impressions, received by the innocent and sometimes bemused eye of a recently settled traveller, and continues to the point where the traveller began to notice so much about the country that he wondered whether he could be certain of anything at all. I hope that in what follows I have managed to prevent my profound love and admiration for France and the people of France from breaking through with too embarrassing a frequency.

I. CRIME AND THE ACADÉMIE FRANÇAISE

===

SARTRE: HIS MOTHER WAS RIGHT

I first became aware of the ghostly presence of Sartre during the month of August, when the Parisians abandon Paris and the city's past returns to life. The characteristic sounds of an August evening in the *quartier* were provided by the Portuguese voices drifting up to the windows of the apartment from the darkness below. Those Portuguese who were too poor to take a holiday pulled out the chairs from their ground-floor rooms and sat around on the pavement, gossiping quietly in the darkness, turning Paris briefly into a southern city. But there was nothing even the cheerful Portuguese could do about the courtyards at the back of the apartments which are the real heart of those buildings. However 'grand standing' the front rooms may be, it all peters out where the back windows and air-vents crowd round that gloomy, tiled space.

Shortly after moving into the 5th *arrondissement* I discovered that Sartre grew up in a neighbouring block. There is nothing outside to show that the most famous French intellectual of the century spent his childhood there. Then I realized that for four years Sartre attended the Ecole Normale Supérieure. The usual route from his apartment to that '*grande école*' passed our front door. Sartre was a boisterous student. He liked throwing things, such as water bombs. In 1924 one might easily have gone out for a baguette, met Sartre and returned home very angry and covered in flour.

One can imagine the little Sartre growing up with his adoring mother (who kept his hair in ringlets, dressed him in frocks and called him 'Poulou'), working hard at school, finishing his homework early and then spending hours of his childhood looking out on to the back courtyard, the few dozen square metres where the pretensions of the wealthiest Parisians are exposed. It is across *la cour* that so many indignities have to be avoided. In a southern city like Marseille or Vigo the courtyard is a place of flowerpots, song and an exchange of information. People know all about each other and make the most of it. In Paris it is a cramped world where neighbours try, and fail, to conceal from each other vital clues: what time they get up, how many of them sleep in the same room, what they argue about, what they are cooking. Perfectly respectable matrons have been caught in the act of turning out a drawerful of socks, and the vendetta which follows can last for the remainder of the lease.

My way to work lay across the Jardin du Luxembourg. Sartre was in there all the time in 1929. He used to meet girls there. Students still do this today. Simone de Beauvoir, who spent her life with Sartre, first really noticed him by the central pond of the Luxembourg. Now Sartre has been dead for thirteen years. He has 'disappeared', in the mournful French phrase. But once you become aware of his old haunts he is hard to escape. He hasn't quite disappeared after all.

I was no longer surprised when, having crossed the park and reached the office, I discovered that Sartre was still with me. The flat where he lived at the height of his fame was in the neighbouring rue Bonaparte, overlooking the terrace of the Café des Deux Magots. If you hope to study the view he once enjoyed you could make an appointment with the dentist who works on the floor below his old flat. Sartre moved into this flat with his mother, to whom he was very devoted. He even abandoned working on his autobiography because he did not wish to upset his mother, who remained a staunch bourgeois all her life. When he wasn't in the flat he was in the Deux Magots or in the Café Flore. He wrote many of his books in cafés. He liked working in cafés because he could watch girls while he worked. Normally you have to be a painter to do that and Sartre was a philosopher but he had unusual powers – concentration, among others.

Sartre's popular reputation today is not based on the *Critique de la raison dialectique*, or even on his novels, still less on his plays. He is instead remembered as a revolutionary, and when you consider the course of his life, so much of which was passed in the bourgeois streets and apartments of the 5th and 6th *arrondissements* and Montparnasse, that is at first sight rather odd. For there was one period in

Sartre's life when he had the perfect chance to function as a revolutionary, yet did nothing. During the Occupation Sartre considered the idea of Resistance, although he was not ideal material for a life spent on the run. Because he had weak eyesight the army had assigned him to a meteorological unit in the Maginot Line when he was called up in 1939. It is one of the less tragic symbols of the Fall of France – Sartre among the defenders of the invincible Maginot Line, pumping balloons full of gas and watching as they rose above the fortifications to indicate which way the wind was blowing.

His war continued in this Tatiesque manner. On one occasion he entered the Vichy Zone, illegally, to gauge support for a proposed Resistance group. He travelled by bicycle. One day he started to think, pedalled too slowly and fell off. The proposed Resistance group came to nothing, so it was back to Paris and the company of the German army. For four years the Germans were garrisoned in the Latin Quarter, among other places in the Palais du Luxembourg overlooking the gardens where Sartre first heard Simone de Beauvoir's unnaturally husky voice. It was German troops who drove him out of the Dôme, the café in Montparnasse where he was working in 1941, and forced him to take refuge down the hill in the Café Flore. It was not the soldiers he objected to. It was the fact that the Germans drank real coffee which they brought to the Dôme with them. And Sartre, drinking some ersatz infusion which was all the French could obtain in 1941, could not stand the smell of the real thing.

Sartre finally got a bit-part in the war in August, 1944, during the Liberation of Paris. As de Gaulle marched triumphantly down the Champs-Elysées shooting broke out. Sartre, reporting events for the anti-Gaullist press, had secured a place on the balcony of the Louvre. He was mistaken for a Collaborationist sniper and so on the last day of the war in Paris he came under fire for the first time, from French guns. By then Sartre had missed his chance to be a real revolutionary. He had contributed to a Resistance newspaper, but his attempt to work for the National Resistance Council, the secret leadership of the Resistance, had been rebuffed because his work had also been published in the Collaborationist press. Although he did not know it at the time he would not have had to walk very far if he had been welcomed by the Council. Needless to say its first meeting was held in the rue de Four, just round the corner from the Deux Magots.

It was only after the Nazis left that Sartre became world-famous as a revolutionary. And then a strange thing happened. Coach parties started to arrive at the Deux Magots or the Flore to watch Sartre watching girls. From a position slightly to the left of the door and to the right of the Communist Party, Sartre defended the Soviets, their secret police and their gulags. He repudiated his play *Les Mains Sales* which exposed the dishonesty of Communism. Then he moved slightly to the left of the Party and taught a generation of French students that, in the struggle with bourgeois democracy, the truth is negotiable. Towards the end of his life Sartre spelt out the reasons why he considered himself a revolutionary. Some have suggested that it was guilt at his inactivity during the Occupation. His own explanation went back to his childhood. He had based his politics on hatred of bourgeois values and bourgeois family life. He still saw, through the eyes of a child, an incomprehensible world of savage taboos, restrictions and false pretences; the world of *la cour*. In his case, the smell of boiled fish escaping through a carelessly opened window had inflicted wounds that endured a lifetime. Perhaps that is why he never challenged the Nazis. They were not really a bourgeois movement.

Sometimes when listening to French intellectuals one gets the impression that their brains have gone to their heads. Sartre did not lack courage but his view of where the enemy lay in his lifetime was eccentric. In 1962 he defended the terrorism of the FLN Algerian nationalists. His reward was a plastic bomb planted by the French nationalists of the OAS. It destroyed his flat in the rue Bonaparte. The neighbours were furious. 'All they had to do was shoot him in the back, as he crossed the road. There was no need to smash up the building,' said one. It was *l'esprit de la cour* once again. Fortunately Sartre and his mother (they were still living together) were unhurt and he had earned his stripes as a serious revolutionary. He moved back up the hill, this time to the Coupole in Montparnasse, his choice of café again decided by the great events of the day; if it was not the aroma of German coffee it was a French bomb.

The last years of his life, the years of the Coupole, were not a happy time. He was known to be involved with five women, including Simone de Beauvoir, the lifelong *maîtresse en titre*. But recently a sixth woman, Liliane Siegel, has claimed that unknown to the others she too formed part of the entourage. She published a book about her experience and called it *La Clandestine*. Sartre, it seems, had asked her to agree to secrecy because the others were mutually jealous and he did not wish to complicate his life any more than was necessary. He already had a fairly crowded social timetable and he was also trying to work; he was struggling to finish what was eventually to become an unfinished three-volume life of Flaubert.

In February 1972 Sartre was thrown out of the Renault car factory for fomenting unrest. Eleven days later one of his followers, a Maoist militant called Pierre Overney, was shot dead by a security guard at the factory gates. These were the years when Sartre was photographed hawking revolutionary pamphlets in the streets, and when he became first the figurehead and then the target of younger 'revolutionaries', few of whom are remembered today. But at the time they were capable of offering a serious challenge to Sartre, partly because they could frequently count on the support of Simone de Beauvoir. At one point de Beauvoir, younger and less enfeebled than her lifelong companion, threatened to summon Sartre before 'a tribunal of Sartriens' if he did not fall into line. It was her revenge for years of public humiliation. The intellectual struggle among the Sartriens was pitiless. The French criminal code contains an offence known as *détournement de mineur* (corruption of a minor). During the battle for the old man's intellectual estate it was said that one of the *combattants*, Benny Levy, should be charged with a new offence, *détournement de vieillard* (corruption of an elder) for having 'tried to steal Sartre's atheism', the bedrock of his thought. Levy had tried to smuggle a religious element into Sartre's philosophy. The disciples were fighting over their master's corpse while he was still slumped on the *banquette* of the Coupole contemplating his last cups of coffee. In this way Sartre died two deaths, the first being announced while he was still lucid and capable of reflection.

It was appropriate therefore that the philosopher who died two deaths should, in the course of time, have two funerals, *'un faux et un vrai'*. The first was an unofficial state funeral, transformed into such by the attendance of 50,000 admirers. The body of the man who had grown up under the shadow of the Panthéon, and who as a child dreamed of being buried there, was taken instead to the cemetery of Montparnasse. His coffin was preceded by a car carrying de Beauvoir and two other members of the entourage, one of whom – Arlette – had been both his mistress and subsequently his adopted daughter, an existential form of incest. The crowd soon dubbed this vehicle *le car des veuves*. Millions of people who did not attend the ceremony followed events on television. It must be one of the few funerals at which applause broke out as the coffin approached the cemetery. In Paris it was one of the great media events of the decade. Two *paparazzi*, disguised as male nurses, tried to break into the hospital room where Sartre's body lay on its death bed. They were repulsed and had to content themselves with shots taken through the hospital window with a telephoto lens. At the cemetery of Montparnasse photographers scored a first when one of them actually fell into the open grave just before the arrival of the coffin. Fighting broke out and some of the mourners had to be taken to hospital. All this for the interment of a man who had said, 'So long as death is not here, I am here, and as soon as death is here, I will no longer be.'

The funeral cortège made a lengthy detour which brought it past the long terrace of La Coupole and it paused silently on the boulevard Edgar-Quinet beneath the windows of No. 22, Sartre's final address. The last view he enjoyed, over the walls of Montparnasse cemetery, could hardly have been more appropriate for a bourgeois old age.

If today one looks at the photograph of the crowd packed round Sartre's hearse in April 1980 there seems to be something familiar about it. And then one realizes that these are 'the '68-ers', twelve years on. Sartre's funeral was 'the last demo' of the '68-ers. As they themselves said at the time, they were burying their youth and their illusions with this blind old man. So it was entirely appropriate that Sartre's quasi-state funeral was in itself an illusion, an empty show mounted for the television cameras. Four days later his body was disinterred and cremated at Père Lachaise in a private ceremony.

Sartre's third death, the death of his reputation, has been a slower process than his corporal extinction. If he was the last of the great intellectuals in the French sense of the term, meaning a politically committed philosopher whose word was enough to form the opinions of a generation, one can see why he has had no successors. It was after all Sartre who defended the ideas of Mao Tse-tung, while identifying de Gaulle as 'dangerous for the nation'. He considered de Gaulle a danger because when he returned to power in 1958 he was 'an honorary great man'. It is, of course, a phrase which could be turned against its author. How many thousands of intelligent people did not bother to think for themselves or lacked the courage to speak their minds on public issues between 1950 and 1980, because Sartre had already spoken?

In the years that have followed Sartre's disappearance history has been less respectful of his intellectual power. 'Bourgeois democracy' marches on, whereas 'Marxist humanism' has fallen by the wayside, and the political errors he committed have dragged an entire profession towards its grave. But one at least of his enthusiasms remains admirable and above criticism; his devotion to his mother. It was not 'Poulou' but his mother who was right all along.

======

RESISTANCE, TERRORISM AND THE PLAYGROUND

Some years before the trial of Klaus Barbie opened in 1987 I used to visit Lyon, intending to find out more about the background to the case. If you take the train from Paris to Lyon you can get off at Part-Dieu or Perrache, both main-line stations. The first was usually more convenient, but if one stayed on to Perrache there was a five-minute journey along the old railway line, past the backs of some of the ugliest and most evocative buildings in the city. Among them was Fort Montluc, no longer the central prison of Lyon but still under guard and in occasional use. The great days of Montluc, when it had its own branch line, ended after the Liberation but the stone walls are the same and the memory of what happened behind them – when the city prison was the scene of many of the worst crimes committed in Lyon – still seeps through.

Further along the track, if you knew exactly where to look, came the short wall beside the Cimetière Israélite. Surprisingly this cemetery was in use throughout the Occupation for the burial of those who had not been deported. The Jews could be buried in public. Here there are also family graves marked with the names of three generations, for instance 'aged 78, 48 and 22' – three men who died in the same year – '*Victimes de la Barbarie Allemande*', or, '*Fusillés par les Hitlériens*'. One Jewish woman who died in 1941 in Lyon was 'exiled from her dear Alsace'. It is a small cemetery which tells a small part of the story, eloquently.

Finally there is the platform at the Gare Perrache from which you get an uninterrupted view across the rooftops to the newer prisons of St Paul and St Joseph. On a hot day the men inside hang out between the bars of their cells and wave to the people on the platform. I did not wave back. It would not have cost much to wave to a man in prison, but an experience I once had after waving to a group of women behind the bars of the penitentiary in south Manhattan has made me wary of repeating the gesture. Instead I just looked at them and wondered if it was true, as I had once heard, that the worst torment of life in those two prisons is the continual noise of the departing trains. Barbie was in St Joseph but one never saw his face at the window. The noises that penetrated the last days of his life were made by the trains leaving the station from which he had sent hundreds of prisoners to 'night and fog' during his first period of residence in Lyon.

One day, travelling on the same stretch of railway line, I noticed a building which made the transition to the uneventful present easier. It stands halfway between Fort Montluc and the Hôtel de Police, it is almost as grim as the prison – concrete walls, slit windows, steel furnishings of the style commonly found in French government schools built in the forties and fifties. It is the Lycée Technique des Industries Métallurgiques, and the road separating it from the railway track is called the boulevard des Tchécoslovaques. One looks at it and wonders what kind of people send children to pass the greater part of their childhood in a place like that.

Lyon has some fine street names, even in the suburbs. The district of Bron not far from the Lycée Technique is known for its military airport although I had been attracted to it by a wartime massacre. One hundred and nine men taken from Montluc were shot on the airfield in August, 1944, after being made to repair damage caused by allied air raids. Today Bron has a centre named after Pablo

Picasso, a rue Salvador Allende, a rue Youri Gagarine, and a square Martin Luther King. Street names like these are a roll-call of the events a community considers worth remembering and they can reveal something about that community. In Bron there is the theme of Progress, with the achievements of mother Russia and the struggle for human rights. There are references to French history of seventy-five years ago, the rue du Poilu, rue de la Marne, rue d'Alsace-Lorraine, rue Verdun; there is even the rue de l'Economie, which runs into the rue de l'Economie Prolongée, which ends just short of the deep end of the borough swimming pool. But there is not much about the eventful years of 1939–45.

So what would one make of life, at the age of fifteen, in the Lycée Technique des Industries Métallurgiques in the boulevard des Tchécoslovaques, growing up in a community which saluted a Russian spaceman but ignored its own recent past? For one boy of that age in 1969 the answer was, bombs. He left the school and did his military service in the army, and he left the army and started making bombs. Throughout this period he was under the influence of the same man, André Olivier, his French teacher at the Lycée Technique, who was only eleven years older than he was. The boy was called Maxime, he was in the disciplined sense always a good pupil and a good soldier, and his obedience eventually took him from the Lycée Technique in Lyon in 1969 to the Palais de Justice on the other side of the river in 1989, where he faced fifty-one charges, including three charges of murder. Maxime became Max Frérot, the bomb maker of Action Directe, a group of French revolutionary leftists who, led by Olivier, sought to impose their views on society by violent means – in the convenient shorthand of our day, terrorists. Between the Gare Part-Dieu and the Gare Perrache one travelled from the France of 1944, a nightmare of violence, betrayal, secrecy and death, symbolized by Fort Montluc, to the Lycée Technique and the France of 1989, and for some at least it all seemed remarkably unchanged. While I had been reconstructing the Occupation, and trying not to overlook its daily banality in particular, Maxime Frérot had been reconstructing the same period in a more practical fashion.

That Frérot was attracted to the legend of the Resistance is known by his notebooks, which were perhaps another sign of his teacher's influence, the fruit of some childhood creative-writing project. Between March 1980 and November 1987, Action Directe, and Frérot in particular, were widely feared in France. The organization carried out numerous armed attacks on banks and business premises, and murdered several prominent people. In 1982, André Olivier decided that the bank robberies were getting the organization a bad name as '*vulgaires bandits*'. He wanted to emphasize the political nature of these crimes and decided that the way to do this was to have the raids carried out by black men. He recruited three new members who had been born in the West Indies, in Guadeloupe, and identified them with the Affiche Rouge, a wartime resistance organization formed by immigrants. In his private journal Frérot wrote at this time, 'Those immigrants [of the wartime "Affiche Rouge"] were the first to take up arms against fascism and Nazism when the great majority of the French population were still collaborating and denouncing each other.'

It would have come naturally to Maxime Frérot, a child of Lyon and living a secret life, to make the connection with the Resistance. His school was four blocks away from Fort Montluc. Having spent months tracing the story of collaboration and resistance through the streets and houses of wartime Lyon, I found the same neighbourhoods and even addresses re-occurring in the story of Action Directe. Frérot's first bank raid was carried out against the Banque Nationale de Paris in the place Jean-Mace near the old Military Medical School, where the Gestapo took their prisoners for questioning in 1942 and 1943. Barbie used to walk there to work, from his apartment off the place Bellecour. The first time Frérot shot a man it was in a bank in the suburb of Caluire, near the house where Jean Moulin, political head of the Resistance, was betrayed in June 1943. Later Frérot shot a policeman dead in a bank raid on the boulevard Anatole France, which is just off the boulevard des Belges where, in 1942, Section VI of the SS installed its headquarters. Before he went underground Frérot lived in the district of the Croix Rousse on top of a hill which is famous for its network of *traboules*, concealed passages which have been used for clandestine activities by the Lyonnais for centuries past. Identifying as he did with the Resistance, Frérot began to behave more and more like the arbitrary killers who had been its opponents.

For twenty-one months after the other members of Action Directe were under arrest, Frérot alone was hunted through Lyon.

Leaving the wartime landscape, he spent part of this time in underground car parks. Underground car parks are a useful post-wartime refuge for *marginales* like Frérot. While he was on the run he contacted his girlfriend, Josette, and they spent their last night together in 1986 in an underground car park near the Palais de Justice. She never saw him again until they were brought into the same dock in the Palais de Justice three years later. Frérot was eventually arrested in the car park beneath the Hôtel Mercure. He was correctly described at the time as 'the most wanted man in France' but the two policemen mistook him for a car-radio thief. They challenged him, he drew his gun, there was an exchange of shots, his gun jammed and that was that. I was interested in this detail of the story because I used to pass the Hôtel Mercure every time I walked from the Gare Part-Dieu to the municipal library. Once, in 1985, I got lost in the labyrinth of walkways and unmarked staircases that makes up the rebuilt district of Part-Dieu and I found myself in the car park beneath the Hôtel Mercure, but I did not see the most wanted man in France down there. It was only later, in Paris, that I had any direct experience of Action Directe and its work.

When the police arrested André Olivier and most of his followers they also found Frérot's notebooks. Until then they had known only that they were dealing with a professionally trained bomber. From examining his bombs they knew that he had been in the paratroops, they even knew that he had probably been in the marine commando section. The French paratroop regiment, once described by the historian Alistair Horne as the 'élite and spearhead' of the French army, also contains a rich criminal seam. Albert Spaggiari, the man who stole £5 million sterling from a bank in Nice by tunnelling up from the sewers was an ex-paratrooper; so were several members of his gang. Frérot's regimental record states that he was 'sporting, disciplined, and took an interest in para-chuting, explosives, assault courses and unarmed combat'. When he was on trial Frérot was able to run rings round three bal-listics experts who had produced a badly prepared report on the weapons used in various bank robberies. It was his professionalism which made him such a frightening man. He had been trained to kill by the state, and his instructors had done their work well. He was wanted for three murders, but the police seemed unable to get any closer to him. He had plenty of money and a large and well-distributed stock of weapons and explosives, but he was alone and presumably getting desperate. The organization for which he had fought for seven years, which represented the ideals he had adopted eighteen years earlier, had been broken. People were expecting him to go out with a bang and were wondering where it would be.

One night in 1987 the police were called to the Tour Montparnasse, the tallest building in Paris, because a stock of explosives had been found in the ceiling of an office fifty-two storeys up in the sky. That was the kind of target that attracted Frérot. Earlier, in July 1986, a bomb exploded with lethal consequences inside the headquarters of the Anti-Bandit Squad, the police section which was supposed to be looking for Frérot. Another bomb destroyed the car of Alain Peyrefitte, who had been Gaullist minister of education at the time of the student uprising in 1968, when Frérot had been fourteen but his teacher Olivier, an unreconstructed '68-er, had been twenty-five. M. Peyrefitte was not in the car but his chauffeur was killed. A third bomb was intercepted before it could explode. It was intended for the examining magistrate who was preparing the case against Frérot's arrested comrades. All these attacks showed a professionalism, a coherence and a style that were associated with Frérot.

By then I had stopped visiting Lyon and had come to live in Paris. One quickly forgets the fear which spreads through a city during a well-organized bombing campaign. At that time, the autumn of 1986, there were six successive bomb attacks in central Paris in a period of fourteen days; 161 people were injured, eleven were killed. Twice the bombers struck inside premises guarded by the police. On one of my first nights in Paris a car was blown up outside my hotel. This proved to be the property of a German tourist and its destruction was the work of nervous policemen, but then we moved to an apartment in the 14th *arrondissement* and I used to walk to work each morning down the rue de Rennes past a shop called Tati where seven people were blown up one crowded afternoon. The police said that the bombers were Arabs, but that their local knowledge was so good that they were probably advised by Action Directe.

Our flat was just opposite the entrance to the Cimetière Montparnasse, where Sartre was briefly buried. We used to take the baby for an afternoon airing among the tombs. It was outside the cemetery that I caught the only glimpse of what Action Directe could do.

There is a high wall around the Cimetière Montparnasse and one night in November 1986 members of Action Directe trapped Georges Besse, the chief executive of Renault, beneath the cemetery wall and opposite his house in the boulevard Edgar-Quinet. Two young women approached him at eight o'clock in the evening as he walked towards his front door and shot him three times with handguns. The first shot hit his shoulder and knocked him down. While he lay on the ground they shot him again in the chest and the neck. Only then, when he was dead, did one say to the other, '*C'est bien le bon?*' and received the reply, '*Oui, c'est sûr.*' Then the girls picked up M. Besse's briefcase and jogged casually to the entrance of a nearby Métro station, scattering some leaflets on the way.

Within minutes, before the ambulance got there, press photographers had arrived on motorbikes to record the scene. The police suspected that the press must have been tipped off before the shooting had taken place. The pressmen denied it. The question was discussed in the left-wing daily paper *Libération* under the unemotional headline, 'How a corpse spread itself all over the front page'. By the time I reached the scene the body had been removed but the bloodstains were still on the pavement, leaking away from the chalked outline on the ground. Those photographers who had arrived too late for the body were snapping the bloodstains, like hounds licking the grass after the fox has been removed. There was a crowd of television cameras in the street with their pitiless floodlights trained on the Besse front door. They filmed the arrival of the prime minister, Jacques Chirac, who had come to offer his sympathy to Mme Françoise Besse and her five children. The family had heard the shooting from inside the house.

It turned out that this particular killing had not been carried out by Frérot; the two women were members of the disaffected Paris branch of Action Directe. The leaflets they left at the entrance to the Métro claimed responsibility for the crime in the name of Pierre Overney, the Maoist Renault worker who had been killed during a demonstration outside the company's headquarters in 1972, many years before Georges Besse joined the company. Besse had the ill-fortune to live on the same street as Sartre and to be the chief executive of Renault. The coincidence was too strong for the last of Sartre's pupils to resist. The women who killed Georges Besse were arrested early in 1987, but Frérot remained free.

★

Some weeks later there was an example of the real fear inspired by Action Directe. The trial of three members of the organization accused of murdering two policemen had to be abandoned after five days because the jury were too frightened to continue. The hearing took place before the assize court in Paris and one of the accused, Régis Schleicher, simply asked the judge, 'For how long will the jurors receive police protection?' Three jurors then produced medical certificates and were discharged. It was months before a new special procedure could be set up whereby terrorists could be tried by seven judges sitting without a jury.

But as these 'terrorist courts' began to work their way through the charges brought against the members of Action Directe the evidence did little to confirm the diabolical view of the organization. Among those charged with membership were a barrister, an architect, a writer, a journalist, a bookseller and two teachers. These people had known each other in some cases since childhood. When one met a terrorist the others became friends, and therefore supporters, of terrorists. The story which unfolded was more a tribute to the strength of personal relations in French society than a lesson in how to organize a secret army.

Charlotte was a barrister who had been at school with a girl who later lived with Andreas Baader, co-founder of the Baader-Meinhof group. Through her schoolfriend, Charlotte met a journalist who contributed to *Le Monde* but who led a secret life as the chief propagandist of Action Directe. Charlotte had a niece called Sandrine. Sandrine's family owned flats in Paris, Nice and Montpellier. Many of these flats were used by Aunt Charlotte's friends, that is they became safe houses for the 'soldiers' of Action Directe, the men and women who did the killing. One day Charlotte and Sandrine found some dynamite in one of the Paris flats. *Tiens!* 'So what did you do with it?' asked the president of the special tribunal which was trying Aunt Charlotte and Sandrine for terrorism. 'We threw it in the Seine.' Didn't they think of going to the police? 'We thought about it for a year.' They were still thinking about it when the police came to them.

Paula, a radio journalist working for Radio-France, the government station, fell in love with Claude, a very attractive young man who occasionally shot at policemen. Once he even killed one. Paula had always been impressed by Claude's knowledge of political literature. During their trial she made it clear that she still regarded him as an idealist and a bibliophile. Claude's old schoolfriend, Daniel, also remained under his spell. In later life Daniel became a novelist. He based one of his characters on Claude. In France people still read new fiction, including people in the police. They arrested Daniel and asked him why he hadn't denounced his friend instead of using his lifestyle as the basis for a plot. Daniel's answer was, 'I thought he was making it up.'

The curious thing about Action Directe is that it was very largely make-believe. Frérot, dreaming of resistance, was lethal but he did not really come from the heroic mould. In January 1982, he had led a raid on the Société Lyonnaise in the Place Bellecour, the vast open space in the heart of Lyon which figures frequently in the wartime histories. In 1943 a man had jumped on to the pavement to his death from the second floor window of No. 33 because he could no longer stand being half-drowned in a bathtub of cold water by members of the French Milice, who assisted the Gestapo. In 1987 Frérot's target was on the opposite side of the square and he was at the head of his black commando from Guadeloupe. Inside the bank he pistol-whipped the face of the assistant manager, M. Sabran, and then stole his identity papers. One month later Frérot led the same group back to the same bank. M. Sabran had just time to shout, 'Here they come again,' before Frérot, shouting his name, dragged him to the strong room, kicked him to the floor, then threw banknotes in his face and took his photograph.

'He justified this behaviour,' said M. Sabran later, 'by telling me that the bank was a subsidiary of the multinational Suez group which according to him exploited the Third World. But I think he was just over-excited.' The truth was less dramatic. That evening Frérot wrote in his journal, 'I, a white man and a para, was being watched by black men, so I had to look good.'

Other raids were almost ridiculous. One friend of Frérot's, called Polack, dropped in for a cup of coffee at Maxime's flat in Lyon and found himself being recruited for a bank raid on the following day. Not having any previous experience of robbing banks Polack decided to do what they did on the movies. 'Stick up your hands,' he said, 'this is a hold-up.' The cashier ignored him and a customer who was ahead of him in the queue asked him if it was a practical joke. Having eventually obtained some money Polack left the bank but couldn't find the getaway car, so he had to walk back to 'the hideout' carrying his motor-cycle helmet, his gun and a plastic bag full of banknotes. On another occasion he noticed that the 'lookout' had gone to sleep on a park bench. The heights of incompetence were scaled in Lyon on 12 July 1985. Frérot's meticulously detailed notebooks recorded that three armed robberies were attempted that day. One member of the 'commando' came down on the TGV fast train from Paris already wearing the wig he was supposed to put on for the raid. Later he produced a notice reading 'Closed for Holdup', but hung it on the back door upside down. When he got to the safe it was empty, and his false nose fell off. Outside a passing fire-engine blocked the passage of the getaway car. Frérot himself once misjudged the strength of the explosives at a savings bank and blew down so much rubble that the money was buried beneath it.

The usual reaction when French acquaintances discuss Action Directe today, after seeing its members in the dock, is irritation. It was *lamentable* or *nul*. People do not always see the comical side. The revolutionary tradition in France demands a little more. Everyone, including the police, was misled by Frérot's ability with bombs into thinking that Action Directe was resourceful as well as ruthless; that it was *sérieux*. But perhaps its followers were not really in the revolutionary tradition at all. Perhaps they were members of an older and less complicated fraternity.

Before the trials of Action Directe began I used to wonder what these mysterious people were like, how they could justify the slaughter of a father within sound of his family or could beat up an assistant bank manager in Lyon because the firm he worked for was a subsidiary of a different firm active in Guadeloupe. They turned out to be quite unlike anything one could have imagined. André Olivier, the schoolmaster, appeared in court as worse than *lamentable* – he referred to Georges Besse as 'butchered pork'. But to his pupils he was obviously someone special. Of the nineteen people with Olivier in the dock, nine were his former pupils. While he was their schoolteacher he kept open house for them, took them for rides on his motor bike, and encouraged them to behave badly (or 'anarchically') at school assemblies. Not very difficult, perhaps, for a teacher to impress pupils by those methods, but eighteen years later Frérot was still prepared to die for him.

There is a clue as to why this should have been so in the story of another recruit, Renaud, whom they picked out of a class for dropouts. He was simply told that his new friends had decided to start 'a movement'. He thought at first it was something to do with the ecologists or pacifism. Then he was told that the movement needed money and they had to arrange for some 'expropriations' from a bank. Renaud was told that he would be at the bank next day 'just for decoration'. And next morning there he was, outside the Banque Nationale de Paris, with a decorative gun in his hand. He liked being trained to use a gun. He had always been hopeless at school, and here was a teacher telling him that he was 'a natural marksman'. In this story is all the warmth and trust and comradeship of schooldays. It is the world of *Le Grand Meaulnes* updated. But these pupils came from the Lycée Technique, with its steel and concrete fittings, not from the *lycée* at Sainte-Agathe with the well and the walnut trees beside the playground. Meaulnes, too, first cast his spell with a forbidden box of matches. But in Lyon the fireworks were replaced with gelignite and the lost domains disappeared beneath streets named after the Marne and Verdun. The time had come for a different pied piper to lead the way from the playground to the Palais de Justice, via the underground car park.

The influence of the classroom was evident even at the trial. There were twenty of them in the dock and as Renaud said in his evidence, 'None of us would be here if it were not for Maxime's notebooks.' Wanting to be rude to the judge, who said that he did not understand some reference to the Resistance, Frérot snapped back one day, 'If you followed with more attention, you might understand.' It was a rebuke which echoed the supreme authority in his life, that of the schoolmaster.

'Do you know what Sartre said?' asked Frérot when he was arrested, hoping to place the officer before a higher authority. But the police inspector did not want to know what Sartre had said. He told Frérot to stop playing the fool, and his dreams of Resistance ended with a life sentence. André Olivier also received a life sentence. They were taken away to the same prison as Klaus Barbie, beside the railway platforms at Perrache. They had been tried in the same courtroom as Barbie, before the same judge, and they were defended – equally ineffectively – by the same lawyer. To that extent, Frérot's fantasy world of Resistance did finally brush the real world of the Occupation. Now he too will be able to hear the trains leaving for Part-Dieu. Perhaps they will remind him of the Lycée Technique.

═══

THE MAN BEHIND THE HEDGE

One week before the vote in the French referendum on the Treaty of Maastricht in 1992, there was a dramatic announcement from the Elysée palace. The president of the Republic, François Mitterrand, at the age of seventy-five, had entered the Hôpital Cochin for an urgent operation. A few days later came a second announcement. President Mitterrand was suffering from cancer. Since one of the surgeons who operated on him was Bernard Debré, a Gaullist member of the National Assembly and an opponent of the Maastricht Treaty, the diagnosis was accepted by a cynical electorate as genuine and the news provoked natural feelings of sympathy for the president. It was generally agreed that his illness made a 'Yes' vote rather more likely. And when the Treaty was eventually approved by only 51 per cent there was speculation that the sympathy aroused by the president's operation may even have been a decisive factor.

But during the last days of the campaign there was another rumour circulating in bars and cafés up and down the country and the first person to blurt it out in public was Jean-Marie Le Pen. The president's prostate trouble was doubtless genuine, said the leader of the *Front National*, but had there been anything 'urgent' about his operation? Could it not have waited a week? By choosing to have it seven days before the referendum M. Mitterrand was attempting to influence the result of the poll. When M. Le Pen said this during a television debate it provoked a walk-out by several leading partisans of the 'Yes' vote. Led by the former Socialist prime minister Laurent Fabius, they formed a dignified procession and moved towards a side door. Unfortunately this proved to be a false door which did not open. As they searched around in some confusion for a door which would let them out of the studio the raucous voice of M. Le Pen continued to bellow his bar room insults through the microphone.

It was a farcical climax to the national debate, the great and the good of France, attempting a principled gesture, in fact groping around for an exit while being showered with verbal abuse by the leader of the extreme-right. But since the broadcast a number of prostate specialists have confirmed that M. Le Pen's suspicions were at least medically respectable, and Prof. Debré has revealed that the operation had originally been foreseen for a later date and was brought forward at short notice. In other words President Mitterrand may well have succeeded in winning the Maastricht referendum by mounting a bogus medical drama. Could this dignified elder statesman be capable of such a thing?

The most certain thing about François Mitterrand is that there are no certainties; he remains an enigma. In character he is deeply ambiguous, in expression he is frequently elliptical. For most of his political career any suggestion that he would one day be elected president of the Republic would have caused widespread mirth. His major achievement in life is to have become the first Socialist president of the Fifth Republic. And yet he has never been a Socialist. The former prime minister, Guy Mollet, who was a Socialist, once said, 'Mitterrand is not actually a Socialist. He has just learnt how to sound like one.' And Antoine Pinay, another former prime minister, now aged 101 and still entirely lucid, summed him up last year. 'When we were in the same administration in the 1950s', said M. Pinay, 'M. Mitterrand was a liberal. He has since made himself look like a Socialist in order to be elected. He is a highly intelligent man and he has a diabolical electoral skill. But he is not a great statesman.'

The contest between M. Mitterrand and the French Right has followed the same pattern for the last twelve years, and the results have been so unfair as to reduce rich men to tears. As each poll approaches M. Mitterrand loses popularity and his opponents sharpen their knives and move in, practising their stabbing motions. M. Mitterrand then somehow evaporates and reappears on the winning side of the poll, and his opponents realize that although he is unharmed they have managed to stab each other several times.

So it was over the Maastricht referendum. It was the opposition leader, Jacques Chirac, who originally demanded the referendum, sensing that this might embarrass M. Mitterrand. The president called his bluff and agreed to hold one. Over the next four months

the majority in favour of Maastricht fell in the opinion polls from 70 per cent to 49 per cent. It was widely said that the president had miscalculated, that he had underestimated his own unpopularity, and that French voters would reject Maastricht because they were so anxious to reject him. Meanwhile M. Mitterrand had the intense pleasure of watching his leading opponents Jacques Chirac and Valéry Giscard d'Estaing campaigning desperately against dissident members of their own parties to win him his 'Yes' vote. Giscard, in what was intended to be a hurtful comment, begged M. Mitterrand to stay out of the campaign because every time he opened his mouth his unpopularity increased. M. Mitterrand appeared to fall into a reluctant and humiliated silence. Only he of course knew about the prostate.

And then came the modest announcement in a single column of *Le Monde* – 'The president of the Republic has undergone a surgical operation'.

Apparently nothing serious. Immediately the speculation started. What was he hiding? Could it be something . . . serious? Silence. Followed by a further modest announcement – 'The president of the Republic is suffering from cancer'. And there he was once more centre stage and in the spotlight without having to utter a word. On the eve of the poll he no longer had to take the dangerous course of urging voters to support his treaty. He merely had to be photographed leaving the Hôpital Cochin, looking tired but determined and making self-deprecating jokes about not having lost any of his brain. For the Right there was of course one consolation. If, sadly, the president was suffering from cancer he might be thinking of immediate resignation. Wrong again. The cancer was, it transpired, not very serious. It was localized and provided it had been treated early there was a good prognosis. The men of France learnt, with a mixture of relief and horror, that 40 per cent of males over fifty had cancerous cells in their prostates. Happily, the president's life expectancy – as far as anyone could tell – could be fifteen or even twenty years. He would be back at his desk within a week.

In calling the referendum the president had taken a colossal gamble, but he had won. The Socialist Party was united behind him on the winning side, while his main opponents the Gaullist RPR and the centre-right UDF had both been neatly split by the poll. He had done it again.

François Mitterrand was born in 1916, the son of a railway worker, Joseph Mitterrand, who rose to become station master at Angoulême, and who ended his life as president of the National Vinegar Producers' Association. The description of Joseph as a railway worker is actually rather misleading since he came from prosperous bourgeois stock, but it is what appears in President Mitterrand's entry in *Who's Who*. Joseph was also a devout enough Catholic to work as a stretcher-bearer at Lourdes. The president's mother, Yvonne, descended from distant relations of the English Royal family, was also a devout Catholic. She loved reading and instilled a love of literature in her seven children. When he was young, François Mitterrand, the fifth child, wanted at various times to be a detective-story writer or the Pope.

He passed his *baccalauréat* at the age of seventeen in Angoulême and in 1934 moved to Paris, first to a Catholic college and then to the Sorbonne where he eventually took a degree in Law and Literature in 1938. He was already showing an interest in politics without betraying a settled preference for any single party. He may have recalled that his maternal grandmother, Pétronille-Zelma, had been the niece of a man who started political life as a Socialist and ended it as an Orleanist minister of the interior. Mitterrand arrived in Paris at a time when French politics were more disturbed and dangerous than they had been for many years. In a demonstration outside the Chamber of Deputies seventeen right-wing demonstrators were shot dead by the police and in a counter-demonstration eleven Communists met the same fate. Among Mitterrand's friends was François Dalle who would later be associated with the leaders of the extreme-right, and extremely violent, Cagoule movement. At least three other close friends were also members of *la Cagoule* (the word means 'mask' or 'hood'). The Cagoule was a secret organization which specialized in criminal attacks and 'provocations' and which imitated Nazi tactics by disguising its outrages as the work of Communists. 'Cagoulards' were responsible for several murders and in 1936 a gang of them seriously injured the Socialist leader Léon Blum. One of those leading the attack on Blum's car was a former school-fellow of Mitterrand's. Today, when recalling the early years in Paris, Mitterrand never mentions the Cagoule. It is a period of his life which remains mysterious.

Mitterrand has often been reproached with his Vichyite past. In

1940 as an infantry sergeant he was wounded by a shell splinter near Verdun and taken prisoner. After eighteen months of captivity in Germany, he was moved to a camp in Lorraine from which he is said to have escaped in December 1941. Three months later he joined the Vichy government's *commissariat–général* for prisoners of war. He contributed articles to an official publication, the *Revue de l'Etat Nouveau*, which followed Vichy propaganda in being critical of Léon Blum and of the pre-war Popular Front. In one article Mitterrand went further, apparently excusing German bellicosity. He set the catastrophe that had overcome *la patrie* in 1940 in the context of France's imperial past. He wrote of France's *ardeur guerrière* and said that his country's triumphalism had led to the humiliations of defeat. Perhaps he was already reflecting on post-war problems of reconciliation with Germany; what the French prisoners of war thought of his views is not recorded.

For his work with the prisoners of war Mitterrand was in the autumn of 1943 decorated with the Francisque, a medal normally awarded for personal devotion to Marshal Pétain. It was given to 5000 people and Mitterrand received No. 2202. Holders of the medal had to take an oath of loyalty to the Marshal. He was sponsored for the Francisque by Gabriel Jeantet who after the war was put on trial as a member of the Cagoule. Mitterrand later claimed that he had been awarded the medal after he had joined the Resistance and while he was actually in North Africa meeting General de Gaulle. Other people claim to have seen a photograph of Marshal Pétain pinning the medal on his chest. What is certain is that during 1943 Mitterrand also started working for the other side. His biographer, Franz-Olivier Giesbert, has claimed that Mitterrand did not join the Resistance until it was clear that the Allies were going to win the war. But the leading *résistant* General Pierre de Benouville, who was at school with Mitterrand in Angoulême, has always defended the president's Resistance record.

What is certain is that at some point in 1943 Mitterrand joined the MUR resistance movement and that in November he was flown to London and then to North Africa to meet General de Gaulle. He did not get on with de Gaulle and was returned to France in February 1944 on a Royal Navy corvette. In the last months of the Occupation Mitterrand undoubtedly operated as a genuine member of the Resistance, organizing a network within the various French PoW associations. 1.8 million French troops had been taken prisoner by the German Army in 1940. Mitterrand had found an enormous political constituency.

It was during this period that he first met his future wife, Danielle Gouze. Her sister introduced them but for Danielle it was not love at first sight – she made fun of her sister's friend, comparing him to 'a Brazilian tango king'. They were nevertheless married in October 1944. If Mitterrand has never been a Socialist there is no doubt that his wife has always been one. She inherited her Socialism from her father, a freemason from Cluny in Burgundy who had been fired from his job as a school headmaster by the Vichy authorities and who had then started to work with the Resistance. After moving into the Elysée in 1981, Danielle Mitterrand founded her own political association, France-Libertés, and started to pursue her own foreign policy initiatives around the world. President Mitterrand once said, 'My wife is well to the left of me, you know.' Whether or not President Mitterrand was ever led by his congenital love of secrecy into embracing his father-in-law's anti-clerical free-masonry is another of the endless unanswered questions about him, although it seems unlikely. The Louvre Pyramid, which he commissioned, has been described by the *mauvaises langues* of Paris as 'the country's biggest Masonic symbol'. On the other hand Mitterrand has baptized all three of his children and once said, 'I was born a Christian and no doubt I shall die one.'

After the war Mitterrand, the former Resistance organizer, spent some time editing a woman's magazine, *Votre Beauté*, which belonged to the cosmetics group L'Oréal. He was given this job by his old friend François Dalle, who had also employed several ex-members of the Cagoule at a time when they were on the run from the vengeance of the Resistance and in fear of their lives. When Gabriel Jeantet was put on trial in Paris, with other Cagoulards, for his pre-war activities, Mitterrand gave evidence on his behalf. Then in 1946 he entered national politics. He chose to fight his first seat in Nevers, a town just to the north of his wife's home region of Burgundy. He was originally sponsored by three aristocrats, local landowners who wanted a centre-right candidate to beat the Communist. Mitterrand scraped in with 25 per cent of the vote. He was thought at the time by many in the constituency to be a practising Catholic, 'bustling everywhere, missal in hand', but this must have been another misunderstanding because shortly after his election he started his long and rather oblique march towards anti-clerical Socialism, becoming at the age of thirty the youngest minister in the government, responsible for former prisoners of war. His first patron was the radical Socialist leader, Henri Queuille.

In eleven years the Fourth Republic saw twenty-two governments and during that period Mitterrand was a minister eleven times, notably in the Socialist administrations of Pierre Mendès-France and Guy Mollet. Although he enjoyed considerable success he did not inspire much personal trust. At various times he held all the most sensitive posts, minister of information (censorship), minister of the interior (police and secret police) and minister of justice (police and control of the courts). He was minister for the colonies during the Indo-Chinese War and minister of the interior – which then included Algeria – during part of the Algerian War. His progress as a minister was pitted with murky *affaires*.

In 1954, while he was minister of the interior, top secret defence information was leaked to the French Communist Party. The prime minister, Mendès-France, decided not to confide the subsequent inquiry to M. Mitterrand. Instead he held an inquiry *into* M. Mitterrand, his own minister of the interior. Mitterrand was cleared of involvement in the leaks but the fact that he had been seriously suspected says much about his reputation at the time.

While he was minister of justice in 1957, Mitterrand was believed to have obtained evidence that Michel Debré, the right-wing politician who would subsequently become President de Gaulle's first prime minister, was involved in 'the Bazooka affair', an attempt mounted in Algeria on the life of General Salan in which another French army officer was killed. The purpose of the plot was to provoke a crisis during which de Gaulle could return to power. M. Mitterrand did not prosecute Debré, allegedly preferring to keep the damaging information for private use at a later date.

Then in 1959 came the extraordinary *Affaire de l'Observatoire* in which, at the height of the OAS terrorist campaign in Paris, Mitterrand's car was machine-gunned in the centre of the city by unidentified gunmen. By this time de Gaulle had returned to power and Mitterrand was in opposition. He told the police at the time that the attack had been carried out at midnight after a furious car chase and that he had only escaped with his life by jumping over a hedge into the gardens in the middle of the avenue de l'Observatoire. Later the former minister of justice was forced to admit that the attack had actually been completely bogus and that he himself had helped to stage-manage the arrangements. He was charged with *outrage à magistrat* (contempt of court) and his parliamentary immunity was suspended, but in 1966 he benefited from an amnesty passed by a Gaullist government.

The amnesty may have been connected with M. Mitterrand's knowledge of the previous 'Bazooka affair', but no one has ever been able to explain how such an experienced politician as Mitterrand came to involve himself in the *Affaire de l'Observatoire* in the first place. His opponents said that it was an attempt to give himself national status by making it look as though the OAS terrorists of Algérie Française considered him important enough to assassinate. He himself said that he had mounted the hoax because 'the gunman' in question, a dubious former Poujadist deputy called Robert Pesquet, had told him that the OAS had said they would kill him – Pesquet – if he did not kill Mitterrand, and that he had felt sorry for Pesquet. Whatever the truth, the image of François Mitterrand leaping over the railings of the Observatoire at midnight after rather a good dinner at the Brasserie Lipp and crouching behind a hedge while shadowy figures riddled his perfectly serviceable Peugeot 403 with machine-gun bullets, remains one of the more high-spirited and informal moments of the president's political career. The *Affaire de l'Observatoire* proved to be the starting point in a steady progress towards respectability, *gravitas* and – finally – the Elysée.

To a Socialist Party dissident M. Mitterrand once said, 'You think that politics is a battle of ideas. You are wrong, young man. Politics is a profession.' To discover to what extent M. Mitterrand is a professional one only has to recall his relationship with Jacques Seguela, the brilliant publicist who wrote to him in 1978 offering his services free. Seguela was granted a weekly audience and successively instructed Mitterrand what to do with his hands on television, how to sit, and how to dress. 'Stop wearing pin-striped suits if you want people to trust you,' said Seguela. 'Dress "*à gauche*".' Mme Seguela made the necessary arrangements with the tailor. Finally

Seguela took a deep breath and told Mitterrand to have his Dracula-like teeth capped. 'You have a terrible problem with your canines,' he said, 'You'll never get elected if you don't get them capped.'

For a fastidious, bookish, rakish, liberal who had been posing as a Socialist for fifteen years, the indignity was a detail and M. Mitterrand went to the dentist at once; but giving the advice took some courage on the part of Seguela none the less. With the fangs capped the publicist could sit back. The last traces of the old shark were erased. The Socialist candidate's way to victory in the presidential elections of 1981 lay clear ahead.

During the twenty-three years of Gaullism and opposition, from 1958 to 1981, Mitterrand worked patiently to rebuild the divided parties of the non-Communist Left into the present day Socialist Party and – removed from the temptations of power – he found that his reputation could be improved with his appearance. It was at about this time that the French people began to hear of a new Mitterrand, the rather solitary man who enjoyed walking in the French countryside, who loved trees and streams and mountains, and who when he was in Paris would relax by strolling to the stalls of the *bouquinistes* on the banks of the Seine; a man who rarely carried any money on him because he had never been interested in it. And it transpired that the political hero of this former *cagoulard* had always been – who else? – Léon Blum! Little by little this new Mitterrand became, 'Tonton' the uncle of his people, the faithful friend who always remembered to send postcards to his old constituents in Nevers when he was attending a world summit conference, even though he could never remember their postcodes.

He is certainly faithful in friendship. The list of government ministers who started out as friends or members of his personal staff includes the prime minister Pierre Bérégovoy and the former prime minister Pierre Mauroy, as well as the foreign minister Roland Dumas (once his lawyer), Pierre Joxe, Jean-Louis Bianco, Elisabeth Guigoul, Michel Charasse and Georgina Dufoix. The first head of his private office was his brother Robert; later he appointed his son Jean-Christophe, then a journalist on AFP, as presidential adviser for the whole of Africa. (The Africans, with their unkind sense of humour, nicknamed Jean-Christophe 'Papamadit'.) The secretary-general of the Elysée, Hubert Vedrine, is the son of another of his old friends, Jean Vedrine – once a Cagoulard. Recurring speculation that President Mitterrand may resign before his term is up, either on health grounds or because he has simply had enough, may be proved correct, but when he goes a vast network of friendship and patronage stretching back over sixty years goes with him and it is not a decision he will take lightly.

François Mitterrand has an enormous patience and a remarkable memory. His political style is that of the chess player who rarely attacks but who waits to take advantage of his opponent's errors. In the case of the Maastricht Referendum, demanded by Jacques Chirac, the president immediately saw the possibilities of using the campaign to divide the opposition. He merely had to agree and the trap closed. There was no legal necessity for a referendum since the constitutional changes involved had already been approved by the senate and the national assembly. According to Franz-Olivier Giesbert, the internal political advantages were the only reason why Mitterrand consulted the people of France.

The referendum may have led to a great European debate but as far as M. Mitterrand was concerned that was not its real purpose. The consequent turmoil on the world's currency markets, the abrupt British exit from the ERM, the beam of light thrown on the true priorities of the Bundesbank, the fresh doubts raised about the future of the Treaty and the future shape of Europe, were all incidental to the president's need to weaken the French opposition before the pending legislative elections.

And to clinch the vote, M. Mitterrand, perhaps leafing through some old dossiers, had an inspiration. Why not mount another false attempt on his life? No machine-gun bullets this time, just a *mild* case of cancer. After all if you look at a map of the Left Bank you will see that the way from the Elysée to the Hôpital Cochin lies by the avenue de l'Observatoire. And it is a curious coincidence that Professor Debré, who operated on him, is the son of Michel Debré whose name M. Mitterrand is said to have kept out of the Bazooka affair all those years ago.

1992

27

CRIME AND THE ACADÉMIE FRANÇAISE

In 1918 an angry French soldier sent a letter from the Western Front to the perpetual secretary of the Académie Française in Paris proposing that the letter 'K' be struck from the French alphabet. ' "K",' he wrote, 'is universally recognized as being grammatically useless in French and is essentially German. Let us replace it with "Q" or "C".' If you glance hastily through a French dictionary it is possible to get the impression that the soldier's suggestion was followed. But closer examination of the *Petit Robert* shows that four pages out of more than 2000 are still devoted to 'K'. (English, one is proud to see, has contributed 'know-how' – pron. noaw – and 'kitchenette'.) Perhaps it is surprising that the abolition of 'K' did not form part of the ceasefire agreement and become a clause in the Treaty of Versailles, for the French language has always formed one of the principal glories of France. 'In order to speak French you must have a deep pool of nobility and sincerity in your soul,' wrote the Catholic polemicist Louis Veuillot, and he believed it.

France has never been an ethnic nation: placed on the fringe of continental Europe its shifting borders to the north and east have, over the centuries, repeatedly burst under the pressure of a rich mixture of heavily-armed or fleet-footed newcomers. 'The French people were born of a Christian mother and an unknown father,' according to the writer and member of the Académie Française, André Frossard. 'I say unknown father because France is a nation of immigrants and always has been. It started with the Franks and the Visigoths and has been going on ever since.' The result has been a people who are so volatile, so quarrelsome and so individualistic, so instinctively and so deeply divided, that it some-times seems as though the nation has to be reinvented every morning as its citizens clamber out of bed. It is then that the Republic's 57 million republicans re-enter their daily compact to pass their waking hours in a minimum of social harmony. They re-enter this compact as soon as they utter their first words of French. 'If I speak French I must BE French ... *Merde*!' And with this ancient oath of loyalty the civic peace is secured for another twenty-four hours.

A nation of immigrants is not defined by its geographical frontiers but by its language, and the frontiers of the French language at least are protected by imposing barricades. The defences include a division of the ministry of education, a deputy minister of culture, a parliamentary commission for '*la Francophonie*', and a standing world conference. France must be the only country in the world in which the state can prosecute you for publishing a foreign word where a native word exists. But the last line of defence, the guardianship of the ultimate purity is entrusted to one of the most mysterious of national institutions, the Académie Française.

The Académie Française was founded by the Cardinal Duc de Richelieu in 1635. It sits in Paris in the Palais Conti on the banks of the Seine and is dedicated to 'Immortality', which is why its forty distinguished members are unofficially known as 'the Immortals'. From the start the Académie's principal function was 'to lay down rules for our language and render it pure, eloquent and capable of encompassing both the arts and the sciences'. After the Revolution the Académie's principal function was redefined as being to purge and fix (*épurer et fixer*) the language, though its principal method of doing this was still to be in the production of a Dictionary. Every Thursday afternoon, for eight months of the year, the forty members of the Académie meet for one hour to discuss the Dictionary. The last edition, the eighth, was published in 1935 and they have been at work on the ninth edition ever since. To date they have reached the letter 'F'.

A Dictionary produced only once a century can be of little help in defining a language but it is invaluable in recording it. A French word, like a French citizen, is by the Dictionary given an official identity, an *état civil*. Its birth certificate is provided by its first entry in the Dictionary and its death certificate by its last. The verbal infantile mortality rate, only one entry in the Dictionary, undoubtedly exists; but it is low. When the ninth edition eventually appears those who have been French between 1935 and let us say 2015 will learn at last what their language correctly consisted of.

The late Duc de Castries, elected to armchair (*fauteuil*) no. 2 in 1972 admitted that the ninth edition would probably not be completed during the twentieth century but he was confident that when published 'it would do honour to the Academy'. The Academy's speed of production is sometimes criticized but when one considers that in say eighty years, at eight months a year, there are only 2,774 Thursdays, and that during this period the Second World War took place, and that to finish within this period the Academy would have to polish off the four pages of 'K' in only five sessions, they seem if anything to be going dangerously fast, particularly when one also remembers that the first fifteen minutes of each meeting are spent in approving the minutes of the previous one.

If the Dictionary exists to purge and fix France's language, the Académie itself exists to purge and fix France's list of great men. During the Revolution God was abolished, the friars were driven out of their cloisters and put to the sword and their churches were requisitioned. But the secular Republic which overthrew the Christian monarchy quickly developed a need for the religious concept of Immortality. Naturally Man had to be worshipped in a temple as grand as the temples of God. So the grandest and newest church in Paris, that of St Geneviève, was converted by the Revolutionaries into a Temple of Reason and renamed the Panthéon, the house of all the gods. Today, fixed above its doors in letters of gold are the words, '*Aux grands hommes, la patrie reconnaissante*', and for two hundred years the Panthéon has been the burial place for the nation's great men.

The advantage of the Académie over the Panthéon is that it allows France to bury its great men before they are legally dead, although it has not always been free from error in bestowing this immortality. The list of those never elected includes Descartes, Rousseau, Molière, Pascal, Stendhal, Dumas, Balzac, Flaubert, Baudelaire, Verlaine, de Maupassant, Jules Verne and Gide. Proust died at the age of forty-nine, before the Immortals realized who he was. Zola was rejected twenty-four times. Today, of the forty members, the only names really celebrated outside France are probably those of Commander Cousteau, Claude Lévi-Strauss, Henri Troyat, Ionesco and Julien Green. It is an odd fact that only two of these *académiciens* are native-born Frenchmen. Among the membership there is generally at least one Duke and a choice of doctors, a sensible precaution in view of the fact that the average age of the Immortals is over seventy-five.

For a great Frenchman to be recognized as immortal he has, with rare exceptions, to apply. Marshal Foch, invited to accept membership after the First World War, was elected unanimously. General de Gaulle was invited to join on the Liberation of Paris but he declined. Voltaire was elected unanimously. But virtually every-one else has had to undergo a humiliating process of canvassing support. First the aspiring candidate must ask the perpetual secretary if his or her candidacy stands any chance at all. Then, if the answer is a guarded 'yes', he or she (three women have in recent years been elected to the Académie Française) must request interviews, tradition-ally at teatime, with the existing Immortals and try to find some-thing to talk about. These visits are notoriously difficult occasions. If the candidate refers to his own books he is regarded as conceited, if he refers to his host's books he is regarded as a flatterer unless of course he criticizes them which is worse; if he does not refer to his host's books it is assumed he has not read them and if he does not refer to his own books his host may not remember who he is – four of the current Immortals are aged over ninety, another four over eighty-five. For each vacant armchair there are normally three or four candidates, the voting is by secret ballot and the winner is elected by a simple majority. It is rare to receive much more than a majority, so many of the votes are by tradition *contre*. The glory of any closed institution lies far more in who does not belong to it than in who does.

The Duc de Castries wrote that when the news was announced of a candidate's election he was drowned in attention, after which a complete silence fell which was to be broken only twice, once on his reception and once after his death. It is true that few academicians distinguish themselves after they have been elected but what could they possibly hope to achieve to equal the glory of immortality? There in their *fauteuils* they sit, the forty Immortals, by some way the grandest as well as the most comfortable assembly in France. And what is the solemn task with which the nation has charged them? The production of a dictionary which is likely to be half-a-century out of date by the time it is published, an event which very few of them will even live to witness. It seems poss-ible that the vitriolic element in their voting may be partly born of frustration.

The sophisticated view of the Académie Française among the large majority of citizens who are not members is that there is something faintly ridiculous as well as something glorious about the tenancy of a *fauteuil*. Before his reception beneath the Coupole of the Palais

Conti the candidate has to order his uniform, the aspect of life in the Académie which is responsible for more ridicule than any other. He is eventually dressed, at a cost of about seven thousand pounds, in a black tailcoat covered in green and gold silk embroidery, a Napoleonic cocked hat and a sword – the pommel of which is made by a goldsmith to his own design. This uniform, designed by David, was inspired by the costumes worn by church ushers at imposing funerals during the seventeenth century. It goes with hearses decked in black velvet canopies drawn by horses wearing tall black plumes. Many of the academicians avoid wearing their uniform whenever possible and it is rare to see a photograph of one of them in his cocked hat, even they find it looks ridiculous. And yet, there is no shortage of candidates seeking the right to wear it.

On the great day, a procession in full costume forms up, the drums of the Garde Républicaine start to roll and the Immortals enter their high-domed chamber once, naturally, a chapel. The new academician then reads out his speech of thanks which takes the form of a eulogy of his predecessor in the same armchair. In reply one of his fellows reads out a speech of welcome, which consists of the new member's eulogy. These are the sole public activities of the Immortals, to praise their predecessors and to receive the praise of their peers. *Le Monde* generally publishes large parts of the two texts.

It is when he first seats himself beneath the Coupole that the new academician may truly appreciate the degree to which the mortality of an Immortal is a delicate question. Costumed as they are like the descendants of a dynasty of funeral directors, besieged by a horde of impatient would-be Immortals just waiting for one of them to die, they meet in plenary session only to commemorate such a death. It is no wonder that Pierre Moinot, when welcoming Jean-Denis Bredin in 1989 warned him that *la Compagnie* was in no hurry to admire one of his acknowledged talents, that of funeral orator. 'Here,' said Moinot, pausing and looking round the neighbouring *fauteuils*, 'we only appreciate the spectacle of that particular form of eloquence at a distance.'

The speeches over, the compliments exhausted, *la Compagnie* exits, once more between the drawn sabres and rolling drums of the Garde Républicaine, the sword saluting the pen. The reception is, in the traditional phrase, '*suivi d'un cocktail*'. *Suivi d'un long silence.*

But if the Immortals are largely silent it would be a mistake to view them as an assembly of the living dead. Where there is crime there is life, and in France it could almost be said that where there is life, there is crime. Even within the illustrious ranks of *la Compagnie*, signs of the criminal life are occasionally emitted. Cardinal Daniélou certainly gave signs of a wonderfully disreputable, if not criminal, life after his election in 1974, dying in Pigalle in a *maison de passe* in the arms of a *fille de joie* before he could be received into the less carnal but equally warm embrace that awaited him beneath the Coupole. The Immortals were not amused by this misadventure and they did not risk selecting another Cardinal for nineteen years.

More recently there was the case of the academician and art historian René Huyghe, director of a museum holding a collection of the Académie's treasures. In 1991 he and his wife, who was the museum's curator, were suspected of being involved in the theft of part of the museum's collection. Academician Huyghe hotly denied the charge, and was eventually able to show that most of the 325 missing exhibits had merely been mislaid in an attic. He suggested that the affair was a vulgar plot mounted by the ministry of culture with the intention of taking over the Académie's invaluable endowment. He denounced it as an event '*scandaleuse pour la démocratie*'.

Then there was the case of the novelist, academician and polemical Gaullist journalist, Michel Droit. In 1987 Michel Droit was summoned to appear before an examining magistrate and charged with '*forfaiture*' (abuse of a public office), the most serious offence in the *code pénal* after treason. The last case of *forfaiture* had been in 1917 when a minister had been charged with providing the German High Command with details of an impending counter-attack during the Battle of Verdun. The penalties include banishment and '*dégradation civil*', loss of all civil rights including pension, vote and passport.

What could Academician Droit have accomplished which was on a scale with betraying the French plan of attack at Verdun? As a member of the national broadcasting commission it transpired that he was suspected of favouring the application of a friend for a local radio licence. A complaint had been made against him by another disappointed applicant. It took Michel Droit 'three years of hell' to clear his name. During the course of his ordeal he was further accused of taking bribes, his bank statements were seized and leaked

to the newspapers and television news programmes and he underwent an eight-hour interrogation at the ministry of the interior. At
one point he applied to the supreme court, the Cour de Cassation,
for the examining magistrate who was leading him such a dance to
be taken off the case. In reply the public prosecutor argued that
Academician Droit was 'a man accused who did not want to be
treated like other accused people' and claimed that he had been able
to bring considerable influence to bear on the supreme court. The
president of the Cour de Cassation apparently agreed with the
public prosecutor, stating that she objected to 'the intolerable and
partisan campaign which discredits the court's decisions and puts the
administration of justice under unacceptable pressure'. None the less
the examining magistrate was replaced, the charge of *forfaiture* was
dropped and eventually Michel Droit was cleared of the subsidiary
charges of corruption arising from the same facts. He said afterwards
that the case against him had been 'a political manoeuvre inspired
by the president of the Republic'. The point of the operation had
been to discredit the national broadcasting commission. He had
been singled out because he was a well-known public figure, a
friend of General de Gaulle, a contributor to *Le Figaro* and a
member of the Académie Française. It had been necessary, he said,
to raise the charges to an Immortal level, which was why *forfaiture*
had been dragged out of the legal history books. In a way the affair
honoured *la Compagnie* whose members could not be accused of
committing the banal crimes of ordinary men.

But the Académie's major criminal period was undoubtedly during
the post-war '*épuration*' when some of its members were accused of
crimes on an appropriately grand scale, crimes that could be punished by the firing squad. Both during the Vichy years and after the
War the Académie Française was profoundly Pétainist. In the heat
of the moment, in August 1944, it responded to the arrival of de
Gaulle in Paris by inviting him to become a member; when he
refused it felt no obligation to pay any further attention to his
advice. It was the beginning of a duel that continues today. Some
members of the Resistance suggested in 1945 that the Académie was
so heavily compromised that it should be dissolved, as it had been
for a brief period after the French Revolution. This suggestion was
turned down by de Gaulle who instead suggested to the Académie

that the best solution would be to elect a number of Resisters to the vacant armchairs, no elections having been carried out during the four years of German Occupation. He noted later in his *Mémoirs* that the Immortals disregarded this advice. The Académie, even in those difficult times, was sufficiently sure of itself to 'wait it out', a policy which proved to be perfectly effective. Four of its members were expelled by the Liberation government for their activities during the Occupation, but even here the Académie succeeded in exercising a parallel jurisdiction to that of the state which is very characteristic of the society it adorns.

In the two cases of Abel Bonnard, the crypto-Nazi academician who had been Vichy minister of education and who was sentenced to death in his absence, and Abel Hermant, the grammarian and novelist, who was sentenced to life imprisonment, the Académie accepted the verdict of a mortal court, acknowledged the exclusions and duly elected successors to the relevant armchairs. But in two other cases, that of Marshal Pétain (sentenced to death, later commuted to life imprisonment) and Charles Maurras (hard labour for life) the Académie made no attempt to hold a re-election. Those armchairs were left vacant until their former occupants had in fact died, and their eventual successors read out their eulogies in the customary manner. For Pétain it was as though he had never been disgraced, and beneath the Coupole he never was. He occupied, after all, armchair no. 18 and was the direct successor to Marshal Foch. There was no question of dishonouring armchair no. 18. God did not recall Marshal Pétain until 1951, when he was ninety-five. He was succeeded by the diplomat André-François Poncet and the eulogy read out that day was undoubtedly the first public statement in favour of the Marshal since the end of the war, coming only two years after the last trial of a Pétainist collaborator in the High Court. The case proved to be a triumph for the Académie's delicate sense of distinction and timing.

In two other cases the Académie found itself opposed to the wishes of General de Gaulle. When he became president of the Republic in 1958 de Gaulle became *ex officio* 'the protector' of the Académie, a role which gave him the theoretical power to block any elections of which he disapproved. It was a power which no 'protector' had used since the French Revolution. De Gaulle used his power twice; it was his revenge on *la Compagnie* for having failed to purge itself after the war. Paul Morand was the first victim of the general's displeasure. Morand, a diplomat and writer, had twice been a Pétainist ambassador and had theoretically harmed the interests of France. More to the point he had actually been *en poste* in London in June, 1940, when de Gaulle first appealed for Resistance. But Morand had ignored de Gaulle's appeal and returned to France. For ten years de Gaulle refused to sanction his election, only relenting in 1968, by which time Morand was aged eighty. In the case of Paul Morand the Académie once again had the last word. Morand died in 1977 and in 1980 the Immortals named their foremost literary prize in his honour.

It must be said that the election of Paul Morand (who had been blacklisted at the time of the Liberation) in 1958, the year when de Gaulle returned to power, was something of a provocation for the general. But in another case de Gaulle had less excuse though more success. Saint-John Perse, also a diplomat and considered to be the greatest poet of his time, had been suspended by the Vichy foreign ministry in 1940 as a known enemy of Nazism and had settled in the United States, an action for which the Vichy government stripped him of his citizenship. But despite his anti-Nazi views Saint-John Perse never rallied to the Gaullist cause. For this omission de Gaulle never forgave him and excluded him from the Académie Française. Saint-John Perse had to content himself with the Nobel Prize, awarded in 1960. It brought him more money, but no uniform.

The relationship between crime and the Académie Française is perhaps most clearly illustrated by the case of Jacques Soustelle, one of the most remarkable, and most criminal of modern Immortals. If you can be expelled for misdemeanours committed after your election, it seems that it is quite in order to have embarked on a criminal career before. You can even receive the cocked hat after a period of time spent in exile or banishment.

Jacques Soustelle had a strange career. The son of a labourer from the Cévenol, he passed out first, like Sartre, from the Ecole Normale Supérieure and quickly won a reputation as a noted ethnologist, specializing in pre-Columbian Mexican culture. He was politically active on the non-Communist extreme-left before the war and in 1940 was among the first to make his way to London to join General de Gaulle. He carried out several secret missions in Occupied

France, eventually became minister of information in the government in exile and then, aged thirty-two, director of all the Gaullist intelligence services, a position of considerable power. After the war Soustelle founded the first Gaullist political party, at a time when de Gaulle himself had retired from politics, and in 1955 he was appointed as governor of Algeria by the Socialist minister of the interior, François Mitterrand.

It was an appointment which was drastically to alter the course of Soustelle's life. His arrival in Algeria was greeted by hostile crowds of settlers who had been led to believe that he was Jewish and that his real name was 'Ben Soussan'. On his recall, one year later, much larger crowds came to see him off and fought with the police to try to prevent him from leaving. It took his armoured car one hour to cover 200 metres on the quayside through the frenzied *'pied-noirs'* shouting *'Ne partez pas!'*, and as his ship moved away from the quay the vast crowd sang *'Ce n'est qu'un au revoir'*. The rest of Soustelle's life was dominated by the emotion of that day.

When de Gaulle returned to power in 1958 it was after years of plotting by Gaullists such as Jacques Soustelle and Michel Debré and it was in the widespread expectation that the general was the one man who could save 'Algérie Française'. Soustelle stood beside de Gaulle on the balcony of the 'Gouvernement-Général in Algiers in 1958 as the general made his triumphant speech to the massed ranks of the *'pied-noirs'* which opened with the words, *'Je vous ai compris'*. Soustelle was subsequently among the first to realize what de Gaulle was up to, the first to resign from the Gaullist cabinet and the first to start organizing the OAS, the secret army which fought a violent civil war against de Gaulle's plans to grant Algeria independence. In 1961 the holder of the Rosette de la Résistance and former head of all Gaullist intelligence services went on the run, proscribed by a Gaullist Government. He said later that he had made his decision to rebel because he preferred 'legal dishonour to the shame of betrayal'. (The journalist Sam White took the more cynical view that it was a consequence of his wartime intelligence work since 'the Secret Service always has a fatal effect on the mentality of an intellectual'.)

It was, in any event, Soustelle's second journey into exile and his second *nom de guerre* – he adopted the name of 'Jean-Albert Sénèque', confident that few border policemen would make the connection with Seneca the Younger, the philosopher, orator and statesman, who was exiled to Corsica by the Emperor Claudius. Once again the full power of the state whose interests he was accused of damaging was deployed against Soustelle, it was just like the great days of the Occupation. An international warrant was issued for his arrest and he claimed later that two attempts were made to kidnap him by French secret agents. But he was never caught and it was to be seven years before he was offered an amnesty. Soustelle refused this amnesty insisting that he had never done anything wrong, and eventually the point was conceded. He was allowed to return and resume his political career.

During his second period of exile Soustelle devoted more time to his original studies in ethnology. He established a business base in Paraguay and defended the interests whenever he could of UDI in Rhodesia, of the South African regime during the years of apartheid and of the government of Israel, three causes close to his heart. General Stroessner, dictator of Paraguay, decorated him with the Paraguayan Order of Merit. He probably thought it was the last distinction he would ever win. And then, in 1982 he was encouraged to propose himself for the Académie Française. At last the Académie had found a Gaullist after its own heart.

There is a tradition in *la Compagnie* that once the day of election comes all public criticism of the candidates is silenced, the ballots say it all. The only time recently when this strict convention was broken was not during the anguished days following the Liberation but on the first candidature of Jacques Soustelle. Just before the vote Alain Peyrefitte, then one of the youngest academicians and an ardent Gaullist, demanded the right to speak and denounced Soustelle so violently that it was hard to see how his remarks could be followed so shortly afterwards by the traditional eulogy. Soustelle was not elected and the Socialist Pierre Moinot was chosen in his place.

The fact that Peyrefitte himself occupied armchair no. 11, in which his predecessor had been the Pétainist Paul Morand, seemed to have done nothing for his sense of tolerance. Peyrefitte had been a Gaullist minister during the early 60s when Soustelle was on the run and when the OAS were trying to assassinate de Gaulle and were spreading terror throughout France, and he could not forgive

Soustelle. But the Académie were not pleased by Peyrefitte's breach with tradition and one year later Soustelle was duly elected to armchair no. 36.

And so, for Jacques Soustelle as well, the day came when he could join the procession clad in green and gold and march between the drummers of the Garde Républicaine. He read the eulogy of Pierre Gaxotte, a firm Pétainist and one of his wartime enemies, and he was welcomed by Jean Dutourd, a firm Gaullist who had almost certainly voted against his election and who had supported Alain Peyrefitte's violent denunciation of the year before. Seven years were left to Jacques Soustelle to enjoy his immortality, and he spent them beneath the Coupole, side by side with Peyrefitte and Dutourd, purifying and fixing the French language. During his time the Dictionary progressed from '*chaîne*' to '*deutéronome*', so he never lived to see the word '*emmerdeur*' ('one who puts you "*dans la merde*" – a pain in the neck') officially welcomed into the French language, although he had done so much to establish its currency.

2. MEET THE MEN IN CHARGE

All this week, France held its breath while the Senate, the upper house of parliament, chose its new president. The previous holder of the office, Alain Poher, is aged eighty and was first installed on his throne in 1968. Since then he had been re-elected six times. There was a feeling in the air that it might be time for a change.

The voting continued throughout Monday night, eight candidates putting themselves forward for the honour. Then at 4 a.m. yesterday, France could breathe again. After three ballots, the new president of the Senate, who ranks third in the French political hierarchy, was . . . eighty-year-old Alain Poher, for the eighth time. If the good Lord spares him – and why not? – he will probably run again in 1992, when the Single European Act will become law and the Senate will need an experienced hand at the helm.

For M. Poher this long-drawn out struggle was something new – on the seven previous occasions he had been elected on the first ballot. But so much the better; not every eighty-year-old survives an entirely new experience so successfully. 'This is the first time anything unusual has happened here since Goering occupied the building in 1940,' one veteran observer was heard to remark. Other senators, responding to M. Poher's insistence that his age was irrelevant, said in that case, why not vote for Senator Geoffroy de Montalembert, who is only ninety-one and was first elected in 1945. (Mysteriously enough, one senator did vote for M. Montalembert in the first two ballots; no prizes for guessing who.) But the others didn't want an entirely new hand on the helm, so they gave it back to Poher.

The French Senate is a curious institution. Unlike the House of Lords it is elected, but it is elected by local councillors, an overwhelming majority of them from small country *communes*. This means that the cities of France are under-represented and there is a considerable right-wing majority, three-quarters in 1986 when the rest of France voted 52 per cent for the Right. There is no question here of 'the swing of the pendulum'. It is in a way rather comforting. Chesterton said that 'tradition is the democracy of the politically dead' but in France 'the politically dead' get a seat in parliament, together with three secretaries each, interest-free loans, subsidized foreign travel and an income of about £40,000, half of which is tax free.

Those who attack the Senate say that it should be abolished, that it is useless and corrupt. Those who defend it say that it represents 'an area of moderation and wisdom in French democracy' and that both are sorely needed. In fact the Senate is important, but for quite different reasons. It represents two fundamental political principles: the first is hierarchy, the second is influence, or *le piston* as it is informally termed. The average age of the senators is just under seventy. This is usually seen as a weakness but it is equally a strength. For what else could so many well-connected old buffers do if not manoeuvre themselves into and around the Senate? When French politicians achieve a certain dignity and experience, and lose a certain up-to-dateness, off they go to the Senate, where the marble floors of the National Assembly are replaced by thick carpets (softer when they fall over) and where the young are kept firmly in their place. The Senate is notorious for closing ranks against any young politicians who try to use it as a springboard for something grander.

As for *le piston*, it is true that three senators have been accused of fraud, bribery and tax evasion in the past three years, but they have all been cleared of these charges, by other senators. And since senators are elected for nine years, it is natural that they should keep in close touch with the local councillors who elected them – they don't want to be completely forgotten. And sitting, as they do, in parliament, but without real power, they are perfectly placed to intervene with ministers who are making decisions which might affect their own region. A mayor who cultivates his senator has a hotline to the ministry, and can always find his niece a job with a pension. A senator who cultivates his mayors will be given useful things to do and will be re-elected.

It is a beautiful relationship. Without the Senate both hierarchy and influence would be seriously weakened in France, and that would leave a lot of people not knowing which way to turn.

October, 1989

There are at the moment eight official *affaires* running in France, which is very good news for the dozens of people involved, since no one can keep up with eight scandals at the same time. But here is the latest in *l'affaire Chaumet*, the story of Chaumet, Chalandon, Chauvy, Chanut, Chirac, Chopin and Chaumet.

Until May this year, the brothers Pierre and Jacques Chaumet headed one of the most respected jewellers in the world. Their premises in the Place Vendôme stood beside Van Cleef & Arpels, Boucheron, Guerlain and Rothschild. The Chaumets were at 12 Place Vendôme, the house in which Chopin died. (Chopin has no more to do with this story.) On the opposite side of the square are numbers 11 and 13, which shelter the ministry of justice.

It would have been difficult to say, until now, which house was the grandest out of numbers 11, 12 and 13. Now the Chaumets are spending their fourth month in prison, and the man who directs the ministry of justice, Albin Chalandon, is not feeling very well either.

The Chaumets ran their house in the old way, that is to say with an absolute discretion, and they specialized in diamonds. Diamonds are a currency all over the world, but particularly in a country where people still keep billions of francs' worth of gold under the bed.

Until 1981 the Chaumets apparently maintained the highest standards of propriety, but then they seem to have been stricken by an illness which afflicted many of the wealthier people in France in that year, the year a Socialist government was elected. They decided that they were living in a 'Versailles 1788' situation, and no holds were barred. There was a feeling among the *bon ton* in 1981 that Mitterrand and his band of cut-throats were about to get their hands on everything they could find. The idea was to get the stuff abroad, but the Reds had passed a law against it. So what to do?

What happened next is not entirely clear, but it is known that the Chaumets had a branch in Geneva and that diamonds, unlike currency, could be exported – by those who knew the ropes. All seemed to be going well, until there was a slump in the price of diamonds, just at a time when Pierre and Jacques had laid in a very large stock. Simultaneously there was a feeling among some of the Chaumets' clients that the Swiss banks were preparing to co-operate with the French Reds, who were getting nosy about French citizens holding bank accounts in Geneva.

So it was back into France with the money, now no longer safe in Geneva, and what with the complications of this unfamiliar business and the rocks going backwards and forwards, and some people having open accounts and some people having pseudonyms, Pierre and Jacques got into a dreadful muddle, and began to run out of money, and so they started offering anyone who would lend them money 20 per cent interest, which is known as illegal banking. And then in May this year the whole thing crashed, and a receiver was brought in and the debts were calculated at £200 million, and Pierre and Jacques found themselves in rather unpleasant surroundings on charges of fraud.

At this stage they had the misfortune to meet François Chanut, the examining magistrate in charge of their case, who seems to be a man with all the time in the world. After keeping the Chaumets in for a month, and before he had even questioned them, M. Chanut went on a little holiday. He does not understand about a jeweller's discretion. He just wants a list of all the clients. So far he has discovered that Albin Chalandon, the minister of justice, once sold diamonds to the Chaumets, and so did his wife, Princess Salomé. M. Chalandon is embarrassed, but he has explained that it was a straightforward sale of family heirlooms, and that the Chaumets actually owe him six million francs.

Pierre, the older of the brothers, who hates prison, has told M. Chanut that M. Chalandon also bought nine million francs' worth of diamonds. M. Chalandon denies this. M. Chanut is still waiting for the list.

Two weeks ago the Chaumets' lawyers applied for them to be released. Amazingly, the public prosecutor, Yves Chauvy, who works in the ministry of justice, said that he had no objection. But M. Chanut objected strongly, and so the application had to go to the Court of Appeal. After listening to prosecutor Chauvy's reasons why the brothers should be released, one of the judges said: 'In thirty years I have never heard anything like it . . .' The court rejected the application, and the Chaumets are still in prison, and M. Chanut is still waiting for his list.

And as for M. Chirac, the prime minister, he has no more to do with the story than Chopin, but his wife, Bernadette, is quite a friend of the Chaumets, and they have been kind to her in the past.

September, 1987

'Money corrupts! Money kills! Money stains man's very conscience!' You are not listening to a bearded loon standing on a soapbox in Hyde Park, but to the man who subsequently became the President of the French Republic, François Mitterrand, addressing the historic founding congress of his Socialist Party in 1971. The energetic programme of nationalizing banks and major corporations, which was one of François Mitterrand's first tasks when he was elected ten years later, was inspired by his very public contempt for money. Nothing that has happened since has suggested that he has diluted the purity of this attitude.

So it made something of a sensation when, last Saturday, *Le Monde* published a front-page story claiming that President Mitterrand has received a 'confidential report' on the Pechiney insider-trading scandal, which stated that one of his close friends, a businessman called Roger-Patrice Pelat, was heavily involved in the affair. For two days there was no official reaction to this story. During that time it was taken up by the rest of the press, not always with conviction. *Le Figaro*, for instance, which is a right-wing paper, ran a prominent piece suggesting that the left-wing *Le Monde* was barking up the wrong tree.

Then on Monday night, after two days of silence, the Elysée denied it all. 'No such report has been sent to the President,' said a communiqué from the head of his secretariat, Jean-Louis Bianco. In another part of Paris, President Mitterrand was telling journalists: 'I'm just like you; I find out what's going on by reading the newspapers,' a characteristically ambiguous comment.

At almost the same moment M. Pelat, who had disappeared for over a week, suddenly reappeared before the waiting television cameras on the steps of his house in Paris. He in his turn denied that he had disappeared, saying that he had been having 'a quiet walk' through the streets of Paris. Then he wished the Stock Exchange Commission well in its inquiries into the Pechiney scandal and disappeared again, this time into his house.

It was with some interest that we waited for yesterday afternoon's issue of *Le Monde*. Stung by the belated denial, the paper proceeded to substantiate its original story. Accompanied by a cartoon showing President Mitterrand as Salvador Dali painting over a picture of a confidential report and declaring himself to be 'maddened by his own surrealistic genius', *Le Monde*'s front-page headline was: 'The Internal Intelligence Service provided the document sent to M. Mitterrand.' If you are going to give away your source you might as well give it away in style.

Although *Le Monde* did not name the individual involved, it made it quite clear that he was a staff member of the Renseignements *Généraux* (the secretive information department of the ministry of the interior) who had been replying to the newspaper's questions with the knowledge and approval of his superiors. The story presented a vivid picture of a presidential palace which was essentially paralysed by the general reluctance to breach national conventions of privacy and respect for personal relations.

Few people think that President Mitterrand himself has been engaged in insider-trading. But the embarrassment the president would feel should one of his oldest friends be found guilty is almost as interesting. *The Silences of Colonel Bramble* are nothing compared to the silences of official France.

Years ago, when the two men were living through a difficult period in a German PoW camp, M. Pelat is said to have deloused President Mitterrand. It would be affecting to think that after all this time the President of the Republic was able, in a sense, to return the compliment.

January, 1989

———

The story of the security police in the French embassy in Beirut who have been buying weapons, smuggling them into France and selling them for a profit gets better. It would probably never have been discovered if police in Marseille investigating a stolen car racket last year had not arrested a 'bent copper', Philippe Nino. Nino, twenty-five, was a humble member of the CRS riot police. He was known in the barracks as 'quiet and dependable but rather right-wing'.

When CRS Nino was not patrolling the beaches of Bandol or the Toulon–Marseille motorway he was nicking hand-built Testarossa Ferraris and selling them to a garage man in Metz. In his bedroom he kept an AK-47 assault rifle which he said he had bought from one of the CRS policemen who had been stationed at the Beirut embassy. But when he also said that he was involved in a regular arms-smuggling operation run by the embassy's security guards, nobody believed him.

Then last July an armoured security van was attacked outside Marseille's main station by gangsters armed with Kalashnikov automatic rifles, magnetic mines and rocket launchers. Even the Marseille police thought this was unusual and they started to pay attention to Nino's story. A number of people in authority today probably wish they had not done that, because subsequent inquiries are beginning to lead uncomfortably close.

Yesterday the seventeenth member of the police smuggling network was charged with 'illegal arms dealing'. The weapons bought in Beirut have been sold on to the *milieu* in Marseille, Corsica and Nice. CRS Nino – now known as *Nino la balance* or 'Nino the grass' – was in touch with men bearing names such as 'Bruno Saccomano' and 'Henri Piazza'. Most of the arms were allegedly supplied by Christian Lebanese dealers to Jean-Claude Labourdette, who until this week was head of security at the French embassy.

M. Labourdette is among those who have been arrested and charged, and that is the problem. Labourdette has been a key man in Beirut since 1985, closely involved in the secret negotiations for the release of many of the French hostages in the last six years. He is now in Les Baumettes, Marseille's notorious prison, where as a marksman and suspected arms dealer he will take his place among the élite, and will be in a position to employ a food-taster, should he so desire.

According to one of the policemen arrested with Labourdette, the weapons were sometimes smuggled out of Beirut in French government aeroplanes. The plane used by France's minister for humanitarian aid, Bernard Kouchner ('Monsieur Earthquakes' as he is sometimes known) has been mentioned. While M. Kouchner would drive round the Beirut refugee camps worrying about powdered milk and emergency blankets, his security guards would be packing the hold of his official plane with American, Russian and

Czech assault rifles. The plane would eventually land at Villacoublay, the military airbase outside Paris where customs activities are minimal. The unsuspecting M. Kouchner would then be whisked off to his ministry and the guns would be whisked off to 'Henri Piazza'.

This week M. Kouchner successfully sued two Paris newspapers for recklessly repeating the rumour that he knew something about the arms traffic. It is clear that the poor man was in fact a dupe. He holds Jean-Claude Labourdette in high regard for protecting him so well and once even recommended him for promotion. The French ambassador in Beirut, René Ala, is also in a state of shock. When the Marseille investigators arrived to arrest Labourdette, the ambassador begged them not to take him away, saying that the security chief was 'essential to the safety of the embassy' due to his 'exceptional local contacts'. How right the ambassador was.

Not all the smuggled weapons were sold to the Mediterranean *milieu*. Some went to Paris where a retired policeman called Alain André distributed them to 'private collectors' who were also members of the Association Bagheera, a group of 2,000 former members of the 11th Shock Regiment. The 11th Shock was a cloak-and-dagger unit, specializing in booby-trap bombs and questionable methods of interrogation, which became notorious during the Algerian war. The regiment was disbanded by General de Gaulle but reformed by General Imbot, then head of the DGSE (secret service). Its veterans now form an employment pool for the DGSE, which is organized within the defence ministry.

The arms-smuggling scandal has come at a wonderful time for the French press since the whole country is on the point of closing down for its annual holidays. Last week Jacques Toubon, a Gaullist deputy, and one-time right-hand man to the former prime minister Jacques Chirac, wrote an article in *Le Monde* in which he referred to the Socialist government's 'banana republic habits'. He listed these as an amnesty for crooked politicians, numerous attempts to put pressure on the courts, insider-trading scandals involving friends of President Mitterrand, the activities of M. Mitterrand's son in Africa (where he is a presidential adviser) including receipt of a cheque for £15,000, his explanation for which no one believed, illegal telephone-tapping and now the national police force covered with shame.

'Where,' asked M. Toubon, 'is the country heading?'

He was answered by the foreign minister, Roland Dumas, who said that he would 'not be astonished if the arms-smuggling investigation led to some surprising revelations which would cause M. Toubon's remarks to be stuffed down his own throat.' This Delphic prophecy might well be a reference to the knowledge Jean-Claude Labourdette has concerning the secret negotiations between the Lebanese hostage-takers and the Chirac government between 1985 and 1988.

Some members of the present government are convinced that Jacques Chirac and his former minister of the interior, Charles Pasqua, mishandled those negotiations so badly that they provoked the 1986 Paris bombing campaign, in which thirteen people died and 255 were wounded, and the bombing of the DC10 over the Sahara Desert last September which killed 171.

They have never said this in public, but they say it in private and they would dearly like to be able to prove it. Meanwhile, Labourdette's prosecution will be conducted by officials of the ministry of justice. Among those highly interested in his defence will be the Middle-East section of the ministry of foreign affairs. And officials of the ministry of defence will be looking on anxiously. Labourdette should not feel too worried – as long as he remembers the food-taster.

July, 1990

─────

The police in Paris have just broken up a ring of forgers who specialized in official documents. They were operating from a printing works in the 11th *arrondissement* under the leadership of Bouboule, known as such from his impressive girth and short stature, who is a veteran of the 'French Connection' Marseille heroin affair of twenty years ago. It is practically *de rigueur* for police officers announcing an important arrest to mention that one of their prisoners was formerly part of the French Connection. No serious criminal dossier is complete without it.

When he was arrested, Bouboule was sitting on, or perhaps rolling off, a mountain of 25,000 false identity cards, 4,000 false French entry visas, 2,000 false driving licences, 3,000 false vehicle log-books, 500 false electricity bills, and three false police cards. The street value of his hoard was estimated at around 50 million francs (£5 million). The police, who are trained not to jump to conclusions, were prepared to say that Bouboule might have been taking an interest in the illegal immigration market.

This Aladdin's cave of forged official papers is an oblique tribute to the importance of the identity document in France and it illustrates the power of French bureaucracy and the consequent helplessness of the citizen. It is impossible in France to lease a flat, or obtain a library ticket, or have one's children admitted to school, without producing a thick folder of official documents. French persons wishing to establish that they are French but lacking an identity card would have to produce a sworn declaration of citizenship, full copy of their birth certificate, their parents' marriage certificate, full copies of all certificates relating to the applicant's marriages, divorces and remarriages, ministerial declarations that the applicant has not previously renounced French nationality, and three documents establishing the applicant's permanent address in France.

And if any of the above documents were in a foreign language, it would have to be accompanied by an official translation, and if any of the above documents were issued in a foreign country it would have to be accompanied by a French consular stamp. And that is just the list you have to produce if there are no hitches. Hence the street value of Bouboule's hoard.

This is madness, of course, particularly when one might just as well have gone to Bouboule instead of to the town hall in the first place. But in France, authority is a slave to this need for documents. Documents equal information and information equals power. Perhaps the most extraordinary thing about the situation is not the French government's lust for information but the willingness of the French people to continue gratifying it. It is odd, for instance, that anyone in France who is either important or crooked should continue to use the telephone.

Generally speaking, the telephone service in France is a model of efficiency. A foreign journalist working in Paris was therefore surprised last year when his new telephone line failed to function after a few days' use. An engineer called twice but still it would not work. It failed to ring, or it rang constantly or it was in some mysterious way hooked up to his other line. The supervisor then sent a third deputation, two engineers who were youthful, athletic and alert. They spent some time working in the junction box in the cellar of the building. They then re-entered the journalist's office and mounted an obvious pantomime in which they claimed the problem was simply that one of the telephones had not been plugged in.

The journalist pointed out that they were fiddling with the wrong telephone, the one that had worked all along. But after their visit, the new telephone did indeed work. The journalist concluded, as is traditional, that he had just met two plain-clothes policemen who had sorted out a botched attempt to tap his new line. His colleagues concluded, as is also traditional, that he was suffering from overwork.

After a while people become inoculated against telephone tapping stories. Those who complain of having their lines tapped are regarded as paranoid, or self-important. When one considers the mass of trivial or irrelevant information exchanged most of the time by telephone, the idea seems ridiculous. Impossible to imagine anyone prepared to spend their life wading through that stuff. Not even with modern techniques such as recorders that operate only when the telephone is in use or, even better, only when certain key words are spoken.

But in France there are such people and a surprising amount is known about their working day. They are employed by the GIC (Groupement Interministeriel de Contrôle) which was set up by President de Gaulle during the Algerian war. Every morning the spooks gather in a vast cellar beneath Napoleon's Tomb in the Invalides in central Paris. Each spook has his or her own desk and each is equipped with an audio-typist's headphones and pedal, a pen and a pad.

They spend the day writing out, in longhand, any interesting parts of the tape-recorded conversations placed in front of them. For urgent inquiries they can go into the room where the tape recordings are made and listen in directly. Their notes are made on white, pink or blue paper depending on whether the information is considered of general, economic or political interest. Most of the spooks are serving or retired military personnel. They all have to sign the French equivalent of the Official Secrets Act.

According to one recent estimate, on any particular day 75,000 telephone lines are being tapped in France. One in every 500 citizens is tapped every year. Every journalist and every politician is tapped routinely. These estimates have been made by Georges Moréas, a former head of the police Serious Crimes Squad, and he was referring only to the taps that had been legally installed by an examining magistrate or a civil servant. Since there are eight separate police forces in France empowered to use these taps or *zozors*, and since telephone tapping has, according to ex-chief superintendent Moréas, become the first means of obtaining police information, many more taps are certainly in use.

The European Court of Human Rights in Strasbourg has rebuked France for its absence of laws on the subject of telephone tapping, but here in Paris no one seems to have noticed. This year the GIC was awarded a budget increase of £2.5 million, as well as fifty extra spooks and 400 square metres of additional space under Napoleon's tomb.

In the battle to be top city in Europe, Paris seems to hold first place for telephone tapping.

September, 1990

———

There was an unfortunate incident on the Paris Métro last Monday evening. A member of the GIPR, the élite sharp-shooters of the Transport Security Police (SORATP), shot a male person of West Indian appearance who seemed to be harassing a passenger at Oberkampf station in east Paris. Subsequent inquiries revealed the bad news, or good news, that the man was not a mugger but another plain-clothes member of SORATP. The good news, or bad news, was that the sharp-shooter was not a very good shot and had inflicted only a scratch on his colleague.

Parisians read this news item, '*flic* shoots *flic*', with only mild surprise, but they were interested to learn that there was such a thing as the GIPR. They knew about the PJ and the DST, the DGSE and the Gendarmerie, the Douanes and the PAF, the DNEF and the DPSD, the GIGN and the GIPN, the RG and the CRS and the PM; but they did not know about the GIPR. Now they do. There is a fourteenth bunch of *flics* who can't shoot straight but who open fire anyway.

51

Everyone has their favourite, but for many, in the land of the police and the parallel police and the shadow parallel police, the RG or Renseignements Généraux is king.

The PJ is what in Britain is known as the CID. The DST is what we once called MI5, and the DGSE is what we once called MI6. The Gendarmerie is a splendid body of men with no British equivalent. Although they act as the police force for most of the country they are controlled by the ministry of defence, an unusual state of affairs in a West European democracy today, but there it is.

The Douanes (Customs) are not to be sneezed at either. They are armed, naturally, and their jurisdiction is confined to within sixty miles of every international port. But since this includes airports it gives them most of France, too.

The PAF (border police) are restricted to the borders, but near the borders it is as well to bow three times and turn out your turn-ups if so requested. Anyone who meets the DPSD is either very unlucky or has hit the jackpot in the I-Spy competition since they are military security and almost never emerge from their bunkers.

If your *flic* belongs to the DNEF you will need to have hit the jackpot, for that is the inquiry branch of the ministry of finance – in other words the tax police, oh dear, oh dear.

Leaving the identities of the GIPN, the FAR, the CRS and the PM to another day, let us return to the RG because one of those working for this most mysterious of all government bodies has just got itself into a bit of a pickle.

It started with the disappearance of a homosexual Protestant clergyman who lived in northern Paris and ran the Centre of Christ the Liberator of Sexual Minorities. On 19 July Pastor Joseph Doucé was dragged from his home by three unknown men and has not been seen since. It was subsequently discovered that at the time of his disappearance he was the subject of a police inquiry and was suspected of using his organization as a cover for a paedophile vice racket involving a number of prominent people. Curiously, the police chosen for this inquiry were not the vice squad but the Renseignements Généraux.

The RG operates from within the ministry of the interior. Its main function is, as its name suggests, to provide the government of the day with 'general information', but it also acts as the minister's private intelligence service.

A police inspector working for the RG, called Jean-Marc Dufourg, was ordered to investigate Pastor Doucé, and tried to recruit a former left-wing extremist now living in the elegant Paris suburb of Sèvres to infiltrate the Church of Christ the Liberator of Sexual Minorities. While persuading this ex-lefty to do his bit for his country, Inspector Dufourg apparently fired a shot in the lefty's bedroom ceiling. Dufourg was recently charged with misuse of his police firearm.

Two weeks after the bedroom-ceiling incident Pastor Doucé was kidnapped. Dufourg is suspected of being one of the kidnappers. While being questioned about the pastor's disappearance, he told the examining magistrate that the RG was not really inquiring into a suspected vice racket but was trying to set one up – on behalf of the government. The idea was to blackmail various prominent people by the use of prostitutes and rent boys.

On Thursday *Le Monde* named two of these prominent people. One was Pierre Arpaillange, the minister of justice who had just resigned for political reasons unconnected with the Doucé affair.

The other was Philippe Guilhaume, director of two government television chains, Antenne 2 and FR3. *Le Monde* added that Dufourg's allegations appeared to be highly unlikely.

Dufourg's story may be fantastic but he appears to know enough to be a potential embarrassment. He was unexpectedly released from custody earlier this week, despite the opposition of the public prosecutor. According to his lawyer, Maître Jacques Vergès, he had not even applied for bail since there seemed so little chance of success.

Next day the minister of the interior, Pierre Joxe, made a statement in the National Assembly about the mystery of Pastor Doucé. In it he said: 'The police have never received orders in breach of the law or their honour. On the contrary, everything which concerns the private life of public men, union leaders, journalists and lawyers is considered sacred.' At this point the spluttering noises from the press gallery were said to have been audible from the floor of the Assembly.

One of the prominent men named in *Le Monde*, Philippe Guil-haume, complained last January, six months before the disappearance of Pastor Doucé, of efforts being made by 'people in power' to destabilize him. Although he is head of the government's television channels, he is not a government supporter. He is a right-winger who was appointed in 1989 by the CSA, the independent governing body of French television. His appointment was deeply unpopular with the government, and in particular with the minister of culture, Jack Lang.

M. Guilhaume said he was the target of a whispering campaign. Each week, he said, new rumours were being circulated concerning his 'personality' and his private financial interests. He complained in particular that police inspectors from the RG had been making indiscreet inquiries among his staff about his past.

Inspector Dufourg remains suspended from duty. Only he knows whether he should consult a psychotherapist or a plastic surgeon.

October, 1990

━━━

In an unusual public relations operation, the French government decided last week to arrange a press visit to its secret telephone tapping centre in an underground bunker in front of Napoleon's tomb in Paris's fashionable 7th *arrondissement*. Having decided that telephone tapping is both highly disreputable and highly effective, the government has chosen to make it less disreputable rather than lose the benefit of it. A bill to regulate telephone tapping and bring it up to EC standards is now before the National Assembly.

The bunker is occupied by the GIC (Groupement Interministeriel de Contrôle) and we now know that its entrance is by the corner of the boulevard Latour-Maubourg and the Place des Invalides. From the outside it resembles the entrance to an underground car park. But an automatic barrier manned by a police guard bars the way to confused motorists. Inside, the gleaming banks of automatic machinery resemble the control panels of a power station. Lights blink, little wheels click and whirr. The GIC is commanded by an army colonel and even the metal wastepaper baskets are polished. In the entrance hall stands a public call box so that the state spooks can make private calls at their own expense.

According to the colonel, 1,092 telephones are currently submitted to 'administrative' taps for an average of four months each. None of these taps has anything to do with routine police work or criminal investigation. They are ordered by the prime minister's office or the ministries of defence or the interior in the public interest for reasons which remain *secrets d'Etat*. A retired head of the police serious crimes squad recently estimated that if police telephone taps ordered by examining magistrates were included, the annual total would rise to 75,000.

In the GIC, each call is automatically recorded, stored and then transcribed by one of the 360 spooks who work with headphones and notepads. These civil servants, unlike most others in France, have never gone on strike, which seems a pity. Maybe they enjoy their work too much. The machinery to record the calls is installed in the deepest basement, the *salle des écoutes*. The transcribing is carried out in the *salles de lecture* where the sun shines through the skylights in the roof of the bunker.

On the grassy banks around the skylights, the tourists who have just descended from the bus from Orly airport sun themselves. Nearby, the children of the Republic bowl hoops or toy with their mistresses, unaware that their future telephone conversations will be transcribed in the vaults beneath. Down the road in the National Assembly, the *députés* debate the new bill and gaze nervously at the minister of the day, wondering how much he knows.

June, 1991

The French word *la gégène* is a curiosity, indicating as it does something which, in France, has never officially been seen. It means the little engine attached to electrodes allegedly used for torturing members of the FLN during the Algerian war. Last year the word *gégène* became less of a curiosity when the former paratroop commander General Jacques Massu, now aged eighty and tired of thirty years of pussy-footing around, suddenly said on French radio that as a matter of fact, yes, his men had used the *gégène* against the FLN in 1958.

Massu is himself the root of another French word which never made the dictionary and may even have disappeared shortly after it was coined, *massuisme*, the doctrine that torture is a legitimate military necessity in times of crisis. The general expounded his doctrine shortly after the end of the Algerian war, although at the time he was a little more circumspect about the details.

But on the radio last year he came right out with it, explaining –
according to the summary printed in *L'Evénement du Jeudi* – that
there had been torture, but it was not real torture, besides which
one tortured as little as possible, and it was mostly done by the
police rather than the army, apart from which the army had every
reason to use torture, and anyway he hadn't started it, that had been
his colleague General Bigeard, the most decorated soldier in France.

The French army is one of the central institutions of the Republic
but it is endowed with a sense of drama which places it apart from
the others. There is a history of military intervention in political
affairs in France; it is not authorized in the constitution but the
constitution has been rewritten several times as a result of it. The
present Republic was after all founded by a retired general acting in
the shadow of a threatened *coup d'Etat*. So when a field commander
like General Massu develops a private theory of military ethics,
nobody is very surprised.

There was another echo of this ancient drama only last week when
Le Monde carried the headline '45 generals called to order after
signing an election petition in favour of M. Chirac'. '45 generals
called to order' presents a nice picture of the minister of defence. A
parade of forty-five generals has probably not been seen outside the
Soviet Union since 1945, although, sadly for the photographers,
Jean-Pierre Chevènement issued his reprimand on this occasion by
registered letter. None the less his targets included a former chief of
the combined general staff and a former head of the army, both still
on the reserve list.

The generals' offence, according to M. Chevènement, was to
have signed an election petition saying that M. Mitterrand's 'ambiguous and contradictory views on defence posed a risk to national
security . . . which could only be assured by the election of M.
Chirac'. Last week M. Chevènement said that it had been a breach
of the generals' professional duty to cast doubt on the president of
the Republic in this way. 'National defence is neither left nor right,
but French,' he wrote. If it happened again, they would be
discharged.

Between the lines of this rebuke one can read another story
written not so long ago, a story of a military coup carried out by
General Massu's paratroopers in Corsica, followed by orders to
trade union leaders to halt any trains heading for Paris if the paras

moved to the mainland. (One of the surprised trade union leaders is supposed to have remarked that the paratroops did not usually attack by train.) As the story continued, foreign legionnaires were to dynamite their own barracks, 2,000 paratroops illegally assembled in the forests outside Paris were to be told to go home by the gendarmes, four generals were to be arrested and tried for treason, and one officer, Lieutenant-Colonel Jean-Marie Bastien-Thiry was actually to be shot in the fortress at Vincennes, after failing to assassinate General de Gaulle. Those events of thirty years ago are remembered today. The political views of the military governor of Paris are still carefully examined before his appointment.

Fortunately perhaps for M. Chevènement, neither General Massu nor General Bigeard signed the petition in favour of M. Chirac. It is a considerable nuisance in France to receive a registered letter: it frequently means a special visit to the post office, which in turn means queuing up for hours before being told to try another counter. If General Bigeard, now aged seventy-two, who led the suicidal final counter-attack at Dien Bien Phu, had been made to queue up at the post office merely to receive a damp squib from young Chevènement, there is no foretelling the consequences.

He might have led a final airborne assault on the saluting stand at next Thursday's Bastille Day military parade.

July, 1988

In January 1977 there was an attempted *coup d'Etat* in Benin, West Africa. An unmarked aircraft landed at the international airport at Cotonou and disgorged a party of ninety white and black mercenaries who were heavily armed. They proceeded to attack the presidential palace and stroll around the streets of the capital city shooting up cars, at the same time sipping lemonade, smoking Gauloises and shouting instructions to the terrified citizens in French. But Ahmed Kerekou, the Marxist president, was guarded by a North Korean battalion and the mercenaries were repulsed. They climbed back into their plane and disappeared into the sky leaving six dead bodies behind them. Their identity remained a mystery.

The raid led to the brief imprisonment of a novelist, the late Bruce Chatwin, who had just arrived to gather material for a book and was suspected of being one of the raiders because of his khaki trousers. He reported at the time that rumours suggested that the mercenaries were either Czech or East German, or had been recruited in Paris by political exiles.

Now, in the fourteenth criminal court in Paris, the truth about this event is emerging. Relatives of the dead Benin soldiers are suing two French former mercenaries who have been charged with 'criminal conspiracy'. Only one of the men is in court, the other, Bob Denard, the supposed leader, is in South Africa and has sent a message saying that he never received his summons. The mercenaries were part of a plot to replace President Kerekou with a pro-Western figure. M. Denard's lawyer does not deny the facts but argues that another important conspirator is absent from the dock – the French government.

September, 1991

═══

In Marseille a man has beaten a Yorkshire terrier to death because it peed on his clothes-line once too often. For this the human has received a one-month suspended prison sentence. Both the terrier and its executioner lived in a tower block in the city. The dog lived on the balcony above, and the problem with the washing-line arose only when the Mistral was blowing.

The man did not plead the Mistral in his defence: the days when it was accepted that this wind could drive men mad seem to have passed. The Mistral is apparently now only capable of causing nervous incontinence in a dog.

Meanwhile, in south-eastern France, a severed head was observed on the conveyor belt in the refuse disposal plant at La Tronche, in the Isère *département*. Two operatives watching the belt, not normally a particularly interesting task, saw this human head moving steadily from left to right (or possibly from right to left: history does not relate).

Their comments are also unrecorded, but it seems that if two men in charge of a conveyor belt which usually carries old mattresses and plastic bags are suddenly presented with a human head, they react more slowly than usual.

By the time they stopped the conveyor belt the head had moved on; into a tank containing 500 tonnes of rubbish. Firemen were called, dressed up in frogmen's suits and lowered into the tank. They groped around for three days before the search was called off. This was either the severed head that got away, or a joint hallucination. It is a sign of the times that in such circumstances no one has yet mentioned the name of Jacques Foccart.

In the anniversary year of General de Gaulle – 100 years since his birth, twenty years since his death, and fifty years since he called the free French to arms – the only false note to date is the publication of a book about Jacques Foccart, said to have been one of the most powerful and mysterious figures of the Gaullist years.

Foccart never sought the limelight or bore a grandiose title. His only notable public post was as secretary-general for African affairs, which meant that he advised de Gaulle on everything concerning the post-colonial French African empire, and also on what was then still called Indo-China. But Foccart was credited with enormous powers, and his reputation spread far beyond France.

At the time of the Biafran war in 1967 it was believed in London that Foccart was behind the whole thing; that he had inspired the uprising in the eastern region of Nigeria, that he was arming it, and that his aim was to set up a French puppet state which would then enjoy Nigeria's vast oil resources. The Biafrans used some mercenary pilots, and it only needed one of these men to light up a Gauloise for the whole Foccart theory to spring to life.

In France Foccart was known as the 'chief parallel policeman'. Starting with a career in the wartime Resistance he had built up a private secret service known as the SAC, which was at the general's disposal and played an important role in bringing de Gaulle to power during the Algerian crisis. It was assumed that a man like Foccart carried on after the war very much as though it had never ended. For assassinations, a bomb in the luggage hold, *agents provocateurs* or the odd severed head, the *barbouzes* took the blame. Foccart was an ultra-Gaullist, the enemies were de Gaulle's political opponents and, occasionally, *les Anglo-Saxons*. A legend grew up about the small, bald man with pointed ears, and it seems it was not all false.

The *barbouzes*, a lawless secret police force, certainly existed, and Foccart was prominent among them. A new book, *L'Homme de l'Ombre*, by Pierre Péan (published by Fayard), suggests that the SAC is still in existence today, twenty years after its founder died.

Foccart, too, is still in existence. He no longer carries out his regular parachute training at Cercottes, near Orléans (he is seventy-seven), but he spends a lot of time fishing and sailing in the West Indies, and of course he has objected to this book.

Among other things, the book reveals that Foccart was something of a mystery even to de Gaulle. It claims that in 1966 the Gaullist minister of the interior, Roger Frey, ordered the prefect of the Mayenne *département*, where Foccart was born, to conduct an inquiry into his family origins. This provided the unexpected information that he may have been descended from Napoleon and from the Grimaldi family of Monaco by the illicit union of a priest and a nun. Foccart strongly objects to these suggestions, and a court has ordered that a note referring to his objections be inserted in every copy of the book. But the court has passed no judgment on another story in the book, which raises the possibility that before Foccart became a fearless member of the Resistance he was involved in collaboration.

At a time when wood and charcoal were at a premium in Occupied France because of the scarcity of other fuels, Foccart sold these commodities to the German army through an organization called Todt. He charged such high prices that in August 1943 the Germans put him in prison at St Malo. After a few days they let him out, but only after he had paid them a million francs. Foccart joined the Resistance a week later.

After the war all the witnesses to this episode disappeared. One of them, François Van Aerden, formerly Belgian consul in Le Havre, was shot in a ditch fifteen days after the Liberation. A police report stated that Van Aerden's body contained bullets of both German and British origin, and that he had probably been shot because he knew too much about the Todt trading organization.

The fact that Foccart has not objected to any of this material – but has instead restricted his complaint to the claim that he may be the son of a priest and a nun – suggests that, as ever, he is dancing to a different tune.

December, 1990

In Arles last week a barrister who had been defending a number of people accused of theft was found on leaving the court room to have concealed under his robes a valuable eighteenth-century painting, which he had removed from the wall of the court. He, too, is now facing charges of theft. Nothing odd about that. In Charleville-Mézières a retired public prosecutor, noted at the Ardennes Assize Court for the severity of the sentences he would demand, has been in prison for the last five months charged with bank robbery.

Before entering the bank Jean Holzer, chevalier of the Legion of Honour, colonel of infantry (retired), pulled a nylon stocking over his head like they do in the movies. As anyone who has ever walked around wearing a nylon stocking can tell you, it is difficult to see out. But M. Holzer found his way through the doors of the Société Générale at Châtillon-Coligny, his local bank, and groped his way over to the counter, where one of the bank clerks offered him a roll of notes worth 15,000 francs. He then left the bank, removed the nylon stocking, climbed into his car and drove home, that is, back to his manor house at Denisière. The gendarmes, following up their clues, knocked at his door one hour later. The roll of banknotes was still in the car, where M. Holzer had left it.

It must be quite tiring spending a lifetime prosecuting people, demanding severe sentences, working oneself up into a cold fury about the misdeeds of others, pinning the wretched criminals down as they make their transparently obvious attempts to disguise their guilt, and at the end of the day, has it been a life well spent? Is the world a juster place?

One sometimes gets the impression that Shakespeare has more devoted readers in France than in England. Perhaps M. Holzer looked back on his career and remembered Lear. 'A man may see how this world goes with no eyes. Look with thine ears: see how yond justice rails upon yond simple thief. Hark, in thine ear: change places; and, handy-dandy, which is the justice, which is the thief?' That is the question they are asking today in Charleville-Mézières.

Early reports suggest that M. Holzer will plead poverty but I am sure his defence counsel can do better than that. Holzer is a veteran of the Algerian war so there is always the possibility of the 'delayed reaction defence'. Or perhaps he was reliving some mission undertaken on government service. There may be evidence of earlier instability. It is said that while still a public prosecutor he once startled the court reporter from the local paper, *L'Ardennais*, by yelling 'Freeze!' and whipping a revolver out from under his robes.

M. Holzer will be tried in the autumn at Orléans Assizes where the public prosecutor will face the unusual task of setting about one of his former colleagues. It will not be a pushover. The barrister-art collector of Arles should be disbarred, if only for misusing his robe. He should know that if a barrister wants to acquire a valuable art collection he does not go around unhooking pictures from the wall. He becomes an expert in wills and testaments. The man is a disgrace to his profession. But, for some reason, I like the sound of M. Holzer, and maybe the jury will, too.

August, 1990

===

'Congratulate yourselves that you are not British' the French prime minister, Michel Rocard, said this week. He was talking to a meeting of public servants about their pay and suggesting that if they had been working for Mrs Thatcher they would have more to complain about. Still, it was an unusually modest way of congratulating oneself on being French, and M. Rocard can normally do better than that.

And there are reasons for the French to congratulate themselves on being French. The whole country is feeling proud this morning of Laure Dussard, a 76-year-old lady who normally lives in a magnificent *appartement* in the rue Félix Faure in the 15th *arrondissement*, which is one of the most expensive districts in Paris.

Mme Dussard is a very wealthy woman who has a criminal record fifty pages long that dates back to 1934, when she was twenty years old. She may be approaching the evening of her days, but there are still a few more pages of her life story left to be written by the clerks in the criminal records department and this morning she is 'on the run' – if that is the correct phrase for the movements of a person aged seventy-six who is avoiding the police.

The Paris fraud squad would like to talk to her about 'organic water', a remarkable discovery she made in her laboratory at

Berkeley University, California, where she was known as 'Dr Forbes'. Last year representatives of Dorlyl SA, a subsidiary of Shell, were fortunate enough to meet Dr Forbes and heard about her amazing invention. She provided them with Japanese manufacturing patents and gave a lucid account of her work to the Shell scientists.

The men from Dorlyl managed to persuade her to sell them the French manufacturing rights. Working closely with her team of international lawyers, they drew up a contract whereby they took the French option and she received a first payment of 1.5 million francs (£156,250). What a bargain! Unfortunately since cashing the cheque she has disappeared. She has not been seen in the rue Félix Faure, nor do they know anything about 'organic water' at Berkeley. Needless to say the Japanese patents were forged.

The details of 'organic water' are not being published, perhaps to save the blushes of the Shell scientists, but its name bears some resemblance to a discredited series of experiments carried out a few years ago at the Institut Pasteur which claimed to provide a scientific basis for homoeopathic medicine. The links with Japan and California were also well-chosen. The mixture of academic respectability and enormous amounts of money is just the right formula to impress scientists and shows all the plausibility which has characterized Madame Dussard's financial puffballs over the years.

There are senior members of the Paris fraud squad who have grown old in trying to keep tabs on Laure Dussard. When they joined up as young men she already had an impressively long record. They say she has become a charming old lady, and a nicer, gentler, more trusting person you could not hope to meet.

But the Dorlyl affair is not the only one they want to discuss with her. There is also the case of an elderly Parisian banker – previously considered a man of the world – who was recently persuaded to lend more than 1 million francs to a lady whose description closely resembles that of this delicious old thing. And there is a fifteen-month prison sentence outstanding on a third matter. Even as you read this, somewhere in Europe, perhaps in Bath or Salzburg, some bumbling male is probably opening the door for her or lifting her case into a luggage rack. Let us hope for his sake that he is stony broke. If not, he soon will be.

One day Mme Dussard will be called to give a final account of herself, and it would be sad to think that while she was pulling a final con trick on the recording angel there was no one left below to carry on her work. Evelyn Emin, the managing director of a Lyon property company, is not quite the right person, but her reaction to a recent problem she had with the police shows that France has reason to congratulate itself on her too.

Mme Emin's property development firm has been accused, no doubt falsely, of making illegal payments into political funds. She was arrested and held for questioning. This can be an uncomfortable experience in any country, but at least Mme Emin has put hers to good use. She has prepared a memo for other property developers placed in the same predicament. It is called 'How to withstand police interrogation for forty-eight hours', which is the usual time the police can hold you in France before they have to charge you or let you go.

'You will be held for forty-eight hours,' she notes, 'without any contact with the outside world. Your only right is to call a doctor. *Do not hesitate to do so.* In theory you have a right to silence, but exercising it leads to inconvenience. Instead, co-operate in an intelligent manner although you mustn't just say the first thing that comes into your head. Remember – you have to hold out for forty-eight hours. Pretend you have a headache. Say you are in no state to reply and make sure that this remark is entered in the statement. Don't tell them everything at once, spin it out. Refuse to sign anything until you have had time to read it carefully. Then ask for a few hours' rest before re-reading it and signing it.

'Make regular references to your poor health. Have no scruples about claiming to suffer from a heart condition and make sure this too is mentioned in the statement. *Counter-attack.* Threaten to lay a complaint of extortion against any political parties which claim to have received payments. Say that such parties are your habitual enemies. At the same time claim to have good contacts in all the main political groups.'

June, 1990

The judges are threatening to go on strike again. Last month they marched out of court and massed behind the tall railings of the

Palais de Justice in Paris wearing their long black robes, silk stockings and white neckerchiefs. Then, chanting and waving not banners but legal scrolls, they set off for the residence of Michel Rocard, the prime minister. 'Rocard,' they shouted, 'you're stuffed. The Law has taken to the streets.' ('*Rocard, t'es foutu, la Justice est dans la rue.*') The shopkeepers on the route of the march put up the shutters as though it was the usual mob of students passing by.

Judges are like everyone else, they want more money, but in France they are more like everyone else than they are in England. They have trade unions – several, of various political hues. You become a judge just as you become a civil servant, by passing examinations. You start as a junior judge and if you behave yourself you end up as a senior judge. Every year the grandest judges of the Court of Appeal mark their colleagues on a scale of six up to one for 'strength of character', 'personal authority', 'industry', 'professional relations', 'public relations', 'devotion to duty', and 'common sense and judgement'.

It is not a good idea for the ambitious young judge to get six for any of these. The independence of the judiciary in France is guaranteed by statute, but you gain no advantage for 'ignoring the wishes of those in power'. In fact if you want promotion you have to be extremely sensitive to the hints that are occasionally handed down in politically sensitive cases. ('Devotion to duty.') But you also have to make it look as though you have reached your decision without receiving any hints. ('Public relations.')

The man who is now sitting in judgment on the judges' demand for more cash is the minister of justice, Henri Nallet. Until last month M. Nallet, who is not a lawyer, was minister of agriculture. When he was minister of agriculture M. Nallet's principal task was to tell the French farmers that they could not have more money, and the judges suspect that he is preparing to read the same speech to them.

They are not pleased about this because 1991 was supposed to be the 'Year of Justice'. That was the slogan chosen by the prime minister to appease judges who were demanding more cash. But in the latest budget Justice has been awarded an increase of only 6.7 per cent, while Culture got an extra 15.2 per cent and the Environment won 43 per cent. The judges, who have all been taught to read and count, have noticed these figures and M. Nallet is likely to be faced with a crowd of men and women at least as angry as the peasants. For once, fear of the annual report may not be enough to keep the judges in line.

The minister's position is even more delicate since he himself may shortly be coming up for trial in a vulgar affair of misuse of election funds. Just after he was appointed minister of justice M. Nallet was accused of being responsible for falsified entries in the official accounts for the 1988 presidential election campaign, when he was treasurer of the fund raised for President Mitterrand. M. Nallet denied any impropriety and in particular denied that he was mentioned in the official record of the preliminary criminal investigation. The minister has recently agreed this denial was untrue and in the normal course of events M. Nallet would now be questioned by the examining magistrate in charge of preparing the case (who is a judge), and in due course, if the evidence was sufficient, would be charged. This would be awkward for any minister of justice, but particularly so for a minister preparing to tell his judges that he is stony broke.

And the judges have another card up their ermine sleeves. Judgment was reached this week in a libel action brought by one of France's most unorthodox bureaucrats against the weekly news magazine *L'Evénement du Jeudi*. The bureaucrat is Jean-Christophe Mitterrand, son of the president of the Republic, who is employed as his father's special counsellor on Africa. Before that M. Mitterrand Jnr was foreign editor of the national press agency AFP. As an experienced journalist his appointment at AFP was uncontroversial. But nobody has been able to discover the grounds for his appointment as a presidential adviser. His eminence as a national expert on Africa had previously been well concealed. And the appointment is not a sinecure. As a presidential adviser J.-C. Mitterrand has almost as much influence over policy as the foreign minister.

The libel action followed an article in which *L'Evénement du Jeudi* suggested that Jean-Christophe Mitterrand was known in francophone Africa as *Papamadit* ('Daddy said') and alleged that he 'prefers the rowdy charm of the red-light districts of Lomé and Libreville to the meticulous consideration of African political questions'.

J.-C. Mitterrand did not take these wild accusations on the nose. He was highly insulted. In court the magazine argued that the article was true but the judge decided that 'on the evidence, it was

gravely defamatory' and awarded damages of 80,000 francs
(£8,250), a large award for France. *L'Evénement du Jeudi* is appealing
against the verdict on the grounds that as 'a person holding public
office' J.-C. Mitterrand should have brought his case in the criminal
court where both sides can call witnesses. The action was actually
heard in the civil court with evidence confined to opposing counsels'
statements. The magazine's lawyers are now arguing that *Papamadit*
demanded his damages on the grounds that the libel was an affair of
state but now refuses to go into the criminal court on the grounds
that he is merely a private individual.

The matter will be decided next month by judges whose independence, as we have seen, is guaranteed by statute. So far the Mitterrand
case has been treated with the consideration one would expect in a
country that has not completely forgotten the importance of personal and family connections. But how far can you trust hungry
judges? M. Nallet may have to throw them a crust after all.

November, 1990

According to Jean-Paul Huchon, M. Rocard's private secretary, the
much-publicized kiss the former prime minister gave Mme Cresson
as he left his official residence, the Matignon, was just playing to the
gallery. M. Rocard's departure was bitterly resented, but he did not
want it to look like that in front of the cameras.

'Of course he kissed the incoming prime minister,' said an
irritable M. Huchon. 'It's a woman. Yes? So you kiss it. NO?'

May, 1991

3. OUTSIDE THE PANTHÉON

The highpoint of the life of Jean-Louis Tixier-Vignancour came in 1962 when, against all odds, he saved the mutinous General Raoul Salan (head of the OAS 'Secret Army') from an expected death sentence for treason. With his deep voice, crumpled face, huge nose and ears and streak of cruelty, Maître Tixier-Vignancour willingly symbolized all that was most demonic about France's extreme-right.

After a brilliant student career at the Sorbonne he was called to the Paris bar in 1926. He started in political life as he meant to go on, sympathizing with Action Française and making his first political gesture at the age of twenty-six as one of the threatening, right-wing mob who were driven back by police gunfire when they tried to storm the Chamber of Deputies in February 1934.

In July 1940, following France's military defeat and occupation by the German army, Tixier-Vignancour was one of the majority of deputies who abolished the Third Republic and voted plenary powers to Marshal Pétain. He was appointed to the post of 'deputy secretary-general of information' in the Vichy regime but resigned in January 1941. He was briefly interned by the Germans in Tunis, then liberated by the Americans. He ended the war holding both the Croix de Guerre and the Pétainist decoration, the Francisque. In 1945 he was arrested by the new government and tried for treason. This charge could not be proved but the military tribunal condemned him to ten years loss of civil and political rights.

He emerged from this period of enforced reflection with a deep loathing for General de Gaulle and when he returned to politics in 1955 he was one of the architects of the revival of the extreme-right, using the popular cause of Algérie Française as a rallying point. When those who fomented civil war in Algeria were brought to trial, Tixier-Vignancour was the natural choice to defend them.

Four of his clients were executed, including Lieutenant Degueldre, head of the Delta Commando, and Colonel Jean-Marie Bastien-Thiry who nearly succeeded in blowing up General de Gaulle and his wife at Le Petit-Clamart in 1962. As their advocate, Tixier-Vignancour had to accompany these four officers to the firing squad, thus witnessing a fate which might have been his own in 1945. He was appalled by the experience. He subsequently popularized his political movement, the Rassemblement National with the memorable slogan – 'Against de Gaulle and Communism'.

During the treason trials Tixier-Vignancour became notorious for a tactic known as 'the defence of blackmail' when he repeatedly threatened to call eminent witnesses such as General de Gaulle and the prime minister Michel Debré, hinting that they too were involved in criminal plots. He pulled this trick once too often against Debré, and was disconcerted one morning to see the prime minister sitting in the witness box, waiting to be cross-examined. Since Tixier-Vignancour did not actually have any questions to ask him he decided to bluff it out to the end. 'You are Michel Debré,' he said in his most sardonic tones. 'That is correct.' 'You are,' (even more menacingly) 'the prime minister of France?' 'Yes.' Long pause. 'Thank you very much. No more questions.' End of the defence of blackmail.

Tixier-Vignancour's success in restricting General Salan's punishment to life imprisonment in 1968 so angered President de Gaulle that he considered resignation. By then 'Tixier' had taken his anti-Gaullist crusade to the point of running himself as a presidential candidate. Without any proper party organization he fought a brilliant campaign in 1965, canvassing the French throughout August 'on every beach from Dunkirk to Menton'. He was eliminated in the first round, coming fourth behind de Gaulle, Mitterrand and Jean Lecanuet. He promptly consigned his 5 per cent of the vote to M. Mitterrand in the second round, a gift which the Socialist candidate happily accepted.

With the disappearance of Tixier-Vignancour one of the last representatives of a distinctive line of French politicians seems to have come to an end. It can be traced directly back to the anti-Dreyfusard cause of the late nineteenth century. Tixier-Vignancour declined to be described as 'anti-Semitic' (he once sued Sam White of the *Evening Standard* for calling him this), but he was in no danger of winning a 'righteous gentile' award. If he had any political heirs they would be Jean-Marie Le Pen, leader of the *Front National*, and the left-wing advocate Maître Jacques Vergès who attempted to revive the 'defence of blackmail' during the 1987 trial of the SS officer Klaus Barbie.

But neither of them can match the pungency of the original, an atmosphere of Beaujolais, cigars and malevolence, and of political or legal plots being brewed in the all-night brasseries of Les Halles. Tixier-Vignancour's declared hobby was collecting lead soldiers.

Jean-Louis Tixier-Vignancour, barrister and politician, born Paris 7 eme, 12 October 1907, married Janine Auriol, one son, died Paris 7 eme, 30 September 1989.

Octave Mannoni, who died on Sunday aged eighty-nine, was never really part of the twentieth century, which of all recent centuries, deserved him the least.

The obituaries said that he was 'a psychoanalyst', so producing the neat label which our times demand. Mannoni was indeed a psychoanalyst, and founder of the *Centre de formation et de recherches psychoanalytiques*, but he was trained as a philosopher, for twenty years he was a colonial official, and he was also an ethnologist and above all a writer. This eclectic background showed in his work, which was marked by originality, imagination and humour to a degree rare in any of those fields.

In 1950, after twenty years' service in the French colony of Madagascar, Mannoni published the book which first brought him to general attention. It was called *The Psychology of Colonization*, later retitled *Prospero and Caliban*, and in it he managed to offend just about all the parties engaged in the colonial wars.

Mannoni's thesis – brutally compressed – was that everyone has a rudimentary inferiority complex and dependency complex. In the colonial situation, the European represses one and the native the other. The native, emerging from the security of an ancestor-worshipping society, attaches himself to the European, a man unaffected by traditional magic, who is therefore a type for master, protector and scapegoat. The European, convinced of his own inferiority, resolves his complex and finds reassurance by surrounding himself with dependants. When self-government is projected, the colonial natives feel abandoned and react violently. In other words, Mannoni was arguing that the conflicts in Africa at the end of the colonial era, in particular the dreadful massacre of settlers in Madagascar in 1947, had a more complicated psychological cause than the conventional politics of decolonization would allow.

Mannoni had to resign from his position as chief government information officer in Madagascar because of his anti-colonial convictions. But no sooner was he back in Europe than he found himself attacked for his 'reactionary' book, in particular by the West Indian poet, Aimé Césaire.

Meanwhile, the colonialists were equally unimpressed. In *Prospero and Caliban*, Mannoni had argued that Western man living under democracy in a competitive situation is made sharply aware of differences between himself and his neighbour which results in the inferiority complex, the key to his comparative energy and success. Mannoni added that for those Western individuals who had exceptional difficulty in resolving this complex by achieving their goals within their own society, the colonial situation had a special attraction.

Perhaps forgetting that Mannoni himself had spent twenty happy years working in a colony, his white critics misunderstood him and abused him for saying that they were inferior, a line of attack which rather confirmed his argument about their psychological difficulties. Meanwhile his black opponents, while objecting to a thesis which seemed to put forward a 'colonial' view of native society, were happy to adopt his supposed description of white colonial inferiority.

Privately Mannoni must have been amused by this dual misunderstanding but he was too courteous a man to show it. His writing is marked by its grace and clarity and by the impression he gives of genuine modesty and openness of mind, not qualities one always finds in either writers or academics. Certainly, despite his gentle manner, Mannoni was not to be bullied into any retractions.

In 1966, he was invited to reconsider *Prospero and Caliban* and in an essay entitled 'The decolonization of myself', wrote that although he would probably no longer use the term 'dependency' as being needlessly distracting, he was convinced that the book had been based on 'valid intuitions'.

It is his use of intuition and imagination which makes Mannoni's work so accessible and persuasive. *Le Monde* subtitled an unusually inadequate notice of his life, 'the spellbinder', and Mannoni is one of the best examples of the psychologist described by Graham Greene as a man working hand in glove with the novelist to throw light on the human condition. He had an unfashionable distrust of theory, noting that the more time psychoanalysts spent on theory the less they devoted to dreams. He was surely right in thinking that his intuitions about the psychology of colonization were valid. They apply just as well to subsequent events in Kenya and to the ultimate fate of the Mau Mau as they did to the French experience in Madagascar. But cant about racism is at least as powerful today as it was forty years ago, which may explain why Octave Mannoni's work has never received the honour that was its due.

August, 1989

====

Charles Hernu, who was President Mitterrand's first minister of defence, will always be remembered as the man who took responsibility for the only peacetime act of terrorism a Western democracy has pleaded guilty to since the end of the Second World War. M. Hernu resigned in 1985 after the bombing and sinking of the Greenpeace ship *Rainbow Warrior* which was moored in Auckland Harbour preparing for a voyage designed to interrupt French nuclear tests in the Pacific. A photographer was killed in the explosion. Two days later New Zealand police arrested two French DGSE (Secret Service) agents who were subsequently convicted of the bombing.

The affair caused a major political scandal in France and was probably an important factor in the Socialist government's subsequent defeat in the 1986 general election. Before he resigned M. Hernu lied five times to the Socialist prime minister Laurent Fabius about whether or not the DGSE had been responsible for the bombing. For two years he continued to deny that he had ever given orders for the bombing. Eventually in 1987 he admitted to *Le Monde*, the paper which had driven him out of office,

'Yes, there were such orders. They were bungled. I covered up and I paid the price.'

For the rest of his life M. Hernu was invariably shown by French political cartoonists wearing battle dress and dark glasses. He did much to encourage this image by his behaviour in his private political fief of Villeurbanne, the town near Lyon over which he ruled as mayor. He was proud of the mayor's official car, which was fitted with special mirrors designed to give advance warning of attacks from any direction. And many of his staff in Villeurbanne town hall were convinced that M. Hernu was tapping their telephones. Even in semi-retirement he continued to play a controversial role, becoming implicated in the illegal export of arms to Iran in 1987.

Before the abrupt end to his ministerial career, Charles Hernu was known as one of President Mitterrand's most loyal followers. He was born in Brittany, the son of a gendarme, and remained proud both of his humble background and of the outstanding scholastic record which enabled him to escape from it. He took part in the wartime Resistance and after the Liberation of France continued to fight with the French army in Germany. But he opposed the return of General de Gaulle in 1958 and worked with François Mitterrand to rebuild the French left as an effective electoral force. His reward came in 1981 when he was given the defence ministry where he quickly showed that, in France, socialism can walk hand-in-hand with militarism without any sense of impropriety.

His patron President Mitterrand never broke off their personal friendship and it remains a mystery how much M. Hernu may have been shielding the president. Yesterday his former political colleagues paid tribute to 'his sense of duty, his patriotism and his courage'. Charles Hernu may have given the orders which led to a lethal explosion on an unarmed ship in a friendly port in peace-time, but in France he was never disgraced.

Charles Hernu, French politician born 3 July 1923, Quimper, died 17 January 1990, Lyon.

═══

A great restaurateur has died and Paris is in mourning. Roger

Cazes, seventy-three, was only the third proprietor of the Brasserie Lipp in 107 years. His father bought the lease from the Alsatian founder in 1919 and Roger said that when he first saw the room's beautiful Art Deco lamps and glass, at the age of six, he 'jumped for joy'. He has kept the lamps burning ever since.

Under the two Cazes, 'Lipp' became the leading political and literary restaurant in Paris. For politicians of all parties, both before and after the Second World War, it was neutral ground. When Georges Pompidou and Valéry Giscard d'Estaing made up a quarrel General de Gaulle told them to dine together and to choose a place where they would be seen: 'Why not Lipp?' he said. 'And don't forget to alert a photographer.'

Roger Cazes was known for his rules. Paris was divided into those who were allowed to sit on the ground floor at Lipp and those who were sent upstairs with the American and Japanese tourists. M. Cazes justified this by saying that Americans made too much noise when eating and that if one Japanese were admitted to the ground floor he would be back next day with 100 friends. Other rules included no pipes, no credit cards and no cheques. The Lipp 'anti-customer' was reputed to be a man who ordered a Coke and tried to pay with an American Express card.

But it was not only strangers who failed to gain admittance. Giscard d'Estaing was turned away when he was Minister of Finance, and Laurent Fabius when he was prime minister. 'No room,' explained M. Cazes.

Roger Cazes kept a record of his celebrated guests in a large school notebook, but, despite the encouragement of Hemingway, Saint-Exupéry and Françoise Sagan, refused to write his own memoirs. The menu scarcely varied. If you were eating braised beef in Lipp it must be Wednesday; any Wednesday since about 1920.

Yesterday Roger Cazes united political Paris in death as he had in life. *Le Figaro* paid tribute in headlines, and in *Libération* J.-P. Genet wrote lovingly of 'the best *millefeuilles* and some of the worst coffee in Paris'. Let us pray that Roger's nephew, Michel, continues to turn the tins of tuna fish through 180 degrees every week, so that it remains marinated in olive oil.

April, 1987

The novelist and engraver Jean Bruller, who died last week, suffered a curious fate. He must be one of the few writers who were, in the professional sense, murdered by their own pseudonyms. The *Independent*'s obituary notice was headed 'Jean Vercors', and the name Vercors was also used last week in headlines in *Le Monde* and *Le Figaro*. Jean Bruller had used this name for his first book *Le Silence de la Mer*, written and distributed at the risk of his life during the wartime Occupation. It became the symbol of the 'intellectual Resistance' to the Germans.

Throughout the Occupation the identity of Vercors remained a secret. At the Liberation Bruller was given the Resistance Medal partly for his book and partly for founding the clandestine publishing house Les Editions de Minuit. From then on he tried to live down the immense success of *Le Silence de la Mer* and to establish a reputation under his real name. He lost interest in the illustration and engraving he had done before the war and wrote thirty more books all under his own name. But no matter what he wrote he could not replace the fame of Vercors, and time and again in order to draw attention to his work his publishers had to recall his first book.

This infuriated him. Last week *Le Monde* went so far as to say that he wrote his later books in an attempt to earn the literary fame which his first work had won for unliterary reasons. Had he read his own obituary this would have infuriated him even more. Two facts about Bruller were not generally known. One was that he was partly Jewish, the other that the walls of his Paris apartment were covered with masterpieces apparently by Picasso and Braque. He had painted these himself and could have made a fortune if he had not signed them 'Bruller' and not, be it noted, 'Vercors'.

Nesta Cox, 'Nanny of Nanteuil', who died last week in Blois, Loir et Cher, at the age of ninety-two, was one of the last surviving British nannies to have started her training in the reign of King Edward VII. She was born in the nineteenth century and brought up to believe in the indestructibility of the British Empire. In the event it was she who proved to be the more indestructible. She lived her life to standards of service, devotion and loyalty which she never questioned and which saw her safely through the German Occupation of France and membership of the French Resistance.

Nesta Ellen Cox was born in Thetford, Norfolk, on 19 December 1899. She had no brothers or sisters and when she was orphaned at the age of three she was taken in by the family of an Anglican clergyman and educated in Farnham. After her training she started work as a fifteen-year-old nursery maid but her exceptional gift for looking after children and her strength of character soon secured her an appointment as nanny. She spent four years with the family of a RIN captain in Ceylon, where there was a white Rolls-Royce for the use of herself and the children. Then after another appointment in Gloucestershire she moved to the house which was to become her home for the rest of her life, Château Nanteuil near Huisseau-sur-Cosson in the Loir et Cher. She was issued with her *carte d'identité* in December 1925, becoming one of the legion of British nannies employed to bring up French children between the wars.

The house belonged to William Gardnor-Beard, member of a wealthy family of mine owners, who had married Anne-Marie Denisane, great-niece of the Marquise de Perrigny, a spirited and patriotic young French woman who earned some notoriety on her honeymoon in Arcachon by publicly slapping the face of Madame Joseph Caillaux, wife of Poincaré's finance minister who was herself notorious for shooting dead the editor of *Le Figaro* after he had suggested that Caillaux was unpatriotic. Madame Gardnor-Beard and Nanny Cox were both extremely strong characters but after a difficult few weeks they became firm friends and everyone in Nanteuil soon grew to love 'N'neee' as she was known in the village and increasingly in the region.

The Gardnor-Beards ran a French language and literature school for young Englishmen and women. There was stag hunting in the forest of Cheverny during the winter months. Nursery tea soon became a high point in the day for children and pupils alike. 'Nanny' had established that it was the one time everyone was allowed to speak English. She herself spoke what the newspaper *La Nouvelle République* – in a ninetieth birthday tribute – called 'an inimitable language all her own made up of English and French in variable proportions'. English visitors and the villagers of Nanteuil became accustomed to such sentences as 'c'est très facile to find out'. Another term, understood throughout the region without difficulty, was 'maintNow'.

After the death of William Gardnor-Beard his wife remarried the Comte Pierre de Bernard. On the outbreak of war in 1939 the English pupils left for home but 'Nanny' refused to abandon her post and remained at Nanteuil throughout the German military Occupation. In June 1940 the de Bernard family immediately became involved in Resistance. They sheltered British soldiers and airmen, the first to arrive being one of their former pupils who had escaped capture after Dunkirk. He reached Britain safely. The de Bernards became members of the *Réseau Buckmaster-Adolphe* of south Touraine and 'Nanny' was listed on the network's roll of P1 agents in 1943. The work was mainly in supporting sabotage, receiving parachute drops and burying arms. At one point German troops were quartered on the house. Later a detachment occupied a block house on the edge of the park. 'Nanny' only once became irritated with the Germans, for frightening the children, and that day arranged for their soup to be served in flat plates.

In 1943 the network was betrayed. Pierre and Anne-Marie de Bernard were arrested by the Gestapo and deported to Buchenwald and Ravensbruck concentration camps. 'Nanny' was left in sole charge of the house and the children. She said that she was so certain that she too would be deported that she never went far from Nanteuil without a toothbrush and a Bible. But she was protected by friends in the *mairie* at Huisseau-sur-Cosson and possibly (she thought later) by certain German soldiers. She remained at Nanteuil until the Liberation, never failing to tune in to the BBC's evening broadcast on the large wooden wireless receiver which she kept in her bedroom.

After the War both Pierre and Anne-Marie de Bernard returned from the concentration camps but their health was broken. Madame de Bernard re-opened the school at Nanteuil and the English pupils returned, bearing their packets of tea. 'Nanny', who was entitled to hold the official French *carte de résistance* never applied for one and never considered that she had done anything worth remarking. Nor did she bear any particular ill-will towards the Germans, remembering that many of the ordinary soldiers had frequently behaved correctly. She regarded the War and the Occupation of France from her personal viewpoint as an episode of extremely bad behaviour which was now closed.

'Nanny' enjoyed occasional visits to England but otherwise never left Nanteuil. She lived to look after the children of her original children and then the children of those children. In her last years it was a regular sight to see old, sometimes very old, pupils of the school at Nanteuil returning to the house and being moved to tears on finding 'Nanny' still there and largely unchanged. If, for the first time in sixty-seven years, tea is not served at four o'clock sharp at Nanteuil this week, 'Nanny's' spirit still watches over the house. At her request her ashes have been scattered beneath an oak tree in the park.

=====

Twelve years on the run have ended for Albert Spaggiari, the man who organized the five-million pound 'Nice sewer robbery' in 1976 – when five million pounds was worth a lot of money. Early on Saturday morning his dead body was delivered in a coffin to his mother's house in a remote Alpine village. Spaggiari had died of cancer.

For his part in pillaging hundreds of safe deposit boxes in the strong room of the Société Générale, Spaggiari was tried in his absence and sentenced to life imprisonment. During his years on the run he became a master of public relations, giving numerous press interviews and once taking part in Bernard Pivot's weekly television books programme (from Milan). He underwent plastic surgery and spent part of his time in France. (Those who knew him said that although he never seemed in danger of being caught, he was depressed because he could not mount any new stunts to match the great achievement of his life.)

Spaggiari was a man whose political views were considered 'sound' by the extreme-right. As a paratrooper in the Indo-China war he was three times mentioned in dispatches. He also served his first jail sentence for robbing the cash-box of a brothel. In 1961, as a member of the OAS, he nearly shot General de Gaulle from the room above his mother's lingerie shop, which was called 'Au Caprice des Dames'. He was armed with a Mauser machine-pistol and was within a few yards of de Gaulle, but he never received the order to fire. He was subsequently sentenced to four years in prison for his political activities.

In 1976, while working as official photographer for Jacques Médecin, the mayor of Nice, he rented a safe deposit box at the Société Générale and discovered that the bank's alarm system did not respond to vibrations. For two months he and his men tunnelled up from the sewers. The tunnel was lined with cork and had its own electricity supply. On a long weekend the gang broke into 317 deposit boxes. The owners later admitted losses of nearly £5 million, but the real total is thought to have been much higher. The farewell message Spaggiari painted on the strongroom wall, 'Without hatred, violence or arms', made him a national hero. Shortly afterwards Spaggiari contacted the CIA and offered to tunnel beneath the Paris headquarters of the French Communist Party. He was arrested but he jumped out of the examining magistrate's second-floor window and escaped on the back of a friend's motor scooter.

Last night his mother's neighbours in the village of Laragne were saying that he had been in the region for some time. He organized the delivery of his own body to avoid embarrassment for those who had been helping him in the last few weeks of his life.

June, 1989

4. THE ARTS

The man who was once responsible for Verdi's *Aïda* being performed at Luxor, Fawzi Mitwali, had the equally original notion of bringing *La Traviata* to Versailles, and the première took place last Sunday night.

The stage was erected on a vast pontoon by the edge of the lake in the park of the former royal palace. This lake, called the Pièce d'Eau des Suisses, is in a natural amphitheatre which is bounded to the north by the Route Nationale 10 and to the south by the main railway line to Chartres and Brittany. Also around Versailles are four airstrips for light aircraft.

The RN10 had been closed by the police but the railway was doing very good business. Once sound enters an amphitheatre, it tends to linger. When the noise of the trains died down there were always the aircraft. As the performance continued and it grew darker, several of the pilots were apparently attracted to the unexpected sight, which was not on their map, of 5,000 people seated by the edge of a lake watching a pretty display of coloured lights. The little planes passed overhead and then banked and circled to have another look. The cast ignored them magnificently. The audience, who had paid up to £350 for a seat and come from all over the world for this unique experience, tried to follow their example.

On stage, Violetta, a *demi-mondaine* of the 1850s, went to her window and sang of her dreams of a love which could cure her of consumption. In the garden, beneath the circling Cessnas, Alfredo gazed up and repeated his devotion.

When the time came for the second act, a slight breeze started to blow. On the pontoon the scene had changed. Violetta had abandoned her fashionable life. She now lived with her young admirer, Alfredo, 'in a country house near Paris'. Perhaps it was this stage direction which first gave M. Mitwali the idea of producing *La*

Traviata at Versailles. That is, after all, one way of describing the palace of Louis XIV.

As the breeze freshened, the audience, who were seated beneath plastic sheeting stretched over scaffolding, realized that some of these sheets had not been stretched enough. They rippled, then cracked in the wind. Along the R N10, metal fencing had been erected to prevent anyone seeing the performance without paying for a seat. Occasionally the wind would rush through this fence, setting up an interesting vibration effect, in *crescendo*. Meanwhile, the hawsers anchoring the seating tribunes to the ground began to move and creak, adding a distinctly nautical atmosphere to the performance.

On the stage, the overhead microphones suspended above the performers, and previously invisible, began to swing from side to side. This did not destroy the remarkable quality of the sound but just occasionally, as the microphones gyrated overhead, Violetta's voice faded a little, emphasizing her fragile state of health.

As the second act reached its climax, Alfredo's father having just persuaded Violetta to break off her relations with his son, a conservatory door behind them broke loose from its fastening, potted palm fronds tossed wildly and the cloth over Violetta's writing table threatened to lift into the air. Enter Alfredo. He finds Violetta's note, crumples it, throws it to the ground and then runs off stage in despair.

Unfortunately on Sunday night he did not crumple it quite enough. On its way down to his feet a gust caught the note and tossed it up again and so Alfredo ran off stage, an anguished lover chasing a piece of paper on a windy day.

M. Mitwali, who thinks of almost everything, had arranged for a full moon to rise above the pontoon for the third act and in the moonlight reflected on the water the audience could clearly see that a bit of swell was getting up on the lake. But by now they were entering into the spirit of things. There was loud applause when M. Mitwali's private chef, in full working rig, walked along the duckboards in front of the pontoon before the performance recommenced. In the excitement, the arrival of the conductor passed almost unnoticed.

The third act starts with a ball which was enlivened in this case by the male members of the chorus with coat tails flapping stiffly in the breeze. The ball is followed by the death scene which takes place in Violetta's bedroom. For this production, the designer had selected a backdrop of diaphanous net curtains suspended from above. They were not attached to the floor. As Violetta repined and waited on the bed for Alfredo, the long line of curtains billowed out like sheets on a washing line.

When Violetta's maid went to the window to look for Alfredo, she had to open the curtains. But the singer chosen for this part happened to be quite small. So the climax of this truly memorable performance of *La Traviata* was the sight of a small professional soprano jumping into the air, grabbing at the elusive material and then with both hands wrenching it along the line.

Thank you M. Mitwali, and I really mean that.

July, 1989

An oil painting which disappeared in 1935 and was reported stolen has just emerged from the shadows into the bright sunlight of Provence. Balthus's lost portrait of his young English mistress Sheila Pickering made in 1935 was listed as the centrepiece of a fine art auction which was due to be held in Avignon last Sunday. The sale, which included works by Buffet, Dali and Utrillo, was widely advertised in the United States and Japan. The auctioneer, Maître Jacques Desamais, also placed a quarter-page advertisement in the *International Herald Tribune* featuring the Balthus portrait and among those who saw it was Sarah White, daughter of Sheila Pickering and of the legendary journalist Sam White. Both Sarah's parents are now dead but she had often heard the story of Balthus's portrait of her mother and of how the artist gave her the picture while she was living in Cagnes-sur-Mer, near Cannes, and of how the portrait had subsequently disappeared during a family move to Spain in 1935. At the last moment she managed to get an Avignon court to order that the picture be removed from last Sunday's sale.

Sheila Pickering's role as an inspiration for Balthus is celebrated. She also appears in the foreground of his picture 'La Montagne' (a study of Cézanne's favourite Montagne Ste-Victoire) which is now in the New York Metropolitan Museum. After the War, Sheila Pickering returned to her former home in Cagnes to search for the picture but nothing was found. She died in 1979 and Sam White died in 1988. They had long given up hope of ever seeing the Balthus again. So it was with astonishment that Sarah White reading the *International Herald Tribune* realized that she was looking at a reproduction of the long-lost portrait. There was her mother as a young woman gazing directly back at her from the page and there was the caption 'Balthus, Portrait of Sheila Pickering, 1935.'

To stop an auction and recover a lost painting is no easy matter in France. To have got as far as Sarah White already has – an injunction for one month to allow her to prove her case – is most unusual. Maître Desamais, the auctioneer in Avignon, is very angry about it; he has bared his soul and it is not a pretty sight. He seems to be particularly angry because he has to some extent fallen into a trap of his own making. 'For the newspaper advertisement,' he said, 'I changed the title from "The Young Girl" to "Portrait of Sheila Pickering". Without the name Miss White would never have recognized the picture as she had never seen it before.' Many people might think that would have been rather sad, but not Maître Desamais. Although he knew nothing about the disputed ownership of the picture he has not hesitated to cast doubt on the sincerity of Sarah White's claim. His argument is that since Balthus's pictures were of little value in 1935, nobody would have bothered to steal one. He is apparently incapable of imagining any interest in a picture beyond its commercial value. Since the dispute arose the auctioneer's estimated price for the painting has risen from 3 million francs (£312,500) to 15 million francs (£1,562,500), and he is now making threatening noises about the extra expense he has been put to. Hell, it seems, hath no fury like an auctioneer deprived of his commission.

Although he was warned that the picture was believed to have been stolen, Maître Desamais refused to withdraw it from the sale until ownership could be established. This forced Miss White to seek an injunction, and when this was granted the auctioneer's rage grew further. He had scored own goal number two. 'I cannot understand,' he said, 'how the court could act on the basis of one handwritten statement from Sheila Pickering's brother.' His rage may be better understood when one considers how such matters are frequently arranged in France. The 'lost' Picasso, 'Les Noces de Pierrette' which went for a world record price in Paris last December, was the subject of a disputed ownership suit as it was being knocked down for £32.54 million. But the sale went merrily ahead with the blessing of the all-powerful ministry for culture.

Sarah White now has one month to gather further evidence. She has said that she would like the picture to be in her family, or in Balthus's family, or in a French museum, but that she does not want it to end up on a Japanese motor racing circuit like Picasso's 'Pierrette'. The purported owner of the Balthus is a member of the Cagnes-sur-Mer police force. According to Maître Desamais, 'he has had the picture in his family for years and had never heard of Balthus when he brought it to the Avignon auction house for identification.' The Cagnes police records for 1935 to 1950, the period in which her mother's complaints would have been lodged, were originally said – by Maître Desamais – to have been destroyed. It now turns out that they were moved fifteen days ago. Where to has not been established. Most of Sheila Pickering's friends (who could have corroborated her daughter's story) have died, but there is one important witness still alive, Balthus himself.

The artist, now aged eighty-two, lives in the Vaud in Switzerland. Sarah White contacted him and he confirmed to her over the telephone that he had indeed presented the picture to her mother. He said he would write a letter stating this but the letter has not arrived and meanwhile Maître Desamais, who claims to be on excellent terms with the artist, has said that Balthus himself wishes to buy the picture back and that he was deeply moved when he was recently asked to identify it.

So Sarah White hopes soon to travel from her home in Paris to Switzerland to solicit the great man's help. The scene unfolds. An elderly artist, touched by the rediscovery of the portrait he painted of a beautiful young girl he loved is confronted by the model's daughter, who bears a striking resemblance to her mother and who is pleading for his help. Will his response prove too strong for the arguments of the plausible auctioneer? Will further witnesses be found as a result of the publicity Sarah White's battle has attracted? Will Maître Desamais have to be rolled up in one of his own Persian rugs to prevent him from doing himself an injury? It is practically a Balzac, let alone a Balthus.*

December 1990

---

* In the event, despite Balthus's letter, the court's decision went against Sarah White

It was billed as 'the sale of the century', the day when a new world record price (about £35 million) was to be paid for a work of art, Picasso's 'Les Noces de Pierrette'. And since it was happening in Drouot's smart new rooms in the avenue Montaigne it was also to be the day when Paris regained its rightful place as the centre of the world art market. One sweet, young thing, a 50s *nostalgique* was dressed as a Picasso portrait in profile, the straight nose, the high cheekbones, the long neck, two blue eyes, the blonde ponytail and the cheerful Mediterranean pastel shades. But she was probably an art student and certainly out of date. It was the chic members of Drouot's team who knew the score. They were inspired by Japan, whitened faces, black suits, and hair pinned back with spiky combs. They were thinking not of the picture but of the client.

Behind the long table on the auctioneer's platform an anxious-looking Japanese male cuddled a telephone handset linked to Tokyo. The overheated salon was dominated by the television monitors which showed the genial features of Maître Binoche beaming at us from across the world. In Paris it was his leaner, meaner side-kick Maître Godeau who would cope with any unexpectedly serious interest.

Before the first bids were taken the room was full of noises. The *on-dits* swept along the rows of reserved seats past Alain Delon and Paloma Picasso and the shade of Nubar Gulbenkian. The picture was a fake. Very little of the original was left. It didn't belong to the mysterious Swede who was selling it. The mysterious Swede was also a fake, or at least a heavily-restored version of the original banker who had acquired this extraordinarily beautiful 'blue period' canvas from a confused French barrister who was in the evening of

---

and the picture was duly sold at auction in Avignon. On the evening of the sale I received a telephone call in my office from a woman who identified herself as Maître Desamais's secretary. In a voice that seemed to be trembling with venomous triumph, she said that the auctioneer thought I in particular would like to know that the picture had been sold for 15 million francs. The Cagnes-sur-Mer policeman may have shared some of the venom, though not the triumph when he heard some months later that 'The Young Girl' had been resold by a gallery in the Faubourg St Honoré to Maître Binoche an unknown purchaser for approximately 30 million francs.

his days. These rumours may have been encouraged by the unusually low lighting in the adjoining viewing room where 'Pierrette' awaited her fate. Outside in the avenue Montaigne, in the pearl-grey light of a bitterly cold autumn morning, the crowd who had failed to get in for the few hours of public viewing gazed at Drouot's security guards posted behind the bullet-proof glass doors. No one threw so much as a pot of paint at them.

The picture they had failed to see was an oil on canvas – six feet long – which, in a series of magical, glowing blues, shows a circus harlequin standing in the twilight and blowing a kiss to a beautiful young girl who is seated at a marble café table beside an older man in a top hat. In the shadows beyond the top hat two more pale young faces gaze intently at the harlequin. A woman with her hair up, wearing a low-cut dress which reveals her back, provides the final figure in the group.

'Les Noces de Pierrette' was never explained by Picasso, who once said that he preferred to number his pictures rather than name them. It was given its title by his dealer and has since acquired a plot provided by generations of critics and scholars and based on that of a Catalan play which Picasso had seen and admired while he was living in Barcelona some years earlier. According to this plot, the older man in a top hat and white scarf is the rich groom: certainly he has a piggy, little face. The girl beside him, Pierrette, his new bride, has turned away from him and is lost in the admiring gesture of the harlequin. The shadowy impassive figures beyond the top hat are usually said to be supporters of this rich pig who has carried off the beautiful girl and dashed the hopes of the young harlequin, who may or may not be a self-portrait of the artist as a young man.

According to the sale catalogue Picasso himself dismissed all such commentaries as 'literary, but viewing the picture, which the public were permitted to do for a few hours last month, one felt that it none the less suggested several stories of its own. It is mysterious, slightly sinister, moving and finally breathtaking. One could say, at the risk of sounding like an auctioneer's catalogue, that looking at it is like opening a book and finding oneself gazing through a window of Chartres Cathedral. But if the colours are those of a mediaeval window the figures are indeed figures on a stage; one wants to remain in front of the painting until they move. One waits anxiously to know what happened next. And in the figure of the woman with her back to us, there is a further mystery. Most of the light in the painting is projected on to her bare skin but by what means, one wonders, did Picasso, using so little detail, suggest such a sense of rejection and exclusion of the harlequin? The harlequin's kiss is launched in defiance of the invisible wall joining this woman's shoulder and the bridegroom's suspicious face. If the artist was irritated by 'literary' interpretations of his work he himself was partly to blame. He shouldn't have painted such dramatic situations.

The auction started quietly with 'Ladies and Gentlemen' a collection of twenty-six portraits of transvestites left to us by Andy Warhol. With that attention to detail which has established the reputation of the *étude* of Binoche and Godeau, the transvestites were actually in Tokyo so the bids could be taken in yen. This ensured that even the little ones were going for millions. 'One million yen', rippled the electronic scoreboard, '43,200 francs, 6,800 dollars, 4,400 pounds'. But the transvestites did not go very well. At the Paris end the expensive reproductions behind the platform were generally quite a different colour from the original pictures on the satellite link from Tokyo, an unforeseen development which might have delighted the artist had he lived to see it.

'*Très joli petit tableau*,' murmured the discreet voice of Maître Binoche wired up to invisible speakers placed in all corners of the salon, 'we'll start at five million yen'. A paralysed silence from the ranks of the beau monde sitting in front of Maître Godeau. '*Très intéressant tableau*,' grated Maître Godeau, 'Five million! Yen! Not dollars.' Titters ran along the seats but few hands were raised. Behind him a brown- or possibly a yellow-faced transvestite, somewhat resembling Josephine Baker, simpered at the silent and paralysed celebrities. Who was he, or she? Holly Woodlawn, 'your typical Puerto Rican drag queen', or Candy Darling, or little Joe Dalessandro? All of them stars of the Warhol factory, but the catalogue did not relate. 'The bid is in Tokyo, the bid is in Tokyo, nothing from Paris,' even with the cheaper Warhols there wasn't much waiting for Godeau. Transvestite number eighteen, estimated at 30 million yen, went for 14 million (£61,600 sterling). 'All these pictures are genuine Warhols. They are all signed by the artist,' prompted Maître Binoche. It made no difference, perhaps they resembled each other too closely. Unlike the signatures the art should be recognizably unique. Most of the Warhols went for 50 per cent of the estimates. For the 'sale of the century' it was a bad start.

After a short pause we came to Lot no. 27, the 'Pierrette'. This time the bids were in francs starting at 100 million. Very quickly it became apparent that there were only two bidders, one in Paris and one in Tokyo. Two people bidding down telephones from opposite sides of the world do not make for much excitement. Looking back on it the Paris bidder, a French dealer representing an unnamed client, merely served to push the price up. It eventually stuck at 300 million francs. When the 15 per cent tax was added M. Tomonori Tsurumaki, a motor racing circuit entrepreneur, proved to have paid the highest ever price for a Picasso on public sale (£32.54 million) and the second highest price for any work of art. M. Tsurumaki said that he intended to make 'Les Noces de Pierrette' the centrepiece of the art gallery he would open at his new motor-racing circuit in the south of Japan. He would thus achieve 'the marriage of sport and art'.

The story of how M. Tsurumaki was allowed to consummate this union to the applause of the massed ranks of the world's motor-racing Picasso enthusiasts has a large cast. There was the minister, the first lawyer, the Italian-American, the second lawyer, the second lawyer's sister, the Swede, the dealer and the first and second auctioneers. There were also the first and second Picassos.

The auctioneers and the first Picasso we have already met. The minister was Jack Lang, the minister of culture, who first refused and then granted the export licence which 'allowed "Les Noces" to realize its international value'. The next five characters all owned or claimed to own the painting between 1985 and 1987. The dealer and the two auctioneers are the ones responsible for establishing the provenance of the painting. It is one of the curiosities of the international art market that the authenticity of the goods is frequently established by those selling them. Since this unusual system seems to satisfy everyone concerned it would be superfluous to question it.

Anyway according to those concerned in this case in 1908, or in 1910, Picasso sold 'Les Noces de Pierrette' to an American collector called Stransky. In 1930 Stransky sold it to Gold, an American dealer, who sold it back across the Atlantic to Georges Renand – one of the directors of the Samaritaine department store. In 1942, Georges Renand sold it to a Parisian dealer called Gerard who gave it to Pablo Picasso's son Paulo Picasso in exchange for several other paintings by the artist. Late in the 1950s Paulo Picasso sold it to the first lawyer, a very wealthy Parisian called Bernard Baque de Sariac.

During all this time the picture was never publicly exhibited, nor was it apparently reproduced in books about Picasso. Six foot long and glowing with life it passed unnoticed from hand to hand and between the barred rooms and private vaults of two continents. It is said that the dealer Gerard paid two million francs for it in 1942 during the Occupation, a good time to be paying cash for Picassos in Paris in view of the lack of international competition and the fact that some of the most active collectors of the period clicked their heels and were more inclined to turn up with a military escort than a cheque book.

The war ended, time passed, M. de Sariac, the first lawyer, grew older and there was a murky episode in 1986 when the Italian-American 'Claudio' enters the story. Claudio apparently acquired ownership for '*un prix dérisoire*' that is £200,000 or 1.2 million francs. There was a court case which was dropped after Claudio returned the painting murmuring '*Scusi*'. In 1986 Bernard Baque de Sariac, the first lawyer, died and willed 'Les Noces de Pierrette' to his nephew, the second lawyer whose mother had taken the precaution of christening him Bernard Baque de Sariac as well. His mother's daughter, young Bernard's sister, who had not unfortunately been christened Bernadette but Valérie, was not pleased by her brother's good fortune and considered that she should have had half the action and sued her brother for part ownership of the painting. This case was still before the courts when the sale in the avenue Montaigne took place. In other words M. Tsurumaki was buying disputed property. But nobody seemed too bothered about that. It did not stop Bernard Baque de Sariac the younger from selling 'Les Noces' in 1988 to Fredrik Roos, a Swedish banker who owns a splendid apartment in the Place des Vosges but who is resident in Switzerland.

Exit the first lawyer, the Italian-American, the second lawyer and the second lawyer's sister quarrelling noisily. We are left with the Swede, the minister and the dealer, above all the latter because he invented the whole occasion. We also have the second Picasso, without which there would have been no sale.

The dealer's name was Didier Imbert and in December 1987 he had purchased the second Picasso called 'La Célestine'. Painted in Barcelona in 1904, the year before 'Les Noces' which was anyway painted in Montmartre, 'La Célestine' is a sombre portrait of a cloaked and hooded woman suffering from a clouded left eye. (That is not the approved description, merely what it looks like.) It is one of the best-known pictures of Picasso's 'blue period'. M. Imbert bought the picture himself from the nephew of Picasso's banker after trying and failing to sell it for several years. From the very start, in 1974, it was made clear by the museum directors of France that 'La Célestine' would never get an export licence.

So in 1988 the situation was that M. Roos, the wealthy Swede of the Place des Vosges, was the possessor of 'Les Noces de Pierrette' an obscure but major 'blue period' Picasso. He had paid 25 million francs for this work, to the first lawyer, on the general understanding that it would never be given an export licence. And M. Imbert was the owner of 'La Célestine' a major and much more famous 'blue period' Picasso for which he had paid the same price on the same understanding. And the minister, Jack Lang, did indeed refuse the licence to both pictures. 'Situation intéressante.'

M. Lang's full title is minister of culture, communication and the national heritage (and the Bicentenary). As minister of the national heritage his duty is clearly to prevent major works of Picasso from leaving the country. On the other hand as minister of culture he has a duty to art dealers as well as to art. Impossible to imagine one without the other after all. There is Picasso, but there is also 'the international art market'. There is major Picasso but there is also 'the centre of the international art market'. Where is that? In London. Or in New York. Certainly not in Paris. Why not?

And that is precisely the question which Maître Binoche put to the minister, with the full agreement of Maître Godeau. How could Paris ever 'regain its rightful place as the centre of the international rat market' if it was impossible to deal with the international rats? The minister wanted major Picassos. The dealers wanted to sell major Picassos. But with two major Picassos under embargo the solution almost proposed itself. France would have one. The rats would have the other. Paris would once again be the place to which

Japanese kamikaze capitalists come when they are bored with playing with their racing cars.

After the sale a claque from a rival international auction house
continued to put it about that the picture was in poor condition.
But the underbidder, Hervé Odermatt, described it as 'a masterpiece'
which his client had been unable to afford. One was left wondering
who his client had been and thinking how very well-informed, as
well as elegant, were the compliments paid by the young ladies
from Drouot.

━━━━━

Dior, Chanel, Balmain, Cardin . . . where are they now? Where
were they then? By then I mean in about 1952, which was the last
time the Paris Spring Collections played any part in my life.

In those days it was from the fashion pages of the *Daily Express*
that the Fourth Form at St Philip's obtained its information about
the Paris Spring Collections. The arrival of 'the Sack', from Dior,
caused such a shock that the Fourth Form were still battling over it
days later.

It has to be said that whether one was or was not *contre le Sac* had
something to do with one's mother's views on this matter, as on so
many others. For it was invariably in the company of mother that
the Fourth Form looked at the Spring Collections. Mother opened
the newspaper and looked at the clothes and the Fourth Form sat
quietly beside her and looked at the mannequins. In order to justify
this close attention the little fellows had to make some contribution
to the conversation about the clothes. That is why the names of the
couturiers became so well-known.

One of the Paris houses was called Jacques Fath. They employed
a mannequin called Marcelle. She looked like all those remote,
extraordinary women. Tall, incredibly elegant, brown eyes, plucked
eyebrows, dark hair pulled back over her ears, quite a lot of lipstick,
not much eyeshadow. She modelled jewellery as well, she had
beautiful shoulders.

In those days the Paris mannequins were the grandest of all. In
the fantastic hierarchy of beauty they were top. Disgustingly rich
men would compete for the company of these remarkable ladies.
When they entered restaurants you could judge from the behaviour

of the waiters the importance of the moment. In the 1950s, Marcelle's life was just one party after another.

Marcelle was twice married and twice divorced. Last year she died alone in her large, comfortable apartment in Montmartre. Some months before she died she had a last moment of fame when she appeared on a television programme about divorce. 'The worst thing,' she said, 'was to go home and find no one saying "Hello darling, what sort of a day?"' Some time after that her gas and her telephone were cut off.

Marcelle was sixty-four when she died and her last forty-five days were spent in starving herself to death. She kept a careful journal of her progress in a school notebook. She limited herself to half a litre of water a day. If she had drunk less water she would have died more quickly. She yearned for some thin soup or one slice of melon. But she had self-discipline. She described fasting as 'the most horrible death possible'. The notes she left were sufficiently precise to be of some clinical interest.

Outside in the rue Championnet life continued as normal. The door-phone of her block buzzed every few minutes. The *concierge* conscientiously pushed the post under her door and polished the brass in the hallway. At Jacques Fath it was business as usual. In another part of Paris the Spring Collections came and went – yet again. Then for some reason, after eight months, a neighbour began to wonder what had happened.

There are people like Marcelle all over Paris. There is a house in the rue Franqueville which was last inhabited by its owner in 1944. The lady is now ninety-three years old and has visited the house every day since she left it. According to the caretaker, the house has not been dusted in forty years and the furniture is beginning to decompose. The owner has refused every offer made for her house. She won't live there, and no one else can either. No one knows where she lives instead. Quite a lot happened in Paris in 1944. It seems that some of it still matters.

On the avenue Montaigne, Marlene Dietrich lives the life of a recluse. Recently she had to sue a photographer who had had the thoughtful notion of hiring a crane, climbing into its bucket and having himself hoisted up outside her bedroom window. The pictures were due to go to *Paris Match*, but Mme Dietrich took out an injunction and won the case.

Even today, the past has a certain power. It can be risky messing around with it. There is a singer called Denise Paul who used to unload vans in the fruit market. Her impressions of the late Edith Piaf were so successful that she turned professional. Last week she was found at 1 a.m. in the Place Edith Piaf, drugged, with her hands tied and the skin of her back lacerated.

She had a placard round her neck signed by 'the committee for justice of the friends of Edith Piaf'. She had been receiving anonymous threats because her voice sounded 'too much like that of the singer'.

Meanwhile, the Spring Collections have been again, the waiters are bowing and scraping before some fresh new faces, and the doorphones are buzzing all over Paris.

February, 1987

The Opéra Comique off the boulevard des Italiens is a pretty little theatre which was chosen last Sunday night by the fashion house of Christian Lacroix as the place to launch a new scent called 'C'est la Vie'. About £25 million was behind this operation. The new scent is to be distributed by Dior Perfumes, part of a group which made £450 million by exploiting *haute couture* names last year. The square outside the Opéra Comique had been transformed into a gypsy encampment complete with brazier, caravan and white horse. There was a gypsy orchestra. The police were everywhere. Bullet-proof limousines full of glittering people kept arriving. On the steps of the opera house Maurice Roger, the head of Dior Perfumes who personally invented 'C'est la Vie', was looking relaxed and happy like a man who knows he is safe when surrounded by so many policemen.

Inside the theatre, before the start of the musical revue, 100 professional Parisian greeters, unnaturally beautiful young men and women in formal dress, were lining the staircase preparing to say *'Bonsoir'* about 750 times. They don't have greeters like this in other parts of the world. It is a profession here, you go to a school to be trained for it. By the time one had climbed up to the third balcony, forty feet above the stalls, one felt that one had stumbled on a long-lost family of elegantly dressed teenage cousins. The show's big name was Sylvie Guillem but the stars on the night were Nathalie Stutzman, the young contralto, and the costumes provided by Peter Brook's designer, Chloe Obolensky. Nathalie Stutzman opened with a wonderful performance of Parry's 'Love is a babble' though one member of the Milanese beau monde described it as gloomy. When the lights went down the predominant scent from the historic red plush seats was of mothballs. But in the ensuing hour another fragrance rose through the darkness. This was 'C'est la Vie'. The organizers had sprayed it on to the army of female greeters and as the girls warmed up we all got the benefit. It is officially described as 'a heady cocktail of orange blossom and Provençal flowers with vanilla, sandalwood and tonka bean' but at the Opéra Comique it was more reminiscent of a bevy of old ladies in talcum powder.

The world of Paris couture is a private place where people communicate in secret codes. But after a week I would say that you can forget about words like extravagance, frivolity, or *joie de vivre*. What we have here is the Midland Bank, disguised as Lanvin, slugging it out in the world luxury goods market with Bernard Arnault who owns Lacroix and controls Dior and Givenchy. Just before the first show M. Arnault won an important skirmish in his court battle to gain full control of the Louis Vuitton Moet Hennessy group. His opponent is Henri Recamier and when the battle is over only one of them will still be on his feet. This is an approach to life which is very appropriate to the world of *haute couture*. As the shows succeeded each other I became aware that all around me people sitting on little gilt chairs were doing despicable, painful, things to each other with charming smiles on their faces. They smile while they are dishing it out and they smile while they are taking it.

Nobody ever shows pain, they just smile and wait their turn. It is more disciplined than a Jesuit penitential exercise. If Madame Ceausescu had realized her true metier she would probably still be alive and running a couture house in the 8th *arrondissement*.

My very first show was Lacroix and, well briefed as I was, I knew exactly what to expect. Sure enough there was someone sitting on my little gilt chair. She was a lady of a certain age, and when she offered to move she opened her eyes wide and looked impossibly fragile. Of course there was no question of moving her.

It would have been too dreadful if she had had to stand merely because she didn't have a ticket.

She placed me on the next seat and masterminded the ensuing musical chairs with practised skill. When the lights went down she was still seated comfortably in my place while all around us furious ticket holders groped desperately for a level surface on which to perch.

The hierarchy of the little gilt chairs is the mark of your standing in the world of couture. In the front row along the catwalk sit the celebrity customers. Nobody seems to think that they actually buy many of the dresses but they represent the idea of the private client, inhabitants of the dwindling world of those who are still prepared to spend £10,000 or £20,000 on a frock which may be worn only twice. These ladies have names like Baronne de Rothschild, Paloma Picasso, the Princesse de Furstenberg and Veronica Hearst.

The best seats in the house are right at the end of the catwalk where the wives of leading politicians are sometimes joined by film stars such as Catherine Deneuve and Mireille Mattieu. As these little groups assemble the photographers set frantically to work adding to the general air of excitement. Also in the best seats are the leading fashion journalists. The fashion editors wield real power in this world. They receive a personal escort to their seats and during the year they are showered with gifts. The little Christmas box from Chanel is awaited with particular interest it seems. One personal client of Emanuel Ungaro's told me that she found the fashion writers' comments totally unhelpful, but that is not a dispute which a lone male would be well-advised to join.

At many of last week's shows the power lineup was the same. There was American *Vogue*, looking lovelier than ever in bobbed hair, tweed jacket and a black mini skirt; she made one proud to be in the same profession. Beside her were the three burly males from Manhattan who lay down the law in *Women's Wear Daily*. They always sat together, glaring into the spotlights and muttering urgently.

Also present was the *International Herald Tribune* who has written hurtful things this week about Dior and Nina Ricci and who nearly did a disrespectful Italian photographer a nasty injury at the Pierre Cardin show when she snapped her personal computer shut within half a centimetre of his pants.

My first impression after watching half a dozen shows is that, for all its emphasis on innovation, the world of couture is deeply traditional. The same lovely collection of girls appears in one show after another. Every show ends with a wedding dress. After the wedding dress there is the appearance of the designer, a man in a crumpled suit who absent-mindedly kisses the nearest girl. Clearly this performance is what the customers want. But is there a slightly unconvinced air about it today, as though making dresses to sell perfume is not as interesting as making dresses to sell dresses? The days when the great couturiers were looked on as members of a wider community of artists are surely over. The mass luxury goods trade has seen to that.

January, 1990

[*In March, 1987, the French government signed an agreement with Walt Disney Inc. for the construction of EuroDisneyland, a 5,000 acre theme park sited twenty miles to the east of Paris near the First World War battlefield of the Marne. As part of the agreement the French government undertook to finance and construct one of Europe's largest motorway and rail junctions at the gates of the park.*]

THE PROLOGUE

Once upon a time there was a beautiful part of the Ile de France called the Briard. It was a land of cheese and honey, flowing with rivers, dotted with villages where the bells rang out from the church towers in the evening and the cattle lowed in the peaceful fields.

In the middle of this region there was a plateau surrounded by five communes. Twenty-five farmers lived upon the plateau, growing their crops, making their Brie cheeses, happy to pass their days in this favoured spot where the topsoil was four metres deep and where much of their business could be done in cash which they could keep where it belonged, under the bed.

Then one day a big car drove up to the plateau and four large men climbed out. They were carrying maps and binoculars and they smiled a lot. In fact they smiled all the time. They loved the plateau and looked all round it and bought lots of cheese. 'We are from California,' they said. 'If only we could live on this beautiful plateau it would be like a fairy-tale come true.' Then they drove away. The farmers waved them off. 'See you next time,' said the four big smiling men. 'I wonder why they said that?' said the farmers.

THE PLAY

The scene moves to the Hôtel Matignon, on 24 March, 1987. A ceremony is being held to mark the signing of the contract between France and Walt Disney Inc. to build the first Disneyland in Europe. It will occupy a plateau in the Briard region, and it will be one-fifth of the size of Paris. The twenty-five farmers will be evicted.

The ceremony is held in a room with chandeliers, Gobelin tapestry, fine gilt work and a photograph of President Mitterrand. At a long table seventeen men are seated including Jacques Chirac, the prime minister of France. They are all smiling. The four big men from America are there and they seem to have made everyone in the room very, very happy.

The signing of this Californian contract, a document which stands literally one metre high, was important enough to take more than an hour of the prime minister's time. M. Chirac said that the Disneys were a prestigious partner for the French government and that their name was a guarantee of success. Then he slowly tore his notes up while the Americans spoke. The pieces got smaller and smaller. M. Chirac has very strong thumbs.

On behalf of Walt Disney Inc., Michael D. Eisner, the president, spoke first. Like so many of those associated with Disney he seems rather larger and rather healthier than life. As a former head of Paramount Pictures one can assume that Mr Eisner is capable of handling a business negotiation in a way that few of those who have negotiated with him will ever forget.

Mr Eisner told us that Disney had chosen to come to Paris because, 'Everyone has two cities in their heart; their own and Paris.' In Hollywood business circles people only make speeches like this when they have just eaten the other side alive.

The second Disney to speak, also an exceptionally tall, gentle and healthy looking man, was Robert J. ('Bob') Fitzpatrick. Mr Fitz-patrick has only been with Disney since the begining of this month. And already they have made him the President of EuroDisneyland! The United States is a truly democratic society.

Why has this mild-mannered, old-fashioned gentleman been snatched from the university campus to head this busy, busy corpora-tion? It turns out that Mr Fitzpatrick has been a university professor of French and he started his speech yesterday with a quote from du Bellay – 'Happy is he who, like Ulysses, completes a long voyage'. Mr Fitzpatrick ended his speech by inviting us, that is M. Chirac and the assembled crowd of reporters and photographers, 'to dream together'. In this kind of operation Mr Fitzpatrick is known as 'the good furniture'.

The Disney who did not smile quite so much and preferred to remain in the background was called Joe Shapiro. He is a lawyer and he was in charge of the last part of the negotiations when one concession after another was successfully demanded by the Disneys. Mr Shapiro looked like a pretty mean operator, but appearances must be deceptive because his press handout said that 'he represents defendants in the criminal courts who cannot afford to pay, without charge', and Walt Disney's PR men would never tell a lie.

As a result of Mr Shapiro's success France will be paying for all the motorways and rail-links which will now lead to Disneyland. And if there are any disputes, under the contract they will not be settled in the French courts but by outside arbitrators. France is doing this because Disney has woven a beautiful dream of 10 million tourists a year coming to France from all over Europe, and even M. Chirac loves to dream. Perhaps he is dreaming that one day he will be invited to become a Disney. He might become president of EuroDisneyland rather than president of France. He would be almost as powerful and much, much richer.

The story of the negotiation between Disneyland and the state of France will probably never make a Walt Disney film. The basic ploy used by the Disneys, who were determined to establish their European Disneyland near Paris, was to get Paris to beg them to come. So yesterday we heard of how the district of Marne-la-Vallée had been chosen out of 200 centres, how 'Barcelona nearly got it' and of how Disney had first been approached by the French (who had heard of their top secret project by chance).

In the business this is known as 'the softening up process'. When it is over the other side find they are begging to give away hundreds of acres of their best farmland and offering to pay you to occupy it.

Unfortunately the twenty-five peasants up on the plateau can't remember the date when the four smiling men arrived in their motor car, but it was probably quite some time before the French government 'heard the first whisper' of this top-secret project in 1983.

After the signatures, a reception at the Conseil Régional, rue Barbet de Jouy. An excellent lunch, speeches, the French negotiating team and the Disneys have now become *chers amis*, there is a cake two metres high decorated with Mickey Mice and Donald Ducks but fortunately cooked in France. Chablis, Bordeaux, Champagne. The Mayor of the commune of Coupvray was there, a retired farmer who lost his farm when it was purchased for development long before EuroDisneyland. A man who is going to see more changes in his commune than two world wars were able to arrange. He was born in France but he now has the chance to die in Cinderella's Castle.

He said that his commune was entirely happy with the arrangement; they were going to see supermarkets, swimming pools and cinemas all within one kilometre of their front door. As for the suggestion that it was turning France into America he found it strange considering that so many parts of Paris had been transformed into Afrique du Nord.

Of course there will always be those who can't join in the fun. Like the American student at Science Po who said yesterday that she had 'come to Europe to get away from all that garbage'. Now it would be 'Hello, cheesecake, goodbye, Brie'. Some people just want to keep Europe living in the picturesque past. They can't see how awkward it is to have countries around who have not forgotten who they are. It makes the big men with big smiles who never really knew where they came from nervous. They don't like going to Paris and finding somewhere different.

THE EPILOGUE

The Tokyo Disneyland has started a national urban development movement. Even Hiroshima and Nagasaki are going to have 'historical theme parks'. These two cities are considering which themes will illustrate their particular history. That is the strangest Disney fairy-tale yet.

March, 1987

═══

To people all over the world Robert Doisneau is probably the supreme photographer of Paris. Many of his most famous black and white pictures of lovers in the streets taken in the 50s used models, skilfully posed to look natural, but they still symbolize the city. Yet according to his friend, the novelist Blaise Cendrars, Doisneau is not a Parisian photographer at all but *'un photographe zonier'*.

He was born on the edge of the 'zone' and he still lives on the edge of the zone, although the zone itself no longer exists. It disappeared in the 60s under the *périphérique* motorway. The zone was originally the field of fire, the open space beyond the ring of defensive artillery forts which encircled Paris. The defences were abandoned in 1919 and the zone became a lawless area. The jurisdiction of the Paris police force ended on one side and that of the Gendarmerie started on the other. As a child Doisneau heard the story of the commissionaire attempting to deliver a summons in the zone who hurried back into Paris still clutching the summons and stark naked, his handsome uniform having been distributed among the children of the zone.

At the age of six Doisneau was taken to school by his Aunt Zoe's maid, who had just left school herself. Instead of going to school they went straight to the fortifications where the girl met an admirer and little Doisneau was told to run along for twenty minutes. The maid was eventually fired when 'her apron strings became too short', that is when her condition became visible. Years later Doisneau took many of his first photographs in the zone and realized one day that he had made his professional debut in the very place where his nurse had become pregnant. In France his most famous book, with a text by Blaise Cendrars, is still *La Banlieue de Paris*.

Doisneau lives today in the same apartment in the suburb of Montrouge which he bought in 1937, shortly after his marriage. He was attracted to it by its north-facing studio with tall windows. Today he is the oldest inhabitant of the building and he lives in the apartment alone. 'The time has passed horribly fast,' he says. 'The apartment was gay in the old days, there were the children and my wife – who was always very funny. Now she has been in a clinic for five years.' But she is close enough for him to walk there to visit her every day, and though his daughters have their own families, one of them lives near by.

Doisneau sees himself as 'a strolling photographer'. He has always followed two precepts. They are the sort of rules which, unlike most rules, are attractive to the young. One is the importance of wasting time. It is only by hanging around, doing nothing, waiting, that the photographer can hope to be there when something unforeseen takes place. 'If I hadn't been playing truant from an advertising shoot in the Tuileries I would never have got that picture of the men moving the statue,' he points out. It is the picture of the four intrepid workmen manoeuvering a massive female bronze figure. They are using her breasts for purchase but she remains unmoved. His second precept is related to the first: the profession of photography is 'the disobedient profession'. If there is a policeman saying 'Move on, *circulez*, there is nothing to see,' there is quite clearly something to see. The photographer is an irritating anarchist who continues to walk against the stream of obedient people.

Doisneau has spent much of his life, and taken many of his pictures, in bars or in bistros. There is one of a girl playing the accordion who was blind. She sang a love song about 'You'll never guess how much I love you, It's so sweet to hold you tight,' and the detail Doisneau liked was seeing all the customers with tears in their eyes: 'They were the slaughtermen from the local abattoir.' He is a cheerful man, and very good company. Even his regrets are stated gently, almost humorously.

One of his chief regrets is the amount of time he spent working for Renault in the enormous car factory at Boulogne Billancourt before the War. Doisneau achieved membership of 'the disobedient profession' slowly. It was a battle. He first trained as a lithographer. But he was dissatisfied with his draftsmanship. He loved photography but he could not afford the equipment so he sought a job as photographic technician, work to which his engraver's training could be adapted. He is proud of the fact that he remains a very good darkroom technician. He has always developed and printed his own pictures.

He was liberated from the darkroom by a new form of servitude, the Régie Renault. He went to work in the appalling 200 acre site of Louis Renault's pre-war empire, *la fortresse ouvrière*, battleground in the pitiless struggle between Louis Renault and the PCF, the Parti Communiste Français. The sirens would howl every morning as the crowds of workers pressed through the high gates. 'As you walked in there were just other men's backs, for as far as you could see,' Doisneau said later. He himself was generally half-asleep.

Doisneau's work at Renault produced some memorable pictures but mostly it was boring in the extreme. He used a heavy 18 × 24 wooden camera on a tripod with copper lenses, glass plates, magnesium powder and thirty metres of thick electric cable. He had to hump all this round the factory all day long, light work compared to most of the other jobs. He worked for Renault's archives department, recording the daily life of the factory. His arrival was usually an amusing diversion for his fellow workers. The magnesium went off with a tremendous flash. 'When you'd exposed two plates there was generally such a cloud of smoke that you had to go away again,' he recalled. It was in these conditions that Doisneau produced his first industrial photography.

His years at Boulogne Billancourt reinforced his lifelong sympathy for the men and women who had to pass their lives in factories. It is a sympathy that he has kept all his life. There is a post-war picture of a carefree boy running down a steep grassy slope towards some factory gates through which he will shortly disappear for the remainder of his days. And years after leaving Renault, Doisneau produced a montage of industrial injuries, six mutilated hands gesturing in front of a landscape of tall chimneys and plumes of smoke. The six men had all suffered their injuries in factories in the same valley in Lorraine.

Sometimes there were more amusing assignments. Doisneau took a series of pictures of bright young things driving the latest Renaults through the countryside. The models used in the pictures were amateurs and they all worked at Boulogne Billancourt. For them it was a day out. The girls were from the typing pool. 'I chose them and I had to be careful to choose slim ones because we had to seat three in a row and make it look as though there was still plenty of room. The pictures were actually taken in the Bois de Boulogne because we were not allowed to go any further. Question of economizing on petrol.'

There is another picture of a large man with a Charlie Chaplin moustache lying unconscious on a slab in the factory infirmary dressed in his boots and working clothes, attended by a nurse in a crisp white uniform – '*un type grotesque*' says Doisneau today. Was he actually ill? 'Oh, certainly. Probably had too much to drink.'

Doisneau was eventually, after five years, fired for bad timekeeping. He had received many warnings and as a last resort he adopted the hopeless expedient of altering his timesheets in ink. Why was he always so late for work? Doisneau has given several reasons. He once claimed that it was because he used to work far into the night mastering a primitive colour printing process. But he told me that he was habitually late for work because he had a young wife and it was obviously more agreeable to linger in bed with her than it was to join the crowd of men pushing their way through the factory gates into the inferno of noise. One summer afternoon in 1939 he was summoned to the pay department and shown his forged records by an unsmiling supervisor. He was handed his cards and a small pay-off and instructed to leave immediately and not to return. He was free, but it was rather a short period of liberty since he was called up a few months later for military service.

Doisneau's war, after he was discharged from the army, was spent like so much of the rest of his life in the *banlieue* of Paris. There was a serious food shortage and he had an infant daughter. The little girl was entitled to a government food supplement, a broth. He recalls today, affectionately, that his *sale gosse* would eat every mouthful of it while her father looked hungrily on. To earn a little more money he would devise photographs intended to illustrate the life of Napoleon, print them as postcards and bicycle into Paris to sell them to tourists outside the gates of the Invalides. Many of the tourists were German soldiers. They would have been interested to learn that the young man with his pile of homemade postcards also did some work for the Communist Resistance as a forger, making documents and identity photographs and occasionally lodging people who were on the run. (Fortunately his forging technique had improved since his days at Renault.) He took an evocative picture of a clandestine printing press in the rue des Petits Champs near the Bibliothèque Nationale. 'The girl was called Olga. All three people in the picture are dead now.'

Doisneau also photographed the Liberation. General Leclerc made his triumphal entry into Paris down Route Nationale 20 which passes the end of Doisneau's street. But his war photographs are still marked by a certain gentleness. There is one of a camouflaged vehicle moving through an eerily deserted street. Two of the occupants, festooned in branches, are scanning the rooftops for snipers. But the snipers are imaginary. The vehicle is a trolley, the camouflaged figures are children. Other photographers were recording the real battle in neighbouring streets. Doisneau – with equal authenticity but greater originality – chose to show the Liberation of Paris as a children's game.

There is another unpublished picture of a crowded open-air swimming pool. A girl with the tumbling, thick wavy hair of the 40s, wearing a very early bikini, is stepping over the sunbathers who are almost all young men. Doisneau, who writes his own titles, has entitled this picture 'La Piscine Deligny en 1944'. That is again typical because one immediately wants to ask 'which month?'. If it is any time from April to mid-August, the bronzed young men with short hair wearing swimming trunks are German, resting before resuming their usual occupations. The girl is a certain sort of a girl. But if the picture was taken in September, the bronzed young men are French or American or Canadian, resting before resuming the same occupations but on the other side, and the girl is perhaps a different sort of girl. Doisneau's point, as expressed in his title, seems to be 'does it matter?' They are after all just young men during a war, enjoying a few hours in the sunshine.

'I've never been very attracted by the military tool-box,' Doisneau says. 'I've always noticed those men who linger in front of shop windows which are packed with weapons. A man who enjoys carrying a tool like that is a man who is no longer bothered by the people who ask him questions he can never answer. When he is wearing his knife or his gun they stop asking him the questions. I like finding subjects like that, things which everyone has seen but no one else has noticed.'

After the war, Doisneau continued to take industrial subjects. The 1946 picture of a steam engine on a turntable looks as though it was taken at dawn, but is entitled 'Full moon over Le Bourget'. It was during this period that he started to work with the Agence Rapho and took on fashion, portraits, reportage and street scenes. He has photographed Picasso, Aragon, Prévert, Giacometti, Simenon, Raymond Queneau, Braque, Léger and many others. When he visited Simenon in Switzerland the world's best-selling novelist came to pick him up at the railway station in his new Rolls-Royce. 'The car broke down about 300 metres down the road. Simenon was not at all pleased,' Doisneau recalls. 'He had to telephone for a second car. I always seem to have that effect on Rolls-Royces. It happened again the other day in the Champs-Elysées.'

Some of his best portraits are of unknown Parisians. Mme Nenette with her magnificent *embonpoint* encased in stretch-nylon leopardskin standing at the counter of her bistro; the master jeweller, an enormous man with fingers like Montbéliard sausages, surrounded by the miniature tools of his exacting craft; the drunken 'Coco' in his black bowler hat, leaning on a bar in Les Halles, attempting to bring the lense into focus. 'He was an ex-Legionnaire. Hard to say if he was French. A lot went into his mouth but not much came out of it.'

And there is the gardener of Gentilly, a little man with the face of a gnome who is in fact standing between two real garden gnomes, a grass rake over his shoulder, proud, ridiculous and sad. 'Yes, well he was quite sad. He detested his wife. They lived together in that tiny hut at the end of the garden but they ate every evening at separate tables.'

One of Doisneau's street scenes taken after the war shows a thin house at the angle of an intersection like the point of a wedge or the prow of a ship. The house is surrounded by the *pavé* which is glinting in the rain, there is a canal to one side and a man in a beret is walking on the narrow pavement carrying a small bucket. It is a bleak, grimy, misshapen scene but, to anyone who can remember, it says immediately 'France – after the war'. The street is poor and foreign and pungent and full of adventurous possibilities. There is one cheerful point in the picture. The front room of the narrow house at the corner of the two streets has a faded sign, 'Au Bon Coin', and the net half-curtains of the café are gleaming white. You know that as you open those rickety doors you will be assailed by the noise of laughter, and by blue cigarette smoke and by the smell of fresh coffee, and fresh bread and cheese and wine and the *plat du jour*.

Doisneau returned recently and photographed the same corner. The buildings are structurally the same but the only man in this picture is wearing a Burberry raincoat and walking a well-fed dog. The *pavé* has disappeared beneath tarmac. And this time the unpopulated street is full of locked cars parked in the road and on the pavement. There is a 'No Entry' sign beside the house, which has been painted a clinical white. 'Au Bon Coin' has become somebody's private front room and is protected by patio shutters. There will be a television set behind those shutters and as you read this somebody will be sitting alone in that room watching on that television set the opening of 'EuroDisneyland' which has been constructed just fifteen kilometres to the east of the zone.

'You know the real change in the streets of Paris since I was young?' says Doisneau. 'They don't smell any more.'

April, 1992

———

A dozen people are standing behind a pane of glass in a steel half-tube which is suspended hundreds of feet above the ground in central Paris. They are looking across a void towards an identical half-tube from which a similar group of people gazes back. Behind them a crowd of impatient visitors await their turn. They too want to press their noses against the cold glass which their breath will, in due course, help to steam up. This is an important new building and the visit is an essential item on the Paris itinerary.

All these people have mounted to this altitude on an escalator. This is the Beaubourg experience. They have come from all over France, from all over the world, to stand behind this pane of glass. Visiting the Multi-Cultural Arts Complex at the Centre Pompidou is the most popular diversion in the city. Nearly twice as popular as visiting the Eiffel Tower. More than seven million people come here every year.

The space beneath them has been improved since the photograph was taken. Now there are bollards and litter bins and street artists. In the evening it becomes one of the most hideous and futile areas of the city, a battleground for warring gangs of teenage dope fiends, understandably avoided by members of the Paris police force. Beneath the piazza is an enormous underground car park where the gangs roam looking for something to steal. Some of the people gazing out of the window will return to the surface of the planet to find that in their absence they too have made a donation. None of these people can stay up there all day. From the area beneath them, the old central market of Paris – what Zola used to call 'the stomach of Paris' – McDonald's is calling; whatever the time of day.

One has only to murmur 'McDonald's', even in a French accent, and one thinks of litter bins. In Paris these have been designed with some care. They are discreet but not too discreet. The outside is durable and easy to clean. When they catch fire they reduce themselves to a pile of ash without causing an unacceptable level of cancerous fumes. The designers never intended the bins to serve as platforms. But apparently they can do so. A man can stand on a Paris bin and give his mime show.

On the pavement below the bin, his ghetto blaster. A backdrop formed by the mindless procession of traffic rushing past. Above his head a lamp standard in the form of an ancient Roman war ship, the trireme. There are thousands of young men like this one in Paris. They will do almost anything to gather a crowd and pass round the hat. It makes a change from the Beaubourg's underground car park. A lot of them do slow-motion mimes. This man does a slow-motion mime standing on a little bin. A mime artist is intimidating. His audience usually avoids meeting his eyes.

Some of the visitors to the Pompidou Centre may mount to the top of the towers of Notre Dame. Up there they will be in the open air beside the gargoyle. In front of the gargoyle they will find that the dean and chapter have erected a net. This net is nothing to do with repair work nor is it an attempt to keep the pigeons off the stonework. It is designed to prevent suicides from jumping off the towers of Notre Dame. If you jump off the tower of Notre Dame the last face you see is probably that of a gargoyle. Suicides have been jumping off for years but recently one of them landed on a fellow tourist who was walking in front of the cathedral's west doors. In the Republic, suicide, even on church property, is an inalienable human right, but jumping on to other people is not. Hence the net.

It is a Mark 1 net. Mark 2 will be more ingenious. In future if you jump you will be caught in a bag from which you will be unable to climb out. You will have to stay there until the fire brigade arrives to retrieve you. You will lose the dignity of the suicide. You will become a public spectacle.

I once saw someone about to jump off the roof of a cathedral. He was standing beside me. He did not move. He was alone. He was looking down from behind the railing like anyone might do. He was also blocking the way. People pushed past him impatiently. He took off his jacket and wrapped it neatly and put it into a carrier bag. Then he hung the bag on the railing and a few seconds later he jumped. There was no net. He did not hit anyone on the paving below. The police cordoned off the space around and put a blanket over him. Up on the roof his carrier bag and his jacket were still hanging on the rail and the tourists continued to walk round the roof, doing what they had come to do, photographing the gargoyles and admiring the view.

August, 1990

———

The Royal Rat Pack received a rebuke on Saturday from an unexpected direction. Having turned up in force at the Moulin Rouge in Paris, to cover Prince Edward's visit to the new show, *Formidable*, the Pack naturally expected a few photographs of HRH backstage with the cast. But a week of hard bargaining with Fleet Street's finest had proved too much for case-hardened Jean Miguel, the director of the Moulin Rouge.

Before he would let the Pack near the Prince, Jean Miguel assembled the sixty gorgeous dancers in the cast and passed round a tray full of bras. Only when these had been placed in position were the Pack admitted for their photographs. Jean Miguel had already caused disappointment by ordering the girl who normally dances a Highland Fling wearing nothing but a mini-kilt to drape herself in a long tartan scarf.

Replying to the Pack's angry squeaks Jean Miguel said: 'You people seem to forget that this is the son of your Queen who is visiting us tonight. If it had been the Emperor Hirohito I would have covered up the girls dressed as Geishas. I am Swiss and we have a lot of respect for Queen Elizabeth. What's more, I have been talking to Prince Edward. He is very serious about the stage and I think you are being unfair to him.'

The shock of being given a moral lecture by the director of the Moulin Rouge left the Rat Pack, for once, quite speechless.

February, 1988

5. OUT OF FRANCE

One of the most famous group portraits of nineteenth-century France is now being exhibited in Paris. It is the painting by André Brouillet called 'A Clinical Lecture at the Salpêtrière by Professor Charcot'. Perhaps this work lacks the artistic merit of Rembrandt's 'Anatomy Lesson' but as an illustration of a dramatic dead end in the history of medicine it has its fans.

In the centre of the lecture hall stands the great professor, long white hair gleaming, index finger extended in emphasis. He is not looking at her but, by his side stands a young woman who has apparently fainted. The most noticeable thing about her, to the non-medical eye, is her magnificent *décolletage*. Her arms hang loose, her head is thrown back. She is leaning heavily against the tall, bearded figure of the brilliant Dr Babinski, then a follower of Charcot, later one of his severest critics and numbered among the founders of neuro-surgery. He bends over her solicitously.

Beside Babinski stands a motherly nurse, her arms held out, ready to catch the *décolletage* if the brilliant Babinski should let his attention wander back to the lecture. Seated in front of the professor are his audience, motionless with attention and all of them male.

But what is wrong with the young lady in the picture? Has she just been told, in the magnificently tactless tradition of the teaching hospital, that she is expecting twins? No; for she has not actually fainted. Instead she is none other than Blanche Wittmann, a *grande hystérique* and one of Charcot's most cooperative patients. For Charcot, who was one of the great medical figures of his time, became obsessed with the study of hysterical illness and his lectures were attended by the *tout Paris* of the 1880s.

Neurology was then a new branch of medicine and Charcot was one of its first exponents but his theories about hysteria were discredited even in his own lifetime. Charcot was working twenty years after the apparitions and the beginning of the pilgrimage to Lourdes; a time when the French Catholic hierarchy – battling against rationalism and the Third Republic – did not scruple to encourage belief in hundreds of miraculous cures every year. Many of these early, uninvestigated miracles were in fact the cures of cases of gross hysteria. In his lecture Charcot could demonstrate identical miracles. He could not only cure spectacular maladies, he could cause them as well. Suggestible women such as Blanche Wittmann would expose a healthy throat. Charcot would, through hypnotism, provoke the hysterical mechanism and in the glowing white skin a bruise would appear which would swiftly turn into an open wound, a fistula penetrating sometimes as deep as the bone. Charcot would then suggest the opposite reaction, and the wound would close up and disappear. Nowadays it would be called great television.

For twenty years before he became one of the most celebrated men in Paris Charcot worked in La Salpêtrière which was among the despised places of the city, an asylum for old ladies and lunatics.

With these obscure unfortunates as his research material the young doctor developed his theories of neurology. In his opinion hysteria was a physical illness. It was caused by patches of fatty tissue in the brain. He proceeded to track down the proof of this theory in the mortuary, finally without success. The trouble with his cures was, as in the case of so many of the early Lourdes miracles, that they did not last. Hysterical illness, even today, is said to be among the most difficult to cure permanently. The audience were not really observing a scientific demonstration. They might as well have been sitting by the baths in Lourdes.

But for one of them at least it was not quite a dead end. The young Sigmund Freud came all the way from Vienna to watch the great Professor Charcot. He was deeply affected by the teacher's personality and he was not worried by the subsequent discrediting of his theory of fatty cerebral tissue. Freud was much more interested in the demonstration of hypnotism and suggestibility, which led him on to his own theory of the unconscious mind.

If Charcot were newly-qualified today, he could start all over again. For just as the painting of his demonstration was being exhibited in Paris the annual Bichat conference, also held in La Salpêtrière, was hearing of a new study in hysteria. According to this, one third of all men are believed to suffer from undiagnosed hysterical illness. It is quite different in its symptoms from the hysterical illness traditionally found in females, and it is an unusually difficult condition to diagnose.

And there is one new development. Hysteria goes in waves, according to what's on the news. Perhaps it is fortunate that Charcot lived before John Logie Baird.

November, 1986

===

In France literature enjoys an indecently close relationship with food. The writer's work is conceived, celebrated, and even executed, in cafes and restaurants. Yesterday was the holiest day in the French literary year, the day when the Prix Goncourt for 1987 was announced, and as always it was announced at the Restaurant Drouant, just off the avenue de l'Opéra.

This year's winner was a Moroccan novelist, Tahar Ben Jelloun, whose book *La Nuit Sacrée* tells the story of the self-liberation of a young peasant woman living in the mediaeval society of modern Morocco. It took six rounds of voting to find a winner, and the result was only reached after the usual hard bargaining among the ten judges, all of them authors who can be counted on to represent the interests of the powerful houses which publish their own work. Tahar Ben Jalloun became this year's favourite as soon as the shortlist was published for the simple reason that he is published by Seuil. Last year's winner was elected by an alliance of judges representing the houses of Grasset and Seuil and they chose a book published by Grasset. It was therefore logical to suppose that this year it would be the turn of Seuil; and so it was.

The announcement was made at the door of the private dining room at Drouant's, a restaurant which was recently sold by its founding family to a large group which promptly spent 70 million francs (£7 million) in making it completely unrecognizable. Outside the private dining room, in a corridor which now resembles the plush interior of a couturier's salon, gathered the usual mob of television crews. At one o'clock precisely the doors opened and a man with a white beard emerged. His lip curling with contempt at the spectacle before him he mentioned the name of the restaurant, announced the winner, stepped back and shut the doors in the face of the mob.

Behind the doors the ten judges could return to their traditional reward of caviare, pâté de foie gras, lobster and venison. Meanwhile, outside the restaurant, such is the magic of the Goncourt, a sizeable crowd had gathered on the pavement under police supervision and at this point, by tradition, the stunned winner is supposed to be led from a neighbouring café and presented briefly to the jury who interrupt their meal long enough to present him with a fifty franc cheque.

But Tahar Ben Jelloun, an unusually self-possessed winner, was nowhere to be seen. He was actually on the other side of Paris in a rival literary restaurant, the Brasserie Lipp, which is still a family concern and in no immediate danger of redecoration. 'I am moved, but I am not knocked out,' he said. His book has already sold 50,000 copies and he can now expect to sell ten times as many again. M. Ben Jalloun said that his prize would help to unite France and the Maghreb and that he wished to associate all his fellow countrymen with the honour. He added that his next book was well underway.

In this he is more fortunate than a previous winner, Jean Carrière, who had a massive success when he won in 1972. His novel, *L'Epervier de Maheux*, subsequently sold 1.7 million copies but the author's life was nearly destroyed by the fame he won. His wife became seriously ill, his marriage broke up, he took to the bottle, he became hooked on tranquillizers, he was on the verge of suicide – and for years he could not write a word. He has told the story in a book published this month entitled *Le Prix d'un Goncourt*. Now he is writing novels again and enjoying his food. But he at least will never be found on some future Goncourt jury.

It is all a long way from the values of the philosopher Emile Cioran who has refused the Paul Morand prize, worth £30,000 from the Académie Française. He said that at the age of seventy-seven such prizes were 'incompatible with what I have written and with my way of seeing things'. His gesture did not make the headlines.

November, 1987

In January 1608 it was so cold that the Communion wine froze in the chalice at the church of St André-des-Arts in Paris. That is a recorded fact. What is not recorded is whether or not this event led to a controversy about the nature of the transubstantiation in extreme weather conditions. As so often, the historians have left the really absorbing questions unasked.

The coldest day ever recorded in Paris was 10 December, 1879, when the temperature reached −25·6°C. One might think that this bitter experience would accustom the authorities to dealing with the cold but, on this occasion at least, they have been almost as incompetent about it as the British. With night temperatures in Paris at −12°C approaching their lowest point since the Second World War, and the capital under twelve inches of snow, there were calls for snow ploughs. It turned out that there were no snow ploughs in Paris.

'Paris is not a ski resort,' said the responsible official showing a characteristic ability to move instantly from verbal defence to verbal attack. What about some grit on the roads? 'It is far too cold for the addition of grit to have the usual chemical effect,' he replied with the patience of a remedial class teacher. Magnificent. Was he doing anything at all? 'Two thousand men of the municipal force are labouring day and night with their shovels,' he said.

In addition, police bulldozers, designed to smash barricades, were being adapted for the current emergency. Only in Paris perhaps would one find a fleet of barricade-smashing bulldozers but no snow ploughs.

Meanwhile, a mystery has developed about the celebrated Parisian *clochards*. When the freeze struck, Jacques Chirac, Mayor of Paris, instructed the public transport authorities to open the Métro stations at night to shelter the *clochards* who are estimated to number between 10,000 and 15,000. And the Cardinal Archbishop threw open the doors of his churches, and the Salvation Army provided thousands of extra beds.

The mystery lies in the fact that the churches have remained nearly empty and the extra beds unoccupied. The homeless prefer to sleep in the streets, even in this weather. Asked why, they have explained that the hostels are full of troublemakers, drunks, lunatics, unemployed people with a grudge against society, and single mothers. Not the sort of company they wish to keep. In view of this it has been hard to follow the Cardinal Archbishop's instruction to go out into the freezing streets and direct the *clochards* to the nearest church.

Certainly one's own efforts in this direction have been a failure. One night driving home I saw a *clochard* lowering himself into a manhole. After supper I began to worry about this man. Was he all right? It was minus God-knows-what outside. A small parcel was prepared marked 'A Gift of the Foreign Press Corps'. I put on my ridiculous fur hat and battled out to the manhole.

What a waste of time. Peering down through the elaborate wire cage which the *clochard* had erected around his shelter I could see a long ladder and a dim electric light. There was a sound of someone coughing beneath the ground and a terrific blast of heat rising into the night.

'Are you all right down there?' I called. 'Here is some claret, bread, fruit, cheese and *chocolats truffés.*' There was a long silence, then a muffled voice replied: 'Can one get no rest, even down here? Get stuffed.'

I left the package resting on his wire cage, but the chocolates would undoubtedly have melted by the morning. These rugged individuals are not always treated with such care. Last week an ambulance drew up at the Nicolas-Flamel reception centre and its crew requested the staff to receive a wounded man who had been discharged by a suburban hospital. The reception centre refused to take him because he was incapable of walking up to the dormitory. He had a leg wound and a face wound, his clothing was stained with dried blood and he was unable to speak. The ambulance crew thereupon lifted their patient out and left him on the pavement.

In the drought-stricken regions of Africa people call famines by different names. So they have the famine of 'Grinding up the water gourd' (to eat it) and the famine of 'Cast off the wife' (save yourself). In France they might call this cold spell 'The winter of the dead joggers'. Two joggers died on the same day, both apparently in perfect health but both overcome without any warning by the temperature.

One was a 38-year-old gastroenterologist who was jogging in the company of a medical professor and a biologist. Not even immediate expert attention could save him. The gastroenterologist died in mid-stride.

People suffering from cold have now been told to take no alcohol. Warm tea with honey and sugar is recommended instead. So an entire breed of mountain dogs has been put out of work, since not even the breath of a mature St Bernard can keep tea warm in a snowdrift.

Babies of less than four months are not to be taken outside at all, if it can be avoided, nor should they be passed rapidly from warm rooms into temperatures of less than $-10°C$. Scientifically speaking, it therefore seems unlikely that the Infant Jesus could ever have survived the journey from Bethlehem back to Nazareth.

Certainly He would have stood little chance if He had relied on some members of the Paris ambulance service.

January, 1987

═══

There was an old lady sitting at a table outside the café near the shopping centre in La Défense. She was reading a hard-cover novel. She was completely absorbed in it. Beside her there was a glass of Coca-Cola. Several things were wrong with this scene.

In the first place, this old lady was not the sort one normally sees reading a book in public. She had a back like a ramrod. Idleness to her would have been a lifelong offence. The days of her life would have been filled with small tasks and sharp comments. She had probably been a *concièrge*; or perhaps the receptionist at the Préfecture.

Further, no old lady drinks Coca-Cola in a country where the cafés sell white port or Dubonnet all day long. Finally, there was the hardback novel, a rarity, even in a bookshop, in France. She was reading it so carefully that I had to know the title. The drink remained untouched as she steadily turned the pages. She never looked up. It was called *Les Courriers de la Mort*. It reminded me of the story of Madame Bidon.

Some years ago a widow of fifty called Simone Bidon (a word of many meanings, including 'tin can', 'belly' and 'rubbish'), living in the Massif Central, found a copy of *Familles Chrétiennes* in the church in the village of Moyrazes. In the personal column she read an advertisement placed by a smallholder, Elie Raynal, who was sixty-two years old and looking for a wife. He was a widower who did not want to die alone. Simone was Catholic, but they married in the *mairie* all the same and went to live on Elie's little farm, like Darby and Joan.

After a time Simone began to find the work too hard and Elie began to grumble. Simone was not happy either. Elie did not want to die alone, and she did not want to eat alone. One day, when he was late for dinner yet again, she complained and he said: 'If it hadn't been you walking up the steps of the *mairie*, it would have been another one.' That remark was probably a mistake.

Time passed, things got worse and Elie started working on another smallholding. But when he came home he expected life to continue as normal. *He still wanted his dinner cooked.* Then Elie became ill. The neighbours noticed that he was only ill when he was living at home. They concluded, privately, that his wife was trying to poison him. When Elie went to the doctor traces of strychnine, then white spirit and then barbiturates were found in his water. The doctor suggested that he should be careful what he ate and drank. One day Elie had a fall and the hospital found traces of rat poison in his mouth. Everyone agreed that this was rather curious.

So things continued, for four more years. Elie became older and weaker but his temper did not improve. *And he still wanted his dinner cooked.* All the work on the farm fell to Simone. When that was finished she had to cook his dinner. One day while she was doing this he told her: 'When I'm dead, I'll leave everything to my children. There'll be nothing for you.' He might have kept this information to himself.

One evening, as the soup was just about ready, Elie, with characteristic timing, heaved himself out of his armchair and stumbled down to the cellar, cursing Simone as he went. 'He didn't come up and the soup was ready,' she said later. 'I was worried about him so I followed him down. He was chopping logs. I said, "I've already eaten. Finish that later."' Elie cursed her and pushed her. She tugged at his belt, the belt snapped and he fell forward on to the pile of logs, where his axe lay.

'He didn't move,' she said. 'His axe was beside him and he had gashed his neck when he fell. So, I took the axe. I placed the blade in the wound. I held the axe by the metal bit. And then I pressed on it. I pressed very hard. Very hard.' By the time the police arrived he had bled to death.

Simone got fifteen years. She said that after seven years of a marriage like hers she looked on prison 'as a sort of old people's home'.

After a while the old lady sitting in the café closed her book and paid her bill and left. Perhaps she had not been wasting time after all. She was probably going home to cook someone's dinner. The French frequently comment on the atrocious nature of the English murder, but they speak as connoisseurs.

February, 1987

A country which is still obsessed with the wartime Occupation has this month paid a belated tribute to one of the strangest members of the French Resistance, Simone Weil, the writer and mystic who died in a TB sanatorium outside Ashford, Kent, in 1943.

Simone Weil is one of those figures who fit into no movements or groups. Her ideas were so awkward and original that most of them were of little practical use, but at the same time they expressed valuable truths. The first volume of her complete works has just been published by Gallimard, forty-five years after her death. In English she is best known for her personal apologia, *The Need for Roots*. In that book one finds the mixture of idealism, personal gentleness and harsh Cartesian logic which is characteristic of her.

Like Dreyfus, Simone Weil was of Alsatian Jewish descent. Her father, a doctor, brought her up without a religious education and with private tutors. Later she entered the Ecole Normale Supérieure and qualified as a university teacher aged twenty-two. In those days the *Normaliens* were fiercely divided between the Left and the Right. She engaged in extreme-left politics, taught philosophy to railway workers and became a syndicalist. She frequently wore a railwayman's boiler suit and caused a mild scandal in the provincial schools where she taught. In Puy, in the Auvergne, she was known as the 'female anti-Christ in trousers'.

It was a wonderful time to be a twenty-year-old revolutionary in France. Hitler had not come to power. The Spanish Civil War was in the future. The most exotic ideas could be tried on for size. Simone Weil's ideas were sufficiently wild for her to attract the attention of Trotsky, who attacked her publicly as 'a prejudiced, petit-bourgeois reactionary'. This was unfair (she was a 'grand-bourgeois') but it amused her and she managed to arrange a secret meeting with the fierce old man who was then living outside Paris under police surveillance.

She was twenty-three, he was fifty-four ... but the meeting merely ended in another outraged attack. This time he accused her of being in the Salvation Army. At the same time the French Communists accused her of 'defeatism' for pointing out the uncomfortable fact that the German workers were being urged to fight with their bare hands.

In 1935 she went to work on the production line in the Renault car factory at Boulogne Billancourt. She always wanted to find out for herself. The following year Simone Weil's voyage around the history of her time took her to Spain with the International Brigade. She had already begun to develop her defence of individualism in the face of the collective. In Spain she was horrified by the lust for blood shown by both sides and she wrote that 'barbarism is a universal and permanent characteristic of human nature ... People are always cruel to the weak.'

Simone Weil was extremely short-sighted and she had to be invalided home from Spain after she had stepped in a bowl of boiling oil. One day a year earlier, while travelling in Portugal with her parents she had watched a procession of women in a fishing village celebrating the feast of Our Lady of Sorrows. Recovering from her experience in Spain, Simone Weil went to Italy and felt the first tug of a conversion to Catholicism. When France fell in 1940, she and her parents fled first to Vichy and then to Marseille. She used the early months of the Occupation to organize her ideas into a synthesis of what still seemed valid in her original convictions. When she and her parents managed to reach New York in 1942, she volunteered as an army nurse, then she wrote to Jacques Soustelle in London and asked to be sent back into Occupied France.

At first de Gaulle did not know what to do with her. Her poor health made it quite impossible to send her to France so he set her to work writing a philosophical blue-print for the Liberation. This turned into *The Need for Roots*. Some of her ideas are very relevant today. She wrote: 'We all know that when journalism becomes indistinguishable from organized lying, it constitutes a crime. But we think it is a crime impossible to punish . . . Where does this strange notion of non-punishable crime come from? It constitutes one of the most monstrous deformations of the human spirit.' Her suggested punishment for lying journalists was indictment before a special tribunal which would oblige the newspapers to report its judgements. In the case of repeated or blatant errors against the truth the offenders could be condemned to hard labour and their publications would be closed. But they would not be prevented from starting others.

Politicians might be pleased by that suggestion. Here is another one, which foresees the fashion for the 'politically correct' opinion. 'Protection of freedom of thought requires that no group should be permitted by law to express an opinion. For when a group starts having opinions it inevitably tends to impose them on its members . . . The intelligence is defeated as soon as the expression of one's thought is preceded, explicitly or implicitly, by the little word "we".'

It was part of Simone Weil's idealism that living as she was in the freedom of England in 1943, prevented from returning to her beloved France, she should refuse to eat any more than people could eat in France. Since she was suffering from TB this was a fatal decision. De Gaulle said that she was mad. She died on 24 August, having asked for a priest. Unfortunately he missed the train. One can see why she has been half-forgotten for so long. She abandoned the Left and abandoned her family traditions, and she opposed the imposition of technology and collectives. But in her intellectual honesty and courage she was close to being a saint.

April, 1988

SuperChannel was launched in Paris with a party at the British embassy. Television sets were dotted around the embassy's beautiful reception rooms for the guests to watch the launch 'live from London'.

The first treat turned out to be a forceful harangue by Margaret Thatcher in an electric-blue silk dress. She always seems to be shimmering in blue, even if the dress is brown. Perhaps it is her eyes. Anyway, this evening she ordered all the Europeans to watch our programmes and then informed them that if they did not already know it, 'British television' was 'something rather special'.

Behind our prime minister, as though to prove the truth of her words, a hideously bloated female puppet wearing a crown and carrying a cigarette-holder was apparently trying to break in through a window while mouthing curses in her direction. Could this be the Queen, or just Princess Margaret? The French guests were unsure.

Knowing nothing of *Spitting Image*, and thoroughly puzzled by this time, the potential customers were then treated to an extract from *'Allo, 'Allo*, the situation comedy which is set in France at the time of the German Occupation. What an inspired choice. The idea of setting a situation comedy in Occupation France has always seemed . . . robust. As part of an attempt to sell a television service to a country which is still waiting for the Barbie trial it was no less than heroic.

In the SuperChannel launch we saw a specially prepared extract from *'Allo, 'Allo* which included the following scenes:

A French barman obsequiously served a fat German officer with free drinks. Their conversation then turned to the black market in food. (We should not forget that some people in France starved to death during the Occupation because most of the food was commandeered for the Reich.) Next, the German officer struck the barman a few playful blows. The barman was then asked to sell his daughter, who was waving enthusiastically in the background, and they started to bargain about the price. Finally, the Frenchman was bullied into saying that he very much hoped the Germans would win the war. It would have been quite fun to watch the whole business of the launch in Bonn as well. All the better if there had been a few Frenchmen present.

Of course, foreigners are a funny lot, and we all make silly mistakes, but you do not have to be a specialist in French affairs to know that the subject of the Occupation is seen rather differently over here than it is in other parts of the world. Quite why the subject should still haunt France is not always immediately clear; every time it comes back into the news there seems to be a different reason. Last week, for instance, a Socialist deputy searching for some insult to throw at Raymond Barre, the new golden boy of the Right in the opinion polls, decided to say that he was 'a dangerous man, more like Pétain than de Gaulle'.

The idea of the twinkle-toed Samba king in any way resembling the dignified, tragic, gloomy old Marshal of France would seem far-fetched. And the reason for the comparison in this case was not very sinister.

It turned out that Barre was like Pétain because he believed in slogans such as 'hard work, the family and our country'. The Socialist considered that such ideals were corrupting the governing class and warned other Socialists to avoid being contaminated by them. The point is not the justice of the comparison with Pétain but the fact that it does not seem ridiculous. It is still an insult.

February, 1987

═══

At ten o'clock on a morning in March three years ago, Frédéric G, then an eighteen-year-old Sixth-Former in a *lycée* in Bordeaux, walked into the school playground during the break and shot a fellow pupil, Anthony F in the back with a sawn-off shotgun. Anthony survived the experience but spent six months in hospital. Frédéric was tried last week. Anthony was in court to give evidence.

'Anthony F,' said Frédéric, 'I am speaking to everyone but above all to you who suffered this violence because I want you to understand what retribution you faced that day.'

At this point Anthony looked at Frédéric and said, 'I would rather forget the whole thing.' He then left the court. In doing so, he missed hearing one of the more original defences to a charge of attempted murder which is likely to be advanced in France this year. Frédéric told the jury that after much reflection he realized he had shot down his fellow scholar because he was suffering from 'a deep existential malaise'.

This had been brought on because he had problems with his family which he had attempted to escape by reading the works of Camus. He had been struck in particular by a study of the Emperor Caligula who, according to Camus, was something of a Left Bank intellectual, being an existentialist who had decided to commit an anti-social act in order to find a meaning for his own existence.

Although Frédéric was not faced with the problems which beset the Emperor Caligula, he did suffer from the occasional *ennui*.

His father, José, was professor of chemistry at the University of R— and described as 'violent, brilliant and intolerant'. Frédéric modelled himself on this dominating figure but felt confused when the professor took up with a girl of his own age, then sixteen.

Continuing to model himself on his father and on Caligula, Frédéric then made an affectionate proposition to his mother, but she had not been reading Caligula so she merely gave him a flea in the ear. Deciding that he must be a failure, as a son and as an emperor, Frédéric started to live alone – but for the company of Camus. Pondering which anti-social act to commit, Frédéric rejected robbery as 'ridiculous'. There is, it seems, a world of difference between 'the ridiculous' and 'the absurd'.

He then considered suicide but decided it would not serve his purpose since he would not be around to watch the effects of the act. He would have given his life meaning, but only by depriving himself of it. That left the urgent necessity of committing an irrational act within three days, the timetable he had set himself.

Frédéric went out and bought a shotgun and some cartridges. He practised firing the gun into a pile of sand. It worked. Then he sawed off the barrel so that he could get the gun into his satchel. He fired it again and was rather dismayed by the size of the hole which a sawn-off shotgun makes in a heavy wooden door. But it was too late to change his plans.

With his preparations complete, Frédéric had one day of freedom left. He decided to enjoy it. He did his washing, tidied up the house and went out to a restaurant and to the cinema.

The following morning he met his victim, chosen because he was popular and brilliant, and arranged to see him in the break. When the time came, Frédéric walked up behind Anthony, removed the gun from his satchel and pulled the trigger. It failed to go off.

At this point it is clear that Frédéric's education was defective. He should have studied Graham Greene. He would then have realized that he was not in a book by Camus, he was rather a character in *The Revolver in the Corner Cupboard*, and he could have skipped out of the playground, bought his mum some flowers and written off to join the Secret Service. But that is one of the basic flaws in the French national character: too much logic.

Turning round so that no one noticed what he was doing, Frédéric reloaded the gun and fired again. With Anthony splattered over a considerable part of the playground, Frédéric then walked calmly along to the headmaster's study, placed the gun on his desk and told him what had happened. History does not record the position of the headmaster in relation to the desk at the time, although it is quite possible that he was under it.

Summarizing his defence, Frédéric explained he had been suffering from an unresolved Oedipus complex which had developed in an atmosphere of physical and moral violence, and that he had taken refuge in a damaging isolation. The court psychiatrist said he entirely agreed with this analysis.

The Bordeaux jury also seemed impressed with his explanation, because they accepted a plea of mitigating circumstances and he was given a sentence which will mean that he can continue his university studies in a year. He intends eventually to become a barrister.

April, 1987

======

Last month *Le Monde* published a photograph taken on the corner of Birdcage Walk with Big Ben in the background. In the foreground a crowd of men in city suits and bowler hats were moving in a body towards Horse Guards Parade. The caption read: 'Businessmen going to Buckingham Palace to pay their respects to Queen Elizabeth II.'

If you were a Frenchman standing on the corner of Birdcage Walk and a brisk body of men came down the street wearing city suits and bowler hats you would hardly expect them to be a company of the Artists' Rifles. You would not necessarily realize that in England when old soldiers assemble in civilian clothes, they choose to wear civilian clothes that are uniform. That would not be *logique*. Either one or the other.

No, you would see what you had expected to see when you got to London – that is to say 300 businessmen doing some form of business that required them to move all at once from Birdcage Walk to Horse Guards Parade. Nothing odd about that. In France such gatherings of old soldiers evoke a little more of the barrack room, a little less of the parade ground. Dress is selected by the individual, anything from jungle combat kit to shiny blue suit and beret.

Lunching with the veterans, after one reunion last November, I was treated to a tactical appreciation of the surrounding countryside by the man who had just carried the Tricolour to the local war memorial. When that was finished he started reminiscing about his old campaigns. He said that he had fought in France, Korea, Indo-China and Algeria and he put his military distinction down to a steady diet of beans. It was these, he claimed, which had propelled him to the rank of corporal.

His neighbour, an even older veteran of the war before the last, asked him how long it had taken him to achieve this eminence and was delighted to be told that it had been no more than seven years. The senior veteran agreed that the Great War had not been very amusing but said that for him the real tragedy had been his inability to father children, added to which he could not get his plastic mustard squirter to work and this was preventing him from enjoying his *entrecôte*.

The ex-corporal helped him to unblock the mustard squirter and surmised that it was obviously the same problem all over again. The old boy had never had any children because he could never remember to remove his *capote anglaise*. He'd better watch out with the mustard now or he'd end up with twins.

This conversation was carried on over two litres of red wine and in front of a puzzled group of infants, several of whom appeared to be drinking tap water diluted in *vin ordinaire*, to purify the water perhaps. A foreigner joining our table might have imagined that this was a typical French scene. And he would have been correct.

A list of the hundred richest millionaires in France reveals that the largest single group among them, twelve, made their fortunes from booze. The French continue to drink more alcohol per person per year than any other country in the world. And most of it is wine. The average daily consumption of wine in France for people over the age of twenty is half a bottle. That is just wine. In addition every French adult over twenty averages per year 102 pints of beer, forty pints of cider and four pints of spirits. That works out at twice as much pure alcohol per head as the English can manage.

There is another superficial impression about the French that they go around smoking Gauloises. They do. A recent campaign by the

French anti-smoking pressure group tried to publicize its discovery that smoking causes male impotence, particularly in young men. This campaign seems to have been a total failure. Although the press conference where this astounding fact was released was well-attended, the French journalists present, mostly heavy smokers, must have concluded that it was either untrue or too depressing to mention.

April, 1987

Case number four in Court No. 1 of the Tribunal de Paris reached its banal conclusion on Monday when the film actor Jean-Pierre Léaud received a three-month suspended sentence for throwing a flower pot at his 82-year-old neighbour, an artist, Mme Yvonne Pradie.

This event occurred on a hot evening last August, when the police in Paris had quite a lot to do anyway. But three *agents* managed to tear themselves away from hunting terrorists to find in the courtyard of an apartment building in the boulevard Edgar-Quinet a bare-chested, handsome man in an excited state, dancing amid the rubble of numerous geraniums. According to one of the policemen, '*son sexe était dehors et à la main*'. According to another, he was 'jumping all over the place'.

The officers knew exactly what to do, they go to the cinema just like the rest of us. The three of them overpowered the star, handcuffed his hands behind his back, gave him a few blows in the stomach, manacled his feet and inserted this conveniently stream-lined shape into their squad car. When they arrived at the police station, they dragged him across the pavement and charged him with assaulting the police. Léaud spent the next fifteen days in La Santé prison. That was Act One.

The action now moves into flashback. Léaud, a vulnerable boy of fourteen, who has spent his childhood in French boarding schools, the perfect raw material for a film director, meets François Truffaut and is cast for world stardom. He is remade in the image of his films. Before long, the only absolutely clear fact in Léaud's life is Truffaut. Truffaut becomes his father, his friend, his banker. Then Truffaut dies and Léaud is very confused indeed.

He finds some comfort in the work of another friend, Thierry Lévy, a barrister. Léaud spends hours in court watching Thierry at work and studying how people behave in the dock. He decides that the dock is the best stage in the world and that all actors should study those who stand there. He even says 'an actor who has never stood in the dock is not a real actor'.

And so, one hot night in August, after Léaud has had a row with his girlfriend, the old lady next door makes too much noise and . . . we move forward into the present.

The scene is a court. Jean-Pierre Léaud is the accused. He is supported by Jeanne Moreau. Today she is blonde. She sits beside him absently stroking his neck, the index finger of the other hand extended along her cheek in a gesture that would make her recognizable in photographic negative. Léaud is defended by his friend Thierry Lévy, naturally. Also present is Jean-Pierre's shrink who has diagnosed what we shrinks call 'a cry for help'.

Only Mme Pradie, the elderly artist covered in potting compost, has failed to rise to the occasion and has decided to settle her complaint in exchange for a pay-off. Perhaps she is confused by all this *Nouvelle Vague*, never seems to have a plot, all the scenes get muddled up and so on. She could easily end up in the dock herself. It might even turn into a war-crimes trial.

The judge reads out the evidence and calls the accused 'Truffaut'. Léaud, for once not confused, gives his evidence in a low voice. He is pale. He denies throwing flowerpots at the old lady. It was just that he was throwing flowerpots around and one of them unfortunately hit her. He absolutely denies the bit about his dress being 'disarranged'. Indeed he swears a separate oath on this point. The police have been getting their movies muddled up.

It is said that in the squad car he threatened the police with an article in *Libé*, that is the left-wing daily, *Libération*, the thinking Parisian's truncheon. Another neighbour, a dentist, recalls that there have been previous incidents; the last time it was not the flowerpots which took the brunt of the assault, it was a letter-box.

It is time for the star of the piece to move to the centre of the screen, Thierry Lévy. He has a crew cut and a tortured expression. He is playing a barrister who is defending his friend who is an actor playing an actor who is defended by a barrister. Lévy's defence turns on the difficulties of an actor's private life. He spends some time on the conflict between the various aspects of an actor's personality. It is a magnificent performance.

The court announces a verdict. It dismisses the charge of assault on the police, who must be careful about overacting in future. But the offence of battery with a flowerpot is proved and will remain on the record. All too soon the lights come up and it is time for case number five. Jean-Pierre Léaud turns to Thierry Lévy and thanks him. There are tears in his eyes. Cut.

May, 1987

Not far from my home in the battle-scarred heart of the Latin Quarter there is a bookshop which is so scruffy that it could almost be English. The name is no longer over the door but by reading the marks left on the paintwork one can just make out what the name used to be – *La Libre Pensée*.

The selection of atheist and humanist tracts in the shop window confirms that this neglected establishment is one of the important shrines of modern France, the historical nerve-centre of rationalism. On the wall of the building there is a marble plaque which commemorates Ferdinand Buisson, who at the turn of the century was the president of the National Association of Free Thinkers of France, and the man who introduced into the National Assembly the laws that separated the French church and state. The plaque was erected in June 1980 by Buisson's admirers in protest against 'the violation of those laws, committed by the head of state, and on the occasion of the visit to France of Pope John Paul II'. Last week a small notice had been stuck up beside the plaque advertising the annual conference of the Union of Atheists, which was held on Sunday in Paris in the Hôtel Nikko.

The Union of Atheists has fewer than 3,000 members, although they are doubtless of exceptional quality, and its meetings usually pass in an atmosphere of cantankerous and contented argument. But this year in the Hôtel Nikko there was a new form of discord. It came to the point where irrational emotions were expressed, and at a conference of Rationalists there can be few uglier scenes.

The cause of all the trouble was member 2,444, a new recruit who in real life is a lecturer in French literature at the University of Lyon.

Three leading members of the Union of Atheists, Senator Henri Caillavet, Roger Boussin, the president of the Fraternal Union of Rationalists, and the director of *La Raison*, a periodical, all said that if member 2,444 was not expelled they would resign. In vain for the presiding atheist, Albert Beaugheon (the irreligious have wonderful names) to point out that under the union's rules he was not allowed either to refuse to admit member 2,444 or to expel him. The uproar merely grew fiercer.

'Atheism is like billiards,' said M. Beaugheon. 'I like to play, so does number 2,444. That's all that matters.' But in the excitement over the unwelcome new atheist the president went unheard, as did the principal speaker of the conference, who had been billed to give an absorbing talk on 'bad moral examples drawn from the Bible'. So who is member 2,444, and what has he done? His name is Robert Faurisson, and he is the leader of a small group of historians known as 'revisionists', who deny that the Nazi gas chambers ever existed. They also question whether there was ever a plan to murder all the Jews in Europe and whether the Jews who died under the Nazis numbered six million. Their arguments have been appearing in pamphlets for several years, but only recently has anyone paid them much attention. Now, thanks to the general preoccupation in France with the wartime years, there has been an attack of national madness, and M. Faurisson has been built up by his opponents until he is seen by them as the potential author of a new *Mein Kampf*.

His pamphlets are banned in schools. Newspapers which inadvertently print letters from his followers attempt to withdraw themselves from the streets. And a man who was distributing a revisionist leaflet on the steps of the Palais de Justice in Lyon last week was chased off by the police.

Nor did the Union of Atheists prove much more cool-headed. As Senator Caillavet's resignation was noted by the meeting one member called out that the senator was the president of the Franco-Iranian Friendship Association, and 'what sort of atheist hobnobs with Ayatollahs?' There then followed a thoughtful exchange of views which, according to the report in *Libération*, included the words 'swine', 'cop', 'Stalinist' and 'Gestapo'.

Meanwhile, the cause of all the trouble, member 2,444, sat calmly in the middle of the meeting having the time of his previously obscure life. 'It's always like this,' he said with an innocent air. 'If I joined an angling club someone would throw me out after three months, and all because I have, on scientific grounds, raised the question of whether or not the gas chambers existed.'

Asked why he had joined the Union of Atheists he said that it was because his opponents had failed to refute his arguments on rational grounds and had therefore taken refuge in attitudes which he considered to be 'religious'.

The sensible, not to say rational, way to answer revisionist historians would surely be to examine their work in public and either refute it or not. Certainly, nothing could make revisionist history more attractive to impressionable young minds than to say that it is so dangerous that it cannot even be discussed.

And what would the first free thinkers have made of such a suggestion? The very idea of a subject which could not be illuminated by the light of reason would have been rejected by them with contempt. One might say that one could hear them turning in their graves, except for the fact that they would undoubtedly have been among the earliest members of the cremation societies.

Clearly atheism is not what it was. It is not just the paintwork of *La Libre Pensée* which is neglected. Atheism has lost touch with its original vision, like so many other revealed creeds.

June, 1987

———

Last week I was tear-gassed while dining in a restaurant in Lyon. As a news item that sums it up, but from the gastronomic point of view there is more to be said.

For a start, this sort of thing never happens to the food correspondents or the inspectors from the *Guide Michelin*. They could easily have been in this restaurant. It was feeding some of the lawyers from the Barbie trial, and some of them know their *Michelin* better than they know their *Code Pénal*.

One moment one was sitting there, toying with one's *moules feuilletées*, the next one was coughing into one's napkin and everyone was in tears. The same scene at every table. Looking out of the window into the pouring rain the sight of many people, oblivious to the rain, also coughing into their handkerchiefs. 'Just some young people,' said the manageress. 'Just a little tear gas. Nothing.' Probably a neo-fascist demonstration being broken up by the police. '*Normale.*'

An hour later, the *lapin chasseur* having come and gone, a glass of Sauternes – with the compliments of the house – still unfinished, there was a violent crash and two young men entered, one dragging the other. They staggered towards the back of the room leaving spots of blood on the floor. 'A glass of water and call the police' – then they disappeared through the swing doors to the kitchen.

Back to the Sauternes, but no, another crash and here is the noisy one again, shouting at the waiter: 'Dial 17. Why haven't you called the police?' This is a good question. At this point, one of the lawyers leans over to the roast beef trolley and removes the carving knife. He places this under his table-cloth. Does he intend to use it? His female guests are reseated with their backs to the wall. There is a certain amount of 'shall we go?' But no one moves.

And so to the Sauternes, but this is becoming quite impossible. Here he is once more, staggering and shouting and knocking the furniture around. This time, he repeats several times and at the top of his voice: 'One does not do that. It's out of the question. One does not just pull a gun like that. Now he's wounded.' He tries to use the telephone himself but he is too drunk and the waiters, looking a little nervous, refuse to help him. Did he say something about a gun? Still no one moves; probably because no one has quite finished dinner.

Eventually the police are alerted by someone else and three small but muscular-looking men in civilian clothes arrive. They too disappear through the swing doors and there is a very long pause indeed. Outside, two police cars draw up and block the road. Inside the cars large Alsatians are barking their heads off. Some more plain-clothes men gather, the uniformed police do not recognize them, offence is taken, introductions are made and there are handshakes all round. They may be working but there is time for formality.

From behind the swing doors, nothing, silence, a shadow occasionally moving across the light that shines beneath the door. How does a smart restaurant remove a body from the kitchen at the busiest time in the evening when too many of the customers want to know whether it is a body or still a person? One begins to imagine how a corpse would look while it was being frogmarched across the dining room. Lyon is the site of the French national school of *haute cuisine*, but they probably don't teach the answer to this one.

The manageress has been on the phone almost continually since the arrival of the bleeding man, but never to the ambulance, always to the kitchen. 'Where are my three *lapins*? You have forgotten the *moules*.' I ask her what is going on. Is it a demonstration? 'No, it's the local gangs. That's why I did not call the police,' she explains. 'The one who was shouting is the one who was throwing all the tear gas. There is a hotel down the road and they seem to be having a little Mafia trouble.'

The Sauternes is finished by now but clearly one can't leave the story, so an Armagnac is sent for and it arrives just before four firemen walk in and then walk out again dragging the bleeding man, who is put into the fire tender and driven away. The police dogs depart, still barking, another police van arrives and three more plain-clothes men emerge from the next building carrying, horizontally, a hairy young fellow with his hands handcuffed behind his back, his legs bound, his trousers ricked up and a muffled sound coming from the opposite extremity to his socks. They throw him bodily into the van, and then walk away.

A suggestion that this part of Lyon is better than Marseille does not raise a laugh. It is time to leave. Some way down the street the youthful *maître d'hôtel*, who has not been in evidence for a while, is hurrying back to the restaurant. 'I don't know why it is,' he says, 'but something like this always happens when the boss is absent. He is not often absent, to be fair, but when he is, this happens.'

I think I know where the boss gets his tear gas, but where did he find such excellent *moules*?

June, 1987

———

The Paris–Dakar rally, which ends on Friday, has become an annual institution to rival the Tour de France. It is accorded hourly news bulletins for three weeks. Huge crowds assemble along the Champs-Elysées to see the drivers off. The idea of racing cars, motorbikes and lorries across the Sahara desert has caught the popular imagination to such an extent that when the inventor of the rally, Thierry

Sabine, was killed in a helicopter crash in Niger two years ago, the sporting nation was plunged into mourning.

This year is the tenth anniversary of the Paris–Dakar, which has grown into a huge commercial success. The Thierry Sabine Organization sells the television and film rights to one channel which then makes a profit from resales. The entrants pay large fees to the organizers and recoup them from sponsorship, and the sponsors are happy to pay for their names to be displayed night after night on the television.

One of the organizers has estimated the turnover this year to be in the region of £50 million. It is one of the great sporting success stories of the decade. It is also, according to its numerous critics, an obscene spectacle. Those who are concerned about the poverty of Algeria, Niger, Mali, Burkina Faso, Mauritania and Senegal consider it wrong to spend, and make, so much money from a sporting event in a part of the world which is so poor. Rumours of the profits have even reached the Vatican and this year the Pope condemned the rally. His disapproval did not deter the organizers. Rally drivers need thick skins.

Of course Europeans did not always go into the desert to make money, even if they loved machines. One of the greatest poets both of the desert and of machinery was a Frenchman, Antoine Saint-Exupéry. But it is hard to believe that his little aeroplane, with its sewing-machine engine, would have caused much disturbance. Saint-Exupéry learned awe and wonder from his experience of machinery. Like many before him, he saw a wilderness as a place of the spirit. The modern approach is a little different. Here is a picture of one of the heroes of the Paris–Dakar.

Jan de Rooy is a Dutch haulage contractor. He runs a fleet of 275 lorries. He lives in a house which he built in the centre of his lorry compound. He recently told a French newspaper that for him 'lorries are like cows to a peasant. I need to breathe them.' At the weekend, in order to relax, he likes to drive a lorry from the Netherlands to somewhere like Italy.

He has built a special lorry to race in the Paris–Dakar. It has two turbo motors producing 1,200 horsepower, it does a maximum speed of 130 m.p.h. and it can go from 0 to 60 m.p.h. in 8.5 seconds. He has one dream in life, which is to beat all the racing cars on one stage of the rally. This year his second lorry crashed, killing the navigator and seriously injuring the two drivers.

The progress of a Paris–Dakar rally is a murderous farce. People have died in nine of the ten years of the race. This year so far four people have died and nineteen have been flown back to Europe in private air-ambulances with serious injuries. The fatal accidents are frequently ridiculous. Two support vehicles go round a sand dune in opposite directions and hit each other. A mechanic goes to sleep beside the car he is servicing. The car tears off on the next stage, the mechanic sleeps on and is run over by another car.

When the drivers kill Africans it is not ridiculous, it is contempt-ible. The dead Africans are always called 'spectators'. The road they are knocked down on is always called 'the race track'. It happened most recently on Monday; a ten-year-old Malian girl, name un-recorded, knocked for six in a cloud of dust outside her village. Everyone was very upset. The race continues.

Also on Monday, another anonymous African apparently made the most eloquent comment yet on the Paris–Dakar. During the night, from the centre of a heavily guarded compound in the middle of Bamako, the capital of Mali, somebody stole the leading car in the rally. The three mechanics who had been guarding it slept on. A special detachment of the Malian armed forces, carrying bazookas, set out to search the city but it took most of the morning to find the car. In Bamako this is regarded as the best joke for some time. If it was not done by a local, it should have been.

At about the time Saint-Exupéry was writing *Night Flight* and *Wind, Sand and Stars*, another desert pilot, a Spanish foreign legion-naire, landed his plane in the Sahara to take his lunch. 'A caravan of Saharan nomads approached. I asked the leader of the caravan how long it would take him to reach Semara. He shrugged and said, "About three or four days." I laughed and said my plane would reach Semara in only two hours. "And what will you do with the extra hours?" he asked.'

It is doubtful if the Thierry Sabine organizers would understand this anecdote. Their new scheme is to run a powerboat race along the rivers of French Guiana, through rainforest still inhabited by indigenous people. Somebody should stop them, but it probably won't be the French government.

January, 1988

A manslaughter case has now reached its second week in the Assize Court in Poitiers. In 1984, Nicole Berneron, the wife of a pitface worker, was taken into the university hospital at Poitiers for a simple operation, the removal of a benign tumour from behind her left ear. The operation was a success but the patient failed to recover from the anaesthetic – which had been administered to her by Prof. Pierre Meriel, the senior anaesthetist at the hospital.

Shortly after Mme Berneron died, Prof. Meriel discovered that the tubes leading from the two gas cylinders used in the operating theatre had been reversed. So when he thought he was giving her oxygen to revive her, he was actually giving her nitrous oxyde, the anaesthetic gas.

Prof. Meriel promptly accused one of his junior colleagues, Bakari Diallo (who he had effectively demoted the evening before), of sabotaging the machine in order to cause him professional embarrassment. This extraordinary accusation was supported by a third anaesthetist, Denis Archambeau, who apparently broke under police questioning and confirmed Dr Diallo's guilt. Dr Archambeau later retracted this statement but none the less he and Dr Diallo were committed to trial for manslaughter, and Prof. Meriel was also sent for trial on charges of causing death through negligence.

Dr Diallo was born in the West African state of Burkina Faso. He is a brilliant man and the son of a Sahelian nomad, and it was not long before rumours began to circulate that there was a racist aspect to the accusations. A committee of support was formed and two weeks before the trial started a book was published attacking the reputation of Prof. Meriel.

The case looked set to fulfil its usual role in French life, as an emblem of all sorts of irrelevant but fierce political quarrels. Had the good Dr Diallo been victimized, or had the good Prof. Meriel been trapped? The political Left, and those who opposed racism, ticked the first box, the political Right, and those who supported professional hierarchies, ticked the second.

Then events took an unexpected turn. As evidence started to be heard it became clear that none of the parties in the case could give an entirely convincing account of themselves. Prof. Meriel said his patient had died from nitrous oxide poisoning. So why had she not turned blue? Furthermore, why did he leave the operating theatre to take a telephone call when it was already apparent that Mme Berneron was not responding to oxygen? And why did he immediately accuse Dr Diallo of sabotaging the machine? Could he have switched the tubes himself to cover up his own negligence?

Dr Diallo claimed that he had nothing to do with the disaster. So why had he gone to such lengths to ensure that Prof. Meriel would have to be present in the operating theatre that day (by organizing a sympathy strike among the alternative anaesthetists)? Why had he come to the theatre wing, where he had no duties, to ask if Prof. Meriel was at work in theatre? And why did he give an alibi that nobody could substantiate for the one time when he could have sabotaged the equipment?

And as for Dr Archambeau, why did he accuse his friend, Dr Diallo, of switching the tubes, and admit that he had assisted in this criminal act, merely because the police suggested that he had done so? Finally, what killed Mme Berneron? Teams of eminent scientists have suggested several possibilities, apart from nitrous oxide poisoning, depending on which doctor they are defending. What had seemed to be a straightforward medico-political battle has turned into a case worthy of Hercule Poirot. Prof. Meriel has been subjected to a pitiless cross-examination. His professional colleagues are brought to court in handcuffs each day and warmly applauded by their supporters. In the middle of the courtroom stands the anaesthetic apparatus. And sitting near it, in a state of anguished shock, Claude Berneron, now a widower, watches as three doctors who he and his wife trusted, display their mutual loathing and contempt.

February, 1988

Ten years ago the *curé* of Saint-Nicholas du Chardonnet, a baroque church on the boulevard St Germain, was surprised to notice that his usual Sunday evening congregation of six old ladies and two tramps had considerably increased. His church was packed with devout strangers. The *curé* finished Mass, gave the final blessing and said the words of dismissal, but nobody moved.

Instead there entered through the west door, like a bad dream, a procession of altar boys in cassocks and priests in birettas, all the horrors the *curé* had thought abolished by the second Vatican Council; and his uninvited guests proceeded to celebrate on his altar a High Mass in the old Tridentine Rite.

The *curé* has never said Mass in his church again. From that day to this Saint-Nicolas du Chardonnet has been guarded and occupied by the militant followers of Archbishop Lefebvre. The rightful tenant is still living behind the church, barricaded in his turn into his presbytery. On Sunday he was grumbling about the difficulty of life under these conditions and complaining about the noise of the bells which ring incessantly to announce the times of services, while the devout usurpers celebrated the tenth anniversary of their illegal action.

Despite the rain the congregation spilled out on to the pavement. Video screens relayed the service from inside the church while enthusiasts hawked copies of *National* and *La France Monarchiste*, the newspapers of the National Front and the Orléanists, and boy scouts in the distinctive uniform of navy shorts several sizes too small for their occupants, marshalled the crowds.

It was a scene which took one back not ten years but forty; a reminder of that France Nancy Mitford once evoked with her vision of every sixteen-year-old French boy being equipped 'with short trousers and a moustache, a hoop and a mistress'.

Following the original occupation of Saint-Nicolas du Chardonnet, the choleric Archbishop of Paris, Cardinal Marty, obtained a court order for their expulsion but this has never been executed. The French hierarchy, recognizing the explosive qualities of religious enthusiasm in what may or may not be a Latin country, decided to leave the traditionalists in peace.

Unfortunately they seem to be strangers to that state of mind. Indeed they are so cantankerous that although France is a place with scarcely a religious thought in its head, this quarrel between a minority within a minority has attracted an unusual amount of attention.

The first point which people always emphasize about the French 'old' Catholics, or 'new' Catholics as they sometimes style themselves, is that they are politically rather right-wing. This must be a peculiarly French phenomenon since there is absolutely nothing about the Tridentine rite which suggests a party political preference. At Saint-Nicolas du Chardonnet, the priest in charge, l'Abbé

Coache, in a recent sermon noted that certain people were plotting to celebrate the two-hundredth anniversary of the French Revolution. He anticipated that when the day came (it will be 14 July 1989), much would probably be made of the Fall of the Bastille, 'that magnificent fortress erected to protect the people of Paris from the English. But,' he added, 'when I think of the Revolution, I always pray for the heroic Swiss Guards who died defending the King.'

The fact is that those in France who set out to defend the Tridentine rite have found themselves heir instead to the most extreme political views of the nineteenth-century French Church, which spent 120 years quarrelling with the Republic trying to recover the property and influence it lost when the Bastille fell. In an obscure way, this is still a live issue in France today. Although 81 per cent of the French call themselves Catholic very few of them play any part in the life of the Church. Yet when the Socialist government attempted to interfere with the status of religious education in 1983 it caused the biggest public demonstrations since 1968, and the measure had to be dropped.

It is very rare to find a Frenchman who does not describe himself as 'a Republican'. Even monarchists, including the pretender to the French throne, the Comte de Paris, describe themselves in some sense as 'Republicans'. So you might think in that case that the legitimacy of the Revolution would be a closed subject; but somehow it never quite is. The ghosts continue to clank their chains. And the affair of Saint-Nicolas du Chardonnet seems to have become one more excuse for listening to them.

March, 1987

═══

In generally high spirits 200,000 *pied-noirs*, the one-time French colonists of Algeria, ended their assembly in Nice today with an open-air Mass celebrated by five bishops, including the former bishop of Oran. The four-day gathering marked the twenty-five years which have passed since the end of the dream of an 'Algérie Française'.

Today's service closed with the singing of the *Marseillaise* accompanied by the band of the Foreign Legion. The exiles had come from as far away as Alicante, Quebec and Paraguay. Their national anthem brought back memories of the battle and the land they had lost, and by the end of it many were in tears.

During his sermon the former bishop of Oran, Mgr Lacaste, said that 'what happened in North Africa between 1830 and 1962 is now part of French history and will finally be settled between God and the individual conscience.' He offered prayers for, 'All our dead, those whose graves we visit when we return to Algeria and Tunisia and Morocco, and those who have no graves, and for the soldiers who died in Africa, ours as well as those from Metropolitan France.'

As he spoke, people continued to circulate among the vast crowd looking for lost friends and carrying home-made placards with the names of the towns and districts where they were born and where they once confidently expected to die; 'Frenda Ain-Kermes', 'Bab-el-Qued', 'Tipasa', and 'Fort de l'Eau'.

From the terracotta-tiled roofs of the Place Masséna, police marksmen searched the congregation for troublemakers; judging by the number of religious gatherings the marksmen are now required to attend they must be gathering an impressive number of indulgences. But the mood remained more festive than political. It was a scene designed to make the exiles feel at ease. Nice itself is home to 80,000 *pied-noirs*, and one can see why they have chosen to settle in a town where there is the Mediterranean, the blazing heat, the palm trees and a large Arab labour force.

At today's Mass the banner of the 'Friends of Our Lady of Lourdes from Oran' was prominent, as were the venerated images of the Black Virgin of Africa and Our Lady of Santa-Cruz – famous for having once saved the city of Oran from cholera. But the priests, one of them wearing a biretta and dark glasses, gave out holy communion beneath another banner, unexpectedly unfurled, that of the 'Former Prisoners of Algérie Française'. And the stewards were all wearing the faded red berets of the 'paras', so identifying themselves as the veterans who nearly brought civil war to France when they backed the generals' putsch of 1961.

Another constant and appropriate feature of the gathering were the white kepis of the Foreign Legionnaires, many of them born since the conflict ended, but members of a unit which would never have existed had it not been for the 132-year adventure 'over there'. At last night's open-air ball the Legionnaires were to be seen belly-dancing together, their white kepis bobbing like distant lumps of sugar above the packed crowd. Today their buglers saluted the Consecration, and at the end of the service when the former bishop of Oran said 'Merci à Nice, et Vive les Pied-Noirs', the crowd called back 'Et Vive La Légion'.

The reunion has been widely ignored by political leaders but Jean-Marie Le Pen, president of the National Front, was to be seen waving to the crowds this morning. His success in this part of France, where he sometimes polls 25 per cent of the vote, is thought to be related to the high proportion of pied-noirs.

Somewhere in the crowd, but lost to sight, were six harkis, representatives of the 400,000 Algerian Arabs who are descended from those who were loyal to France and who had to flee their country at Independence. Many are still living in miserable conditions in French refugee settlements. The six harkis are walking from Rouen to Monte Cassino (where 20,000 French colonial troops died during the Second World War) in an attempt to draw attention to the plight of their people.

June, 1987

═══

In the barber's shop of the Carlton Hotel, Cannes, an enormous man whose hair is dyed brown, wearing a baby-yellow cardigan, is undergoing a double manicure. The girls sitting on low stools at either hand appear to be in some physical danger. The man looks as though he might burst out of the steel and leather chair at any moment and congeal all over the tiled floor like an outsize gob of chewing gum. The girls carry on fearlessly, each working on a surprisingly small, pink hand which, when left to its own devices, begins to curl inward, as though it wants to start digging something up.

It is 6 p.m. in Cannes on day four of the film festival. In thirty minutes, the hired limousines will be lining up outside the hotel to carry this enormous man, his attractive young lady and several dozen other transatlantic visitors the short distance along the esplanade to the Palais des Festivals. The paparazzi are already in the lobby, the crowd are in place outside the revolving doors. In the bar near the barber's shop an anonymous but possibly important

Japanese drains his whisky and starts towards the door. He is wearing Bermuda shorts in distressed denim, a skimpy tee-shirt and two-tone leather dress shoes, without socks.

The lobby of the Carlton seems once to have been a spacious area of pillars and mirrors. For the film festival, it is crowded with placards for third-rate American films and now looks like a tacky amusement arcade. The stars emerge from the lift, and pass through a security screen and the frantic faces on the pavement outside. This year the stars include Meryl Streep, Marcello Mastroianni, Alain Delon, Anthony Quinn, Sophia Loren and Yves Montand.

None of them are in *Dreams of a Voyeur*, *Kill Me Again*, or *How to Make Love to a Negro Without Getting Tired*, the posters which have been selected for the lobby, perhaps by the blob of human chewing gum. Just by the lift serving as a backdrop for every emerging star is a poster for *Il Frullo del Passero*. This is a twice life-size study of a female bum. The *paparazzi*, who are very quick, have already noticed the possibilities. A blonde girl with a pleasant face, escorted by an older man in a long-sleeved waistcoat which appears to be made from silk mattress-ticking, runs the gauntlet. Sometimes the stars, who get younger every year, are hard to recognize. But this blonde cannot be a star, because no one is taking her photograph. She is just a girl who has a painful-looking sunburn. One can see the holes pierced in her ear lobes, and one can see why they are empty tonight. She is wearing a rather attractive black frock and fiery red tights. No, they are black – the red colour is bleeding through from the legs beneath them.

At last a star. *Il y a strip* . . . already? No, no, the *paparazzi* are referring to Meryl Streep, and she doesn't do that sort of thing. A lady appears in a red dress. The flash guns go off all over the lobby. My God, if this is Meryl Streep my name is Henry Porter and it is time I hung up my notebook. It is not Streep, but I have seen this lady somewhere before. It is . . . Danielle Mitterrand, the president's wife, and like everyone else she is posing right in front of the outsize bum. This sort of thing would never be allowed in France, but France starts outside those revolving doors, continues along the Esplanade la Croisette and stops again at the doors of the Palais des Festivals, *hélas*. 1989 is the year when more than half the official competitors at Cannes are in the English language, but none of them is an English film. It is also the year when the mayor of Cannes allowed a property developer to demolish the Palais Croisette (where the festival started in 1947), the Blue Bar and the Hôtel Gonnet et de la Reine, all of which formerly adorned the esplanade.

It is also the year when two of the selected Italian films are about small-town cinemas which are about to close down. One of these, Ettore Scola's *Splendor*, was received with enthusiasm. It had Marcello Mastroianni, as the owner of the condemned cinema, and the delicious Marina Vlady, playing a veteran cabaret dancer transformed into a heart-throb usherette. For Cannes, in the year of the property developers, *Splendor* would be an appropriate winner of the Golden Palm.

May, 1989

=====

'My name is Francis Leroy, I am forty-nine years old, I am an only child and I was born in Laon.' The man introducing himself in this way is standing in the dock at the Assize Court of the Dordogne and he is accused of murder. His defence is that he is, in the original meaning of the word, a lunatic. Locally he has been dubbed 'the madman of Bergerac', or in the local press 'the wild beast of the forests of Périgord'.

He is a tall, gangling figure, his face dominated by the size of his nose, a pronounced chin and awkward but powerful hands. All told, he has something of the air of David Warner in *Morgan, a Suitable Case for Treatment* but without any of the underlying friendliness in the eyes. In manner, M. Leroy is withdrawn and polite. He finds himself the principal figure in a murder case which is in style at least 200 years out of date, which might indeed have been the raw material for a sequel to a mediaeval mystery story such as *The Return of Martin Guerre*.

The story starts on the evening of 1 December 1978. A young man returning home by the light of a full moon is stopped by a gigantic masked figure carrying a sawn-off shotgun. The giant talks to him wildly of horses and death. When the young man's mother opens the door of their house in Bergerac, the giant locks the various members of the family into separate rooms then wanders around the house searching for something but finally leaving with just a watch and a lighter.

Two years later, almost to the day, it is once again a full moon. The masked giant attacks a young mother. He ties up her son and binds her husband with sticking plaster. Then he orders the young woman to walk up and down her living room and imitates the gesture of stroking her breast. Her husband reacts violently and tries to burst out of the Elastoplast. The giant flees.

In 1981, there were four more attacks, all of them near Bergerac. Two of them took place early in the morning and terminated in rape. The giant has by now updated his act slightly and carries a tear-gas canister. Despite the regional nature of these crimes and the unusual size of their perpetrator, the police succeed in making no arrests.

On 26 August 1983, the night of a harvest moon, the giant is abroad once more. This time he has changed his mask and now wears a grotesque caricature of the face of an old man. He forces his way into the house of a rear-admiral on the active list and takes the children hostage. The rear-admiral comes home and is faced with the hideous sight of a very tall, deranged old man carrying a sawn-off shotgun and threatening his children. He notices that it is a single-barrel shotgun which has to be reloaded after each round. He decides that this is a risk worth taking and grapples with the monster. As they struggle his opponent mutters at him through the mask, 'Your house is surrounded.' Finally the rear-admiral is wounded and the giant escapes, running at full speed across the fields, his huge silvery shadow capering behind him in the moonlight.

During a period of five years seventeen attacks take place, almost all of them at the time of the full moon. Then the creature's frenzy reaches a climax. Breaking into a house on his usual manor, centred round Bergerac, the masked giant ties up three women and then prances around aimlessly, occasionally spraying his victims lightly with tear gas. Fortunately his revels are interrupted by a coura-geous friend of the three women. The two men close on each other and struggle violently. The friend is stabbed in the liver. He collapses and dies. The *gendarmes*, aroused at last from their trance, hand the case over to an officer who has read Simenon's *Le Fou de Bergerac*, published in 1932, the story of a lunatic who terrorized the neighbourhood of the town. 'There is a madman loose in Bergerac,' says Maigret, 'a madman who is only mad now and again, and who, the rest of the time, talks just like you and me.'

In 1978, the year when the attacks started, a film based on this book was made in Bergerac and the local people took parts as extras, among them, M. Leroy. Combing the archives, the *gendarme* came across the case of Francis Leroy, sentenced to twenty years' imprisonment in 1961 for murder and rape, crimes committed in a town far from Bergerac at the time of the full moon. The accused had claimed to be under astral influence. He used to steal cigarette lighters and sunglasses. Leroy was released shortly before the arrival of the giant and came to live in Bergerac, where he was regarded as a pleasant neighbour, chiefly interested in breeding horses. Today he admits the facts alleged against him but claims that he cannot control his impulses when the moon is full.

There are more things in heaven and on earth, my masters, than you will find in a Dordogne estate agent's particulars.

June, 1989

=====

'All over the world there must be people who, at the sight of a remote manor-house in wild and empty country, are instantly reminded of *Le Grand Meaulnes*.' So wrote Alan Pryce-Jones in his introduction to the novel which is still best known in English as *The Lost Domain*. The mysterious and romantic figure of Augustin Meaulnes casts a spell over the narrator of Alain-Fournier's masterpiece. And this spell, as the English translator Frank Davison pointed out, was also cast over 'a whole generation of French readers'. It works from the moment of Meaulnes' arrival in the very first sentence of the book. 'He appeared at our house on a Sunday in November 189 . . .'; and continues up to his final disappearance in the last sentence: 'And already I pictured him, in the night, wrapping his daughter in a cloak, to carry her off with him on some new adventure.'

The Lost Domain is a quest and a love-story which cries out for a sequel. The reader rejects the idea that he has been abandoned by Frantz and Valentine and François Seurel and cannot bear the thought that he will never re-enter their world again. But sequels often disappoint and in any case, one year after the publication of *Le Grand Meaulnes*, its author too disappeared, posted 'missing in action' at the age of twenty-seven in the opening weeks of the First World War.

It is safe to say that *The Lost Domain* would be just as popular if nothing were known about its author but there is an extra interest in the book due to the legend which has grown up around Alain-Fournier's own life.

Henri Alban Alain-Fournier, like his hero, suffered an unhappy love affair, with a real-life 'Yvonne de Galais' before he too disappeared for ever 'on some new adventure'. And it has always seemed bitterly appropriate that a man whose only published work evoked the lost world of rural France before the Great War should himself have been one of the first victims of the conflict which destroyed that world for ever; and still more appropriate that the manner of his death should have remained such a complete mystery. Now, seventy-five years after the event, an essay has appeared which purports to offer a description of how Henri Alain-Fournier died. And the new account is not very romantic at all.

According to an amateur historian, Michel Algrain, who claims to have spent ten years researching the mystery, Lieutenant Alain-Fournier of the 288th Infantry Regiment, was probably executed by German soldiers on 22 September 1914, after his company had opened fire on a German field ambulance and killed a number of medical orderlies and wounded. The allegation has scandalized the still numerous body of Alain-Fournier's readers, who find it both offensive and incredible. The engagement in the beech wood at St Rémy took place in the first 'chivalrous' days of the Great War, when cavalry were still being deployed and long before the brutalizing effects of mustard gas, mechanization and mud had destroyed the idea of military chivalry for ever.

What has always been agreed is that Alain-Fournier disappeared late on a Tuesday afternoon after his company, among others, took part in a confused engagement with German forces in a beech wood known as St Rémy, fifteen miles south-east of Verdun. Michel Algrain's new discovery is that during this engagement, a German field ambulance which was sheltering in the thick wood came under fire from French infantrymen standing fifty yards away and suffered eight dead and sixteen wounded.

Shortly afterwards, a nearby German unit captured a party of two French officers and ten soldiers whom they suspected of attacking the German wounded, and shot these French prisoners on the spot. The execution was noted in the German company's report and subsequently approved at brigade level.

Leading the chorus of indignation against this ignoble hypothesis is the academician Etienne Wolff, who protested to *Le Figaro* which has just publicized Michel Algrain's research. M. Wolff points out that Algrain has not given a complete list of his sources and notes that most of his evidence apparently comes from German witnesses.

'I am scandalized,' he wrote, 'that an article like this sets out to discredit such a celebrated French author. Let us not slander our past glories. And let the dead bury their own dead.' M. Wolff objects to the idea that French troops deliberately opened fire on a German field ambulance, pointing to the confusion which prevailed and the poor visibility in the wood. But clearly what he finds quite insupportable is the suggestion that Henri Alain-Fournier might have led such an attack.

As though anticipating such objections, Michel Algrain has in fact tried to pin the blame for this action on Alain-Fournier's captain, an officer whom he eloquently describes as *exalté* or 'carried away'. But there is no more hard evidence against this unfortunate nonentity than there is against one of the most romantic figures of French literature. Seventy-five years later, the truth of what happened in one of the innumerable actions between the French and Germans around Verdun cannot be established.

October, 1989

═══

'Heavy sentences', said *Le Monde*. 'Light sentences', said *Libération*. 'Bonjour tristesse', said *France-Soir* above a photograph of the novelist Françoise Sagan lying in a corn field. The last comment was the least accurate since Mme Sagan certainly got a light sentence, six months suspended and a fine of approximately £4,000 for possessing, with the intention of re-selling, 300g of cocaine and 300g of heroin. The great Paris drugs trial, which was actually held in Lyon, ended this week. All things considered the Press has been very tactful.

By putting everyone in the same dock, smugglers, dealers and users, the trial provided a cross-section of the Paris drugs trade. As one of the main dealers said: 'I only sold to responsible people. I've never seen a syringe nor the misery of the addicts that's always described. It's not a case of evil dealers on one side and exploited addicts on the other.' Françoise Sagan (who produced a doctor's certificate) was the absent star of the show.

Among the dealers there was Albert Le Gallo, aged seventy-four, a former sergeant-major in the French colonial forces, who won two *Croix-de-Guerre* and the Legion of Honour. He had one previous conviction, for drunk driving in 1936, but, as he explained, that was when he was working for Pernod. Now suffering from lung cancer, he had to take frequent breaks for treatment in an oxygen tent. He said that his first experience of the drug trade was with the French army in Indo-China in 1937 when he transported opium out of the Golden Triangle for his general's secret hoard. On being demobilized he set up as a lorry driver in Cochin. In 1976, after forty years in Indo-China, he was repatriated to France only to find that he could not make ends meet. So he took to 'do-it-yourself' drug dealing, teaming up with his old friend Shu Luangpra-seuth, 'the honourable M. Shu', a Laotian who had retired to Alsace with his family of ten children. They were so successful that they made the Interpol wanted list. When Le Gallo was finally arrested he had £60,000 in his current account.

Another of his partners was André Trihan, sixty-three, also a former sergeant-major (the sergeants run the French drug trade just as they ran the colonial army) and a pilot who was parachuting tons of opium into Cambodia in 1961. He subsequently became involved in the 'French Connection' heroin ring.

Then there was Lucien Carrel, fifty-five, '*le Gros Lulu*', a friend of Sagan's who boasted to police that he had supplied '*le presque tout Paris*'. 'If you were going to charge everyone who shoots up in the Parisian jet-set,' he told the Lyon judge, 'you'd have to hire the city football stadium. My clients went about their respectable daily business with two grams of coke up their noses. They talked of coke because it sounded better – like champagne – but what they really guzzled was heroin.'

The unrepentant Carrel, born in Belleville, the toughest district of Paris, had started out as a butcher's apprentice and had then been attracted to the Latin Quarter in its 1950s heyday, where he got to know Françoise Sagan. During the Algerian war he worked with Bastien-Thierry, the army officer who was eventually executed for trying to assassinate President de Gaulle. He first came across drugs in Thailand in 1974 and made his Paris connections with the help of his daughter-in-law, Maryse Abadie, a chemistry graduate whose training qualified her to cut and grade the stuff. They did business in the select 'Nap' district of Neuilly-Auteuil-Passy.

There, they met Rolande Kienlen, fifty-three, a former professor of couture turned international businesswoman, who worked in what the police called the 'Lola' circuit between her home in Neuilly, her villas in Goa and Ibiza, and her bank in Zurich. 'Lola' was a Neuilly neighbour, Nicole Guigou d'Almeira, fifty-eight, a part-time astrologer and full-time coke dealer, straight out of a Sagan novel, who stored 400 kilos of 'grass' in her loft, wore Chanel suits, and provided police in the interview room with their first experience of the marvellous drawling mock-English accent which the smartest Naps affect. Nicole's boyfriend, the Englishman 'Bobby' ('il est adorable'), Robert Landry, alias Donald Jones, alias John Minor (no relation), is still on the run. Rolande's boyfriend, the German Klaus Roder, alias Charly Soloway, is also 'adorable' and also on the run after two arrests and two escapes.

The stuff, imported by the sergeant-major and Lucien Carrel, and supplied in large quantities to 'Lola', was eventually taken up at the third level – by users who were also small-time dealers. Heroin can be an expensive habit, even for a best-selling novelist, and after examining Françoise Sagan's bank account the police decided that she fitted this category. Among the thirty-five enthusiasts they placed with her were François Debré, son of de Gaulle's former prime minister Michel Debré, a composer, Jean-Marie Cadoret, a writer, Philippe Cardinal (now cultural attaché in France's Yemen Embassy), Jean-François Chaussaing, professor of legal history at the University of Paris, three journalists, one playboy and the former wife of one of Picasso's grandsons.

Unfortunately the trial had a disruptive effect on this small, friendly world. Rolande and 'Lola' had a mental blank about their star-gazing sessions beneath the Ibizan sky and denied they had ever met before. The intellectuals all presented themselves as victims of the dealers and claimed they had started to take drugs only during 'a difficult period' in their lives. François Debré had been threatened with the sack. Philippe Cardinal had been 'inundated with work'. Professor Chaussaing had suffered 'a personal crisis'. Gérard Lumbroso, a journalist, had been in a road accident. All this infuriated Lucien Carrel: 'Isn't it marvellous? Before they met me, none of them took drugs. After I was arrested they all stopped. I hope the head of the drugs squad gets a medal for catching me.'

But, for Carrel, the greatest treason was Françoise Sagan's medical certificate. Albert Le Gallo is dying of lung cancer. He was in the dock. Maryse Abadie is very ill with multiple sclerosis. She was in the dock. But the public prosecutor, who had insisted that they were both present and had twice refused bail to Abadie, made no objection to Sagan's 'state of fatigue'. In vain Carrel's lawyer pointed out that the novelist had been photographed three days before the start of the trial at a gala film première. The public prosecutor works for the minister of justice and the minister of justice works for President Mitterrand. And Mme Sagan and M. Mitterrand are old friends.

Lucien Carrel got twelve years, Rolande Kienlen nine years, 'Lola' six years ('Adieu, Chanel'). Françoise Sagan got some marvellous copy and her former friends will now have the time to read it.

March, 1989

=====

'Apostrophes', the French television book programme, dies next Friday night and this is the moment to honour it. When Bernard Pivot announced that the current series would be his last and that the programme would end with his departure, there was shock and disbelief. For a programme devoted to an intelligent discussion of books to run for fifteen years is extraordinary enough. But Pivot has made it one of the most widely watched regular programmes on television. The commercial importance of 'Apostrophes' is well known. Its audience of between 3 and 6 million would add between 25 per cent and 30 per cent to the sales of a featured title.

At first sight it might seem less surprising to have achieved this success in a country where books, despite the commercial structure of modern publishing, still have a semi-magical status, and where writers are accorded a respect that would astonish the countrymen of Shakespeare. But it is precisely that elevated status which makes Pivot's popular achievement the more unusual.

One of his early interviews was with Vladimir Nabokov, a year before Nabokov died. Nabokov started by explaining that there was no possibility of an impromptu session. He never uttered a word in public, whether orally or otherwise, that was not carefully [weighed and] polished beforehand. After some thought Pivot agreed to [break his iron rule and to] provide Nabokov with a list of the questions. 'Good,' said Nabokov. 'And I will provide you with my written answers. Then we will each read out our remarks in front of the camera.' Protests were useless. Pivot recalls that Nabokov also required to be supplied with a particular brand of Scotch during the performance. But in order not to alarm his readers this had to be poured from a teapot. So it came to pass that Pivot and Nabokov sat there holding an apparently impromptu discussion and that every now and then Pivot would depart from the script to lean forward and say, 'A little more tea, M. Nabokov?' Nabokov, who thought of everything, had also arranged for a piss-pot to be placed under his chair but decided to manage without this prop in the event.

At least twice 'Apostrophes' became the centre of noisy political rows. In 1979 Pivot invited the president of the Republic, Valéry Giscard d'Estaing, on to the programme to discuss his favourite author, Maupassant. Giscard did this with such fluency and charm that Maupassant became the best selling author of that summer holidays. But the Left were furious and Pivot was violently abused for 'toadying' and 'literary prostitution'. The memory still rankles with Pivot today and he suggests that in the excitement of the moment *Le Monde* went so far as to concoct an abusive letter from a non-existent reader.

Then in 1982 Régis Debray called him a 'monopolist and a self-appointed cultural referee and dictator' in an interview with French Canadian television. Debray had just been appointed a special adviser on cultural affairs to President Mitterrand. Questions were asked in the National Assembly, the president had to dissociate himself from his counsellor's first piece of advice and Debray himself later issued a profound apology. Meanwhile Pivot, who had been on the point of abandoning the programme out of lassitude, was stimulated to sign on for another seven years.

His reason for leaving now is a return of that lassitude. He says that he is exhausted by reading for ten hours a day, that he has lost all his pleasure in modern fiction and that he finds that authors have become too well-behaved. They will no longer conduct their rows in public. In the past there have been some wonderful moments on

'Apostrophes'. Leaving aside the time when Pivot fell in love with Jane Fonda ('*Profondément intelligente*') on the air and forgot all about his other guests, there was the time when the American Charles Bukowski, swigging from a bottle of rather good Sancerre, fell asleep with his mouth open, thereby allowing some of the wine to make its escape. Reviving and finding himself in the middle of an interminable literary discussion in a language he could not understand, Bukowski first tried to join in the debate and then tried to seduce the serious young lady to his left, causing her to leap to her feet and readjust her dress while exclaiming, 'Oh, *that* takes the biscuit.' ('*Ça, c'est le pompon*').

'Apostrophes' broke its own records, taking 17 per cent of the total audience against four other channels, when Pivot managed to get Boris Yeltsin and Alexander Zinoviev to sit opposite each other for ninety minutes while they refused to meet each other's eyes and talked instead, in Russian, to Pivot.

But while such highlights were no disadvantage to the programme's reputation, its weekly success lay in Pivot's ability to involve his viewers in the work of the writers under discussion. The philosopher Vladimir Jankélévitch said that in the weeks following his appearance on 'Apostrophes' he sold more copies of his work than in the whole of the rest of his life. The same thing happened on different occasions to a mathematician and a professor of linguistics. The instinctive English reaction to such stories is to exclaim that the French are a nation of pseuds. But Pivot finds nothing reprehensible in the idea of a book as a talisman. Perhaps most of those who bought Jankélévitch's book never read it, and never intended to read it, but they bought it because they saw on 'Apostrophes' that he was a wise old man of great moral courage and they were grateful to him for that and wanted to show their recognition and gratitude.

Pivot, now aged fifty-four, remains a modest and private man. After fifteen years as a television star he still describes himself as 'a journalist' – again the bias in favour of the written word. He is the editor of a literary magazine, *Lire*, and the author, at the age of twenty-four, of a novel. No doubt his celebrated preference for Beaujolais is connected with the fact that he was born and brought up in Lyon.

His greatest achievement may not be what he has done for

French writers but what he has done for television. He seems to be the only person in the world who has fused the mutually hostile activities of reading books and watching television to the honour and benefit of both. He did no damage to reading or writing by inviting a mass audience to think about books whose existence they would never otherwise have suspected. And he invented a new form of popular television. At the same time he made television an intelligent means of communication. How he did it is the secret of his talent. Unfortunately, he is probably unique.

June, 1990

A poignant letter in *Le Figaro* last week spoke for all those who feel that life's rewards have passed them by. Maurice Gad, a Parisian, wrote to let the world know that he was 'sickened' by the inequality of promotions in the Legion of Honour. Some members of the order, according to M. Gad, are constantly promoted, whereas he has never advanced beyond the junior rank of *chevalier* since 1966.

This letter evoked the anxiety felt all over France as the moment arrives for the publication of the next promotion list. There was another such list published this week, and M. Gad's name did not appear yet again. No doubt the eruption of spluttering over the Gad breakfast *croissant* was echoed behind the impassive stone façades of several neighbouring buildings.

There is no justice in the recognition of merit, as events in another part of Paris demonstrated only last week. The story took several days to unravel – the most important point in it being that the chief executive of Rank-Xerox (France), Olivier Grouès, had been taken hostage in his office by a former employee, then shot and seriously wounded. For nearly two days it was reported that it was his kidnapper, Daniel Vielle, who had shot him. Then the authorities summoned up the courage to reveal the rather more complicated truth.

Ten years ago, Daniel Vielle was a Rank-Xerox salesman who won a company competition for selling more products than any of his colleagues. The prize was a world tour. By all accounts Daniel Vielle was a brilliant salesman. He was also ferociously ambitious. In fact he modelled himself on Olivier Grouès, who had also once been the company's leading salesman. So when Daniel Vielle won the world tour he decided he did not want to take it. He preferred to get on with selling. With the company's agreement he traded his prize in for a family holiday in the West Indies.

But he never went on that either. Instead he took the money, produced false bills and stayed at work. When Rank-Xerox found out what he had done, he was fired. Daniel Vielle could not believe his misfortune. As he saw it, he had not claimed a penny more than his entitlement and had been fired because he preferred to keep on selling rather than take a holiday.

He became obsessed with the injustice of it. He did not want compensation or another job. He wanted to be reinstated, to be recognized once again as the number one salesman and to continue his ascent of the Rank-Xerox ladder.

He sold his house, he left his family, he went bankrupt and eventually he lived on the streets of Paris as a *clochard*. Daniel Vielle tried to take his case to the European Court of Human Rights. When his lawyer advised him recently that he had no chance, he despaired. He broke into Mr Groуès' office and made his final demand for reinstatement, this time at the point of a gun.

Events then took an unexpected turn. The municipal police were the first to answer the call for help and they laid siege to the nineteenth floor of the prestigious Rank-Xerox building at the *La Défense* skyscraper complex. Eventually M. Vielle forced his former boss to make a run for the lifts. They were not operating. The chief executive then grappled with his former employee and seized his shotgun. The watching police ran forward. Daniel Vielle was overpowered and a jubilant Olivier Groуès ran down the stairs to the eighteenth floor accompanied by a plain-clothes policeman carrying the shotgun.

As they emerged from the staircase on to the eighteenth floor, another policeman, who had been talking on the radio and had lost touch with events, saw running towards him the chief executive of Rank-Xerox accompanied by an unknown man carrying a large gun. He immediately drew his own gun, aimed at the armed man and fired. The bullet missed his colleague, who was the target, ricocheted, and hit Olivier Groуès in the stomach. When the policeman realized what he had done, he tried to throw himself off the eighteenth floor of the Rank-Xerox building and had to be dragged back by other members of the original rescue party.

So much for the heroic view of history and so much for the reward of merit. If *Chevalier* Gad is a reflective man he may decide that he does not have much to complain about after all.

January, 1990

═══

A Picasso has been stolen, and only the French Communist Party has noticed. Yesterday before a large crowd in the Musée Picasso in Paris, an exhibition was opened which is devoted to 'Les Demoiselles d'Avignon', a painting which belongs to the New York Museum of Modern Art. 'Les Demoiselles' is the picture with which Picasso is sometimes said to have invented both Cubism and modern art, and the New York Museum says that this is the last time it will be allowed out on loan.

Picasso took six months in 1907 to complete 'Les Demoiselles', a study of five girls who once worked in a brothel in Barcelona. The new exhibition contains hundreds of preparatory sketches, letters and other documents relating to the picture, and occupies four rooms and a long staircase. But yesterday, while crowds of bourgeois art lovers followed the minister of culture, François Léotard, round the exhibits, Michel Boué, the critic from the Communist Party daily newspaper *L'Humanité*, ever mindful of the class struggle, was engaged in a tour of his own. He was looking for the only exhibit which mattered; Picasso's communist party card.

'A Picasso has been stolen,' he wrote today, 'and not the least important one. Picasso's pink period is still in the museum, Picasso's blue period is there as well, but the red Picasso has evaporated . . . The showcase displaying his party card and his public appeals for world peace, the indelible evidence of a lifetime consecrated to Communism, have been thrown into the dustbin of history . . . Could it be that the museum directors do not at the moment wish to remind the electorate that this genius was one of ours?'

The story made the front page of *L'Humanité*. Faced with the museum's admittedly rather curious explanation that Picasso's party card is on loan to a gallery in provincial Saint-Etienne, *L'Humanité*'s man became more indignant. 'This is a premeditated and stingy disinformation; it is like erasing the communards from the life of Rimbaud or the Dreyfus case from the life of Zola . . . Is Comrade

Picasso to be buried for ever in the cellars of the Museum? We will keep you informed.'

February, 1988

━━━━━

The VéloSolex light motorcycle, whose demise was announced last week after forty-five years and sales of 6 million machines, was a throwback to a more picturesque era when much French technology seemed to have been inspired by a Gallic Heath Robinson (the late-lamented Citroën 2CV is another example).

The Solex, invented in 1942, was a machine of ingenious simplicity. A very quiet two-stroke motor, approximately the size and shape of two thermos flasks, was fixed above the front wheel to a frame that was only slightly heavier than a pedal cycle. It was advertised as 'the bicycle that goes by itself'.

The result was a motor vehicle that even the philosopher Jean-Paul Sartre was able to handle. The engine was started by pedalling vigorously. When mounting a hill the Solex could be kept going by pedalling the rear wheel while the little engine drove the front one. There was no passenger seat but two pannier baskets strapped either side of the rear wheel accommodated several litres of very ordinary wine and the necessary number of baguettes.

Many visitors to France in the days before motorways will remember happy hours spent driving down minor roads in the track of some blue-overalled, purple-faced agriculturalist whose weaving course at 15 m.p.h. made it inadvisable to overtake. Just when a hill cut his speed to the point where he seemed bound to fall off he would start pedalling, and so remain triumphantly ahead of the growing procession all the way to the top. Another evocative sight was that of girls in billowing skirts attempting to start their machines by pedalling vigorously while the rear wheel was still raised on its stand, in the belief that this made things simpler. The consequences were frequently sufficiently interesting to draw a small crowd.

At the height of its popularity in 1964, 380,000 machines were sold in France; last year the figure had fallen to 2,742. Its original maximum speed was 15 m.p.h., rising to 22 m.p.h. in the final, supercharged version. Engine and frame were designed to last ten years. The Solex would do nearly 200 miles to the gallon, and for most of its life it was only available in black. Its final price of £300 was half that of its nearest rival, the Mobylette.

MBK (Motobécane), which bought the VéloSolex firm in 1980, itself became a subsidiary of the Japanese company Yamaha in 1983. The company has said that the Solex will be on sale for the rest of the year and that spare parts will be available for ten years after that. When production ends the Solex factory in St Quentin in northern France will switch to making 'Rough Riders' and 'Fun Bikes'. The Solex is thought to have lost much of its appeal when crash helmets became compulsory, despite its low maximum speed.

A Solex distributor in Courbevoie, where the machine was first produced, Jean Granet, finds it hard to believe. 'After the Liberation you had to wait six months to a year to get a Solex,' he said. 'Everyone wanted one. After all, in those days there was nothing else like it.' And another distributor said, 'Just two days ago a seventy-year-old gentleman came in to buy one. It was his thirteenth.'

The television journalist Alain Duhamel, who has ridden one for thirty years, pointed out that in Paris traffic it is faster than a Ferrari. But a Paris-based American father of three sons, Russell Melcher, disagreed: 'They were terribly dangerous in wet weather or on bad road surfaces. You could ride them from the age of fourteen and I cannot remember how many times one or other of my boys would come in bloodied from a fall. I'm glad to see them go.'

But the French feel rather sad about the disappearance of the VéloSolex. It was cheap, simple, reliable and quiet, and if men made machinery for its benefits instead of for increased profits, its life would be assured for another forty-five years. In fact its life *may* be assured for another forty-five years. Yamaha are rumoured to be negotiating to sell the necessary patents and machinery to the Chinese government which has been interested in manufacturing millions of Solexes for some time.

September, 1988

═══

Michel d'Ornano, who died last week at the age of sixty-six, was a former minister whose political career appeared to have finished in 1977 when he ran for mayor of Paris and was defeated by Jacques Chirac. But he remained one of the key politicians in the country. As Valéry Giscard d'Estaing's closest adviser, he was involved in the powerbroking that preceded the second presidential election victory of François Mitterrand in 1988, and which resulted, more pertinently perhaps, in the defeat of M. Chirac.

He was also the man behind the extraordinary resurgence of M. Giscard d'Estaing, to the point where the former president is once again seen as a serious contender for the presidency in 1995.

M. d'Ornano's death is a tragedy for his family and friends, but it is also a disaster for the *Giscardien* cause. On hearing of his death, M. Giscard d'Estaing spoke of 'an irreparable loss' and he was not exaggerating. M. d'Ornano was killed in a road accident. In Britain about 100 people a week are killed on the roads. In France, with the same population and the same number of vehicles, the figure is twice as high. This situation is the subject of numerable official inquiries, although to any visitor from another country the explanation is obvious – in France, dangerous driving is a national passion. This is not the nation of frogs, but of Mr Toad. M. d'Ornano was killed while trying to cross the road on foot. He had just bought a postage stamp and was mown down by a passing van in the beautifully named district of St Cloud. In Paris, half of those killed are pedestrians, and 30 per cent of those die on pedestrian crossings. The last public safety campaign urged pedestrians to use these crossings, though it is easy to see why so few bother to do so.

A motorcyclist who killed a girl on a pedestrian crossing recently in Versailles was tried for manslaughter. He was let off with rapped knuckles after the judge suggested the dead girl was partly to blame since she should have noticed that the motorcyclist was going so fast. He also pointed out that in France pedestrian crossings 'are not the safe havens they are in other parts of Europe'.

When the motorists are not racing their cars between pedestrians, they are trying to park them. There are 180,000 legal street parking places in Paris, but 280,000 cars are parked in the streets at any given moment. The situation is made worse by increasing the number of available parking places, and it is also made worse by reducing them. This is another of the absurdities imposed on humanity by the motor car. The greatest brains in France are meeting this month in the Ecole Nationale des Ponts et Chaussées in the Latin Quarter to work out a solution to this problem. No doubt while they are doing so several of them will have left their cars illegally parked outside in the congested rue des Saints Pères.

Meanwhile, other brains, smaller perhaps but not to be despised, have been working out how to make money from the parking crisis. These are the people employed by the City of Paris to collect the coins placed in parking meters. There are 8,000 parking meters in Paris, and they were, until recently, emptied by a well organized team of uniformed *fonctionnaires* (or crooks). Twenty-seven of these men, including their mastermind, the director of the service, have now been relieved of their duties. Nobody is quite sure how many millions they stole but the city was left with 400 million francs a year after they had finished.

The system has now been reorganized. The coins are no longer emptied from the meters in the street. Instead the money is taken in sealed boxes to a central counting house in an underground bunker. The location of the bunker is a state secret, but it is believed to be disguised as an underground car park. It is defended by guards armed with automatic weapons, by radar, by video cameras and by a series of armoured doors.

The teams that bring in the boxes are reshuffled constantly and none of the personnel knows who he will be working with next. The men who collect the money have no contact at all with the men who work in the bunker. In order to ensure that no money is stolen it is imperative to prevent any opportunity for personal relations; it is assumed that friendship always leads to frivolities.

Inside the bunker all operatives have to wear specially designed blue overalls which have no pockets. The sealed boxes are opened inside a machine that counts the money automatically. Three tons of coins are counted each day and then placed in an armoured lift that rises to the surface. An armoured car takes the money directly to the vaults of the Banque de France. Of course, it can only be a matter of time before the alternative brains of the century work out how to beat this system. Taking the pockets out of the men's overalls may not be enough.

March, 1991

Professional rivalry has led to one of the leading shippers of Muscadet, the white wine made at the mouth of the river Loire, being charged with adulterating his product. The quarrel has shed unaccustomed – and, for the producers, unwelcome – light on some of the less reputable practices of the wine trade.

René-Claude Martin will stand trial after an investigation by the Service des Fraudes, a government body which investigates food and wine. He is the owner of Martin-Jarry, a major wholesaler and a long-established family firm which specializes in wine for export. It is situated in La Chapelle Basse Mer, near the city of Nantes. There has been fierce competition in recent years among those exporting Muscadet. Worldwide sales have increased sharply but in some mysterious way local production has managed to keep pace with demand. Recently M. Martin's annual production of 80,000 cases of wine has been on offer at prices other merchants could not match, and his success seems to be responsible for the current investigation.

The Muscadet region produces a slightly inferior white wine from a different grape called *Gros Plant*. This wine is rated as 'VDQS', one grade lower than the 'AC' Muscadet. Last month M. Martin was charged with selling 7,800 cases of inferior wine as Muscadet.

He is now suspected of a further offence concerned with the use of the chemical potassium ferro-cyanide. This is a dangerous product that can only legally be introduced under specialist supervision; it is employed to remove iron from some wines.

M. Martin is accused of treating 11,000 cases of wine, without the assistance of a qualified specialist. There may also be charges that he has adulterated local wine with an inferior white wine imported from Italy, and then labelled it as regional wine. Finally, the examining magistrate is to be presented with evidence that M. Martin may have been concerned with mislabelling inferior wine from other regions and selling it as 'AC' Bordeaux, Beaujolais and Touraine.

In Nantes yesterday one of those who admires M. Martin's wine said that whatever he had done to it, 'it still tastes pretty good'. There is a feeling among the more cynical citizens of Nantes that

M. Martin may be the victim of jealous competitors who have sometimes used the same tricks themselves.

April, 1987

═══

At 4.15 in the afternoon there was a queue of thirty empty lorries waiting for passengers by the bus station at the Porte d'Orléans. An hour later there was a much longer queue of frustrated passengers and not a lorry in sight.

This was route 621 to Cachan, Bourg la Reine and Antony, the short-haul route, running less than half-way down line B4 of the RER suburban railway, which has been closed by a strike of maintenance men who are members of the Communist-led CGT union. On day two of the army's intervention the novelty has not yet worn off. The Porte d'Orléans was swarming with soldiers, and young girls were streaming up from the Métro towards the pick-up points with an uncustomary light in their eyes.

The first hazard of the army lorry is the queue. The Renault trucks give off an astonishing amount of thick diesel smoke, arranged to hit you at about chest level. By the time you reach the set of kitchen steps which the army have placed beneath the five-foot tailboard you are already feeling rather sick. Mounting is a hazardous business for ladies wearing skirts and several of those ahead of me refused, like tiring showjumpers, before being urged on by the military attendant. 'They told us to wear trousers,' sighed Colette as she mounted the ladder, 'but in my office we have to dress properly.' 'Courage, *chérie*,' replied her friend, 'after two days they are probably getting used to the shock.'

Once inside, the passengers are arranged back-to-back on two wooden benches running down the centre of the lorry. Thoughtful as ever, the soldiers had placed a thin blanket over the slats. When twenty passengers were seated the tailboard slammed up and there we sat beneath a rubberized canopy, in the gathering dark for ten minutes more. 'Perhaps the soldiers are also on strike? Which regiment is this? 25th CGT?' Our marine was not amused. It turned out that we were waiting for the next lorry to be loaded.

We were going to travel in convoy. 'Why?' 'Because they only have one map?' 'No, because they are trained to go in convoy.

Unless there is a lorry in front and a lorry behind they go round in circles.' At that point the lorry behind moved up to the loading point, mounting the kerb and narrowly missing a stationary chestnut tree, and shortly afterwards we were off.

The average army lorry driver has achieved 3,000 kilometres which is not enough to master clutch control. There are no handles to grab and the sides are too far away to wedge any but the longest legs. As a result it's quite a cosy ride, particularly since the army keep their brakes in superb condition. A further advantage is that the lorries stop when you ask. Provided you live on RN 20 between Paris and Antony, it's a door to door service.

The girl sitting beside me had brought her home-video camera to record this historic experience. Through the open space at the back of the lorry she filmed the headlights of the cars behind, framed by the profiles of her fellow passengers. The marine in command was recounting his adventures in Beirut, Djibouti and Chad. 'I tell you one thing about this lorry,' said a gloomy voice from the darkness. 'It has no indicators.' 'Of course not,' said his neighbour. 'They don't want to give away our position.'

After an hour of threading our way through the heavy traffic we reached Antony. Not bad on a day when even the head of President Mitterrand's staff was caught in a traffic jam for over two hours. As I started the journey back a stream of lorries went past. By some chance the soldier travelling in the back was always seated opposite a pretty girl. This strike could be less unpopular with commuters than the government thinks.

December, 1988

═══════

The academic year has come to an end and the curtain has fallen once again on one of the strangest sights in Paris – the public lectures given by the Collège de France. The college is a noble institution set up by François I in 1530 to encourage French scholars to come to grips with the Renaissance and a world where scholarship would no longer be conducted entirely in Latin. The idea was that it should teach not what was known but what was still being discovered. It is composed of fifty-two of the most eminent professors in France who are elected by their peers and who set no examinations and award no degrees. Their sole duty is to give an annual series of public lectures on their latest discoveries or notions. The key to the whole arrangement is that these lectures should be 'free and open to all'.

And that is why they are such a bizarre sight. On the podium, one of the most eminent men in France, a leader in Sanskrit or nuclear physics; before him a wide assortment of the human race. On a cold winter's day half the *clochards* in Paris seem to crowd into the grey-columned halls of the neo-classical building with its statues and amphitheatre, as is their absolute right. Beside them a coach-load of retired people and students from the neighbouring Sorbonne, near the front perhaps the only two people in the country who understand a word of what the professor is saying. Sometimes there are five in the audience, sometimes 500.

Pensioners, often highly educated and once powerful people, find a series of lectures in history or palaeoanthropology one of the best ways of passing their retirement. Other professors attract a sort of film star following. Pierre Boulez has been professor of musical technique since 1976. But many of the professors hope to attract colleagues and to start a learned discussion on, say, problems of post-nuclear east European strategy, which can demand a certain amount of patience if they are joined by one of Paris's numerous professional eccentrics.

To avoid this kind of problem, Roland Barthes, the structuralist *penseur*, used to start his lectures at eight o'clock in the morning. And the professor of Chinese in the 60s was so irritated by the invasion of hairy Maoists that he switched to giving his lectures in Mandarin, which successfully got rid of them at once.

Now it is July so the *clochards* are reduced to arguing among themselves on the lawn in front of the college before they, too, abandon the city and set off on the long trek south towards their pavement in the sun.

July, 1991

For *nostalgiques de la boue*, and the lost city of the 30s and 40s, there are still a few corners of Paris which have stubbornly refused to be exterminated. Here one can find the fruitier Parisians who used to

give one's arrival in this city such a memorable flavour. Appropriately they still flourish in the streets around the great railway
stations, most of which remain unshadowed by the twenty-first
century which Paris's hyper-energetic mayor is imposing almost
everywhere else.

This is not always the case. One can no longer receive in the Gare
de Montparnasse any sense of the world evoked by the nineteenth-
century commentator who said that on any day of the week you
could watch the devout Breton peasants descending there from the
train on their first visit to Paris and losing their faith before they
reached the end of the platform. But in the streets to the north of
the Gare de Lyon improvements are not yet complete. On a rusting
steel door in the rue Jean Bouton, a page from the *Bulletin Municipal*
has been pasted up explaining that this building, formerly, according
to the faded paint on the wall, a *laboratoire électronique* (in other
words the place where you got your lamp repaired) is under an
expropriation order. For the rue Jean Bouton lies within the
'ZAC Chalon', a zac being a *zone d'aménagement concertée*, and it is
due to go. One wonders if they have told the old lady who sits in
the window of no. 18 peering through the unwashed windows, past
the empty flower pots towards the traffic and bustle of the avenue
Daumesnil.

Nearby, in the rue de Chalon, the Hôtel Grande Métropole is
still advertising its running water and charging £16 a night for
the experience. But the door of the restaurant 'La Rose de Porce-
laine' has been breeze-blocked up, and the Impasse Chalon has
disappeared completely within the chain link fencing of a temporary car park. The Passage Chalon still exists, but the authorities
have removed its name, and the numbers have disappeared from
its remaining houses. People still live in these houses, officially
condemned, and although these people are poor they continue to
live in the hope of something turning up, a letter for example.
That is why they have chalked up the street numbers again, to
assist the postman.

Walking along the Passage Chalon my eyes filled with tears
caused, I later discovered, by the spray from the municipal cleaning
truck which uses an extra-strong dose of disinfectant in the ZAC
Chalon. An old Alsatian dog, muzzled, fat and almost blind,
wandered along beside me, attracted by the smell from behind the

door of the *halal* butcher. This is one of the few streets in Paris where the Muslim butchers could slaughter goats in the street and no one would notice let alone object, certainly not the blind Alsatian, who must be one of this abandoned quarter's oldest residents.

One corner of the street has already been rebuilt and renamed the Place Rutebeuf, after a thirteenth-century poet. A succession of African pedlars made their way past this new street sign to the unmarked door of a pedlars' wholesaler, stocked with wooden carvings, cardboard suitcases, plastic bangles and cheap beads, modern Africa's revenge on the ghosts of generations of European traders. These Africans do not need street names or numbers, they pass on information by word of mouth. They are members of a temporary, oral culture which springs up in the cracks between two written cultures. Rutebeuf will never be part of their Paris.

The Africans have also taken over Le Nouvel Hôtel in the Passage Basfroi, off the avenue Ledru-Rollin. Its owner has departed but his guests remain, fifty-five of them, in a ramshackle building which they have successfully defended from occupation by the police. They have formed a club and continue to pay a weekly sum towards their electricity, gas and water bills. No one is quite sure whether or not the money includes something towards the rent and the local taxes. The occupants are African, Senegalese and Malian. There are also people from Martinique, Algeria and Morocco and at least one lady is of French origin. Le Nouvel Hôtel is the only place where they can find a room in which to live. It is not ideal.

Madame Traore has room 46 on the fourth floor. This is a medium-sized sort of hotel room which contains one large bed and two single ones. Just inside the door an area has been partitioned off to house the cooker and sink. The place is spotlessly clean. Room 46 is home for Mme Traore, M. Traore and their five children, the youngest a boy of ten months. Mme Traore says that she has been looking for a three-room apartment in Paris for seven years, during which time her family has become more numerous. Somehow her name has never yet reached the top of the waiting list kept by the Hôtel de Ville.

Just down the corridor in room no. 41 is her friend, also called Mme Traore. This is not a device to confuse the tax collector; the ladies come from the same village in Mali, near the city of

Kayès. Presumably the president of Mali, General Moussa Traore, is from their region.

Last week when Mme Traore and her friend were kind enough to receive me in room 46 they were also entertaining several younger members of the family as well as a third lady also of Malian origin. She too lived in the 11th *arron-dissement* but the possibility that she too might be called Traore could not be tested since she explained, most charmingly, that she would prefer to be described as 'a friend'. This was perhaps a tactful way of establishing that she was in what the French authorities describe as '*situation irrégulière*'.

But Mme Traore, the mother of five, is not in '*situation irrégulière*'. She is an entirely regular resident of France. Her husband has a job. Her children go to school. Once a year she buys a seat on a charter flight to Bamako and from there makes the even longer journey to Kayès and so on to her village. She can take holidays, she explains, because she still has a permanent address in Paris. Until recently she had a legal agreement to occupy room 46. (If she had never held a lease it would have been very difficult for her to come and go between Mali and France.) Life now would be fine, says Mme Traore, if she could just get a little three-room apartment.

Families like the Traores are certainly not at the bottom of the human heap in Paris. Below them come other foreigners, frequently other Malians who are illegal immigrants. While they wait to receive a residence permit they are at the mercy of authority in the form of the town hall, the police, the landlord, a sweat-shop employer or any passing, bad-tempered stranger. The illegal immigrants are generally housed in much worse conditions. In the case of the Africans, most of them are single men living four or more to a room in a building which has been condemned and which is awaiting demolition.

The Passage Raguinot, a tumbledown backstreet in the ZAC Chalon provides several examples. Until 1986 this was the centre of the Parisian drug trade. Known simply as 'the Chalon', this network of 'passages' and 'impasses' was beyond police control. One day there was a big police raid. The district was sealed off. Everyone was turned out into the streets. Numerous illegal immigrants were caught and deported and the authorities decided to demolish the whole maze. But today there are buildings owned by the SNCF, the French national railways, which appear to be derelict fire-traps but are in fact occupied. Surprisingly the SNCF still seems to be demanding rent for some of these buildings.

Inside the wiring dangles from the rotting plaster. The staircases are coming away from the walls. There is no rubbish collection. The drains gape with holes. The days of those living in the Passage Raguinot are characterized by waiting, usually in a queue outside the doors of the numerous local bureaucrats these men have to deal with. Many of these Africans start their life in France by earning money as pedlars. They are the men you meet in the Tuileries or outside the Centre Pompidou, or indeed in the centre of any French town, selling cheap mirror sunglasses or paper mechanical birds or bangles or ornaments which may or may not be made from Mauritanian silver. They buy their stock from pedlars' wholesalers, other Africans who make a handsome profit on the colourful junk which they import in their turn from sweatshops in Taiwan or the Philippines.

What brings these men to the Gare de Lyon to live in the charmless surroundings of the Passage Raguinot is the dream they still dream on the banks of the Niger or the Senegal rivers. As the Senegalese writer Sembene Ousmane put it, Europe was 'beaches where the great of the world lay in the sun . . . cities where the nights flashed with many-coloured lights'. For some that dream still comes true. The pedlars' wholesalers exist as well as the pedlars. But they are separated by a great distance.

Mme Traore is somewhere in the middle. When the police came to the Nouvel Hôtel they wanted to get into the cellar to turn off the water and electricity. According to Mme Traore the police beat the men who prevented them from entering, even though they had children in their arms, and they also beat a pregnant woman. If they had succeeded in entering the cellar the building would have become uninhabitable and everyone would have been turned out into the street. But the police failed. An immigrant defence organization, 'SOS Racisme', was alerted, the police were called off, and the Nouvel Hôtel continues to play its essential role on the long weary road between Kayès and an imposing new life in central Paris.

1989

6. THE BLACK MUSEUM

A CONVENT DORMITORY

In an attic of the National Police College outside Lyon behind a locked door there is a carefully assembled collection of horrible objects, mementoes of some of the darker corners of the human mind.

The collection is housed in a very large room which is kept locked. The room stands at the top of a remote staircase in what was formerly an Ursuline Convent. The assistant-curator produces the key and unlocks the door. We find ourselves in an airy studio, well-lit by large skylights. It might once have made a suitable dormitory for the Ursuline novices. They would not much enjoy spending the night in there now. The exhibits are attached to the walls or suspended from the partition which runs down the middle of the room. One moves round anti-clockwise.

It was started in 1931 by Dr Edmonde Locard who founded one of the first scientific police laboratories in France and who became the college's first criminology lecturer. In the early days criminology was largely about the nuts and bolts. Locard originally used the collection as a teaching aid during his lectures and there is a rather homemade air about it even today. It is still the work of enthusiasts, rather like a restored railway branchline.

The first table provides little impression of what is to follow. Two curved glass tubes and a small bottle are laid out in a neat wooden case. The label says that this is the prototype of the breathalyser invented in 1952 by a French forensic scientist, Dr Jacques Locard, Edmonde's son. The assistant-curator explains that in November, 1952, Dr Locard was invited to read a paper about his invention to the British Association of Forensic Pathology, meeting at St George's Hospital, Hyde Park Corner. On returning to Lyon from that meeting, Dr Locard suffered a heart attack and died before he could patent his device. Shortly afterwards a somewhat similar device was put into experimental use in England. The suggestion of professional foulplay★ is just touched on, no over-emphasis on the part of our guide, there is quite enough crudity in this room already.

Through long familiarity with his subject the assistant-curator has adopted the manner of many museum guides. He sometimes faces his audience and describes an item behind his back, his voice has a slightly sing-song intonation. 'You will have noticed the three skeletons hanging in the glass case adjoining . . .' 'And now we pass to the finest piece in the collection . . .' The curator is himself a policeman and has seen a thing or two in his time. He once prevented a man standing in a telephone box from committing suicide by means of an ornamental cannon filled with grapeshot and gunpowder which the man had strapped to his head. The man in the telephone box wished to benefit mankind and to dispose of himself in a way that would enable as many as possible of his bodily organs to be used for transplants or other scientific purposes. He had chosen to do it in a telephone box because he wanted to summon the ambulance just before he died. Then he could be rushed to the slab and transplanted while still in peak condition. The assistant-curator, then an inspector, calculated, cor-rectly, that the air temperature was too cold for the gunpowder to go off and was therefore able to disarm the man, who is still alive. Now the assistant-curator teaches other people how to be policemen. The collection is his hobby.

We pass the tall glass display case containing the three human skeletons, the remains of three men who were guillotined in the early part of this century. On each skeleton the fifth cervical vertebra, discreetly identified by a red thread, has been crushed, a tribute to the Lyon executioner's art since it is said that to ensure a painless dispatch the blade has to strike the fifth cervical vertebra. (But how do they know?) Beneath the skeletons is the collar of a prisoner's coarse cloth shirt. It has been roughly hacked off with

---

★ After this article was first published I received a letter from the Secretary of the British Association of Forensic Medicine, Dr M. A. Green of Leeds University. He enclosed the minutes of the 1952 meeting and wrote, 'I have also checked the attendance register. All those present were medical rather than scientific graduates. I don't think anyone would have had the skill to pinch poor Locard's idea — so "perfidious Albion" for once is guiltless.'

scissors. This was usually done minutes before the execution to ensure that the true fall of the blade was not impeded. For the condemned man, a poignant moment. Two guards would hold him. A third would approach with the shears and start hacking. The prisoner would then feel the sensation of cold steel against his neck as the blades cut through his shirt. Moments later he would be led outside.

The last official guillotining took place in France in 1979, although there was very nearly a nasty accident last year during preparations for an exhibition in Paris connected with the Bicentenary of the French Revolution. The blade of the antique machine chosen to illustrate life in 1789 descended without warning, narrowly missing the neck of one of the technicians engaged in erecting it. The odds against the blade hitting the workman's fifth cervical vertebra would have been fairly long.

The skeleton on the extreme left of the tall glass case has an unusual history. It represents one of the major triumphs of Professor Lacassagne, another pioneer of French forensic science. In 1899 a number of people in Lyon were murdered in their bedrooms by an 'axeman'. The police held a suspect called Annet Gaumet but there was no conclusive evidence against him and he denied it vehemently. However the murderer had the habit of fouling the bedsheets of his victims. By dedicated analysis Prof. Lacassagne discovered that the man carried a very unusual intestinal worm. Gaumet was found to have the same affliction and was duly convicted and sentenced to death. He proclaimed his innocence until he was on the way to the guillotine when he noticed Prof. Lacassagne among the official witnesses and asked to have a word with him. The professor subsequently said that during their murmured conversation Gaumet admitted his guilt and paid tribute to Lacassagne's brilliance. He had also made an unusual last request. Would the professor do him the honour of keeping his body close by him for the rest of his life? Lacassagne promised to do so. In due course he suspended Gaumet's skeleton on the wall of his study. The anecdote makes one wonder a little about Prof. Lacassagne.

Before the introduction of fingerprinting, the police used other means to identify suspects. Several of these were developed by the ingenious professor. One depended on a study of the shape of the ears. One's ears, if it is any consolation, age more slowly than other physical features. Not everyone knows this but Lacassagne did and he made a systematic study of ear shapes. He eventually produced a chart of ninety different 'ear types'. He was also interested in the connection between crime and tattoos. Lacassagne thought that certain sorts of criminal might favour certain sorts of tattoo. He started to photograph tattoos during his early days as a military doctor and maintained this interest throughout his life.

Had he lived to see the introduction of fingerprinting he might have been driven to despair, or crime, by the sheer tedium of it. There is nothing in fingerprinting to match Prof. Lacassagne's barmy collection of 'the ageing process arranged by occupation', which was also used by the turn-of the-century student. So we have 'the ageing process among slaughterers', 'the ageing process among carters', and 'the accelerated ageing process among short-sentence prisoners'. As is frequently the case, to the non-scientist, scientific dead-ends seem far more imaginative (and amusing) than the one true way.

We come to a display of French banknotes. Something of the difference in the English and French approaches to crime is suggested by the case of the master forger, Bojarski, the man who forged banknotes with such skill that not even the Bank of France could always detect whether or not his work was genuine. He was sentenced in 1966 but national admiration for his artistry helped him to win a presidential pardon, after which he was offered a senior position with the Bank of France where his advice on the design of new notes made it impossible for anyone else to emulate him. A triumph of rehabilitation.

A characteristic of the French criminal investigation is the ritual of 'the reconstruction of the crime'. This starts with a sort of scrapbook, a map of the region, a map of the street, a plan of the house, photographs of the body. Later the suspect is taken back to the place where it all happened. He may be asked to act out his version of events. Or he may be asked to act out the police version. He can be questioned, invited to consider the difficulties with his own version, invited to deny the more incriminating version. The reconstruction is also carefully photographed. Its usefulness is shown by the case of Jacqueline Guebin, found dead in a canal near St Quentin in northern France in June 1965. A police inquiry swiftly reached the conclusion that she had drowned herself. Her stiletto-heeled shoes had been found on the terrace of her parents' house. She had apparently kicked these off, walked the half-mile to the canal and jumped in. The officer on the case was on the point of retirement and may have been getting a bit slack. His successor re-opened the file ten months later. He noticed that in the photographs of Jacqueline's body the soles of her stockings were in good condition. He looked over the ground she would have had to cover without shoes. It included a railway track and a muddy bank. Jacqueline once had a boyfriend, Alexandre Naud. The new police inspector called Alexandre Naud in for questioning. In due course Naud admitted everything. He had gone to bed with Jacqueline and drugged her with ether. Then he had wheeled her in a little trolley to the banks of the canal and chucked her in. The trolley had been a bit small and Jacqueline's feet had dangled over the edge. On his way back from the canal Naud had found her shoes. He had picked them up and instead of chucking those too into the canal he had made the mistake of replacing them tidily on the terrace. That was the slip which took him to the guillotine.

The beauty of the exhibit on this case lies in the snaps taken of the reconstruction. Once Naud decided to co-operate he did it with enthusiasm. Jacqueline's part was played by a young policewoman. So in the photographs we see Naud and the policewoman lying on the bed, beneath a devotional image. Then we see Naud applying a rag to her face. Then we see him carrying her down the stairs, but she has not been breathing ether and is smiling broadly, so is he. Perhaps they are looking forward to the trolley ride.

One of the melancholy aspects of a black museum is that it is overwhelmingly a record of failure, of carefully-laid plans which culminate in disaster because they were not laid carefully enough. Armand Féravy was once an athlete, a basketball champion. Then, abandoning the jock-strap for the *capote anglaise*, he won a second reputation as a drinker and *dragueur*. One of the girls he seduced decided to take her revenge. She got him drunk, set to work with the chopper and threw the larger parts of his body into the Canal St Denis. The smaller parts of Armand were wrapped up and left in various railway luggage offices around Paris. But the girl was charmingly naïve as well as very angry and it did not occur to her that when the police find a severed left hand at the Gare de Lyon they tend to go to the Gare du Nord to look for the right one. In the luggage office at the Gare d'Austerlitz they hit the jackpot, as Armand's head, pale but recognizable, emerged from the brown paper parcel. We inspect the photograph of Armand's head.

Another case shows how important it is for cold-blooded murderers to spend plenty of time in the public library. The small snake, 40 centimetres long, which is now preserved in a bottle, is identified as a European asp. This is sometimes said to be confined to Tuscany but it apparently also exists in southern France. This one was placed in the bed of an unsatisfactory husband by his wife, both citizens of Argenteuil. The husband survived because, when his foot descended into the sheets and brushed against the asp – which is by far the most poisonous of the European species – the little brute was fast asleep, the wife having overheated the bed. (Her suggestion that it must have got in from the garden was also rejected since the asp's range does not extend to Argenteuil.)

About the only successful crimes recorded in this room are the suicides. The 11-centimetre nail which one man succeeded in driving into his own brain with a mallet. Or the extraordinary arrangement which the assistant-curator eventually did describe as 'the finest piece in the collection'. This was a hunting rifle used by a man who wished to shoot himself but who was frightened of the noise made by guns. He did not wish this noise to be the last noise he heard. He therefore decided that the thing to do was to shoot himself while he was unconscious. And this difficult task he accomplished, with the aid of an alarm clock, a low-voltage transformer, a rubber collar to hold the barrel just so and a bottleful of tranquillizers. The hunting rifle is a handsome weapon to which the Shilba 4 × 15 coated-image telescopic sight is still attached. The alarm clock was only a cheap two-jewel model, but he had done his homework and it served.

May, 1990

DOCTOR PETIOT

A handsome and comfortable *hôtel particulier* in the rue Le Sueur in the 16th *arrondissement* just off the Champs-Elysées was knocked down by its owner, the Prince de Collorédo-Mansfeld, after the war and replaced by a nondescript block of flats. There was no trouble in getting a demolition order and the purpose was not to increase the rental income. The mansion was demolished because such atrocious things had occurred there during the Occupation that no one wanted to live in it again.

No. 21 had never been occupied by the Gestapo. Most of the buildings requisitioned by them – almost all in the expensive 16th *arrondissement* on and around the avenue Foch – still stand. Instead 21, rue Le Sueur had been used by a kindly doctor, Marcel Petiot, who was believed to be involved in the Resistance and whose speciality was enabling Jews and other fugitives to escape to Argentina. Why Argentina? Well, why not? It might as well have been Cloud Cuckoo Land, because Dr Petiot did not help people to escape at all. He persuaded them that he was going to save them from the Nazis, then murdered them and stole their money. He probably told them they were going to start a new life in Argentina because he frequently arranged to meet them at his local underground station, Métro Argentine, one down from the Etoile on the Neuilly-Vincennes line. The special thing about Dr Petiot was that all his life the sufferings of others made him laugh. He was that sort of doctor.

On 11 March, 1946, Marcel Petiot was charged in Paris with the murder of twenty-seven people and convicted of killing twenty-four of them. This score made him the greatest French murderer of the century, but at his trial – when he pleaded not guilty – he claimed he had actually disposed of sixty-three people. His defence was that he had done it for France – that his victims had been collaborators, or Germans. The jury was unconvinced and he was guillotined. But before the verdict *le tout Paris* flocked to the central criminal court on the Ile de la Cité to hear the doctor's one-liners. Sartre went, so did the Begum Aga Khan and Prince Louis of Monaco. If you had lived in Paris from June 1940 to March 1946 you may have felt that you had lived through a horror film anyway and Dr Petiot's performance in the dock provided the final touch.

Most of the facts about Marcel Petiot were established at the time of his trial. He was born at Villeneuve-sur-Yonne, a town of 3,640 inhabitants which is about eighty miles south of Paris. His father worked conscientiously for the post office. From early childhood Marcel was cruel. He had a pet cat which he apparently adored.

One day he dropped his pet into a tub of boiling water and screamed with laughter while the animal screamed in pain. At the age of three he strangled this cat after insisting that it should spend the night in his bed. Later he poked out the eyes of a caged bird with a needle. The effect of this operation on the bird also made him laugh a lot. From early school-days he used to steal from the desks of other children. Thus was the pattern of his life mapped out. One could add that he was a good-looking little boy, bright enough to pass his *baccalauréat* with distinction at the age of fifteen, and that as he grew older he developed a powerful hypnotic charm.

Marcel Petiot volunteered for the army in 1916 but unfortunately for his fellow citizens he was not among the one and a half million Frenchmen who fell on the field of honour, *morts pour la France*. After the war, at the family dinner table in Villeneuve, he announced that he had a vocation for surgery. He told his brother and his parents that he wanted 'to palpate wounded flesh, listen to the groans of the dying and make some money'. Then he let out a blood-chilling laugh. His father chased him out of the house. None the less Petiot qualified at the University of Lyon in 1921, returned to his native town and set up in practice. By 1927 he had managed to get himself elected mayor of Villeneuve on a left-wing ticket. He was a powerful orator who described himself as 'the worker's doctor, the people's friend'. He married an attractive girl and they had a son. Neither his wife nor his son ever suspected that there was anything strange about 'papa'.

Mayor Petiot left Villeneuve-sur-Yonne in 1933 and moved to Paris. The little town had become too hot for him. He had almost certainly committed three murders there while he was mayor. First a young girl, Louisette, his maid and mistress, had become pregnant and then disappeared. Later the wealthy proprietor of a shopping complex was found clubbed to death near her burning property just after withdrawing a large sum of money from the bank. On the following day an old man went round Villeneuve market telling people that he had seen Dr Petiot in the building just before it went up in flames. What happened later that morning was the first sign of the true Petiot touch. The doctor – and mayor – went down to the market, approached the old man in front of everyone and told him, '*Mon pauvre ami* . . . come back to my surgery at once. I have just received a new medicine from Paris which will cure your rheumatism.' The old man, hypnotized, unable to resist his fate, went back to the surgery. Petiot gave him the miracle injection and shortly afterwards the only hostile witness was dead. Petiot even filled in the death certificate. 'Natural death following heart failure.'

As mayor, he got away with this. But when he was discovered sabotaging his electricity meter and stealing electricity he had to resign his post and leave town. That the citizens of Villeneuve failed to object to their mayor murdering three of the electors but threw him out for fiddling the electricity bill is the essence of provincial France. In a final speech before a crowd of still loyal supporters Petiot produced a memorable example of his popular oratory. 'The higher up the tree the monkey climbs,' he said, 'the more the crowd watching from below has to focus on his bum.' And so, to a final cheer, Petiot continued his ascent. He was only thirty-six years old and his friends were convinced that one day he would be a government minister.

In Paris, Petiot set up at 66, rue Caumartin near the Gare St Lazare. Today the district is run-down and the house is surrounded by cheap clothes stalls and fast-food trolleys. The only plaque on the wall of no. 66, which must have been there in Petiot's day, records that a long forgotten Rumanian *tragédien* died in the building in 1924. Shortly after his arrival Petiot turned for help to his father-in-law, who had a restaurant specializing in the pâté and pigeons of Périgord in the rue Solférino near the Chambre des Députés. Influential gourmets arranged for the young doctor to be re-appointed to the staff of the *état civil* for the 9th *arrondissement* – which meant that Petiot was once again responsible for death certificates. His telephone number was PIG (alle) 7711 and his practice boomed. He became an *habitué* of the Drouot auction rooms and a noted collector. Many of his patients were grateful to him and he was regarded as a considerate and skilful doctor. The source of his wealth at this stage is not entirely clear but it is likely, in view of what happened next, that some of it came in unwitting donations from his grateful clients. If he was left alone with the body Dr Petiot was in the habit of going through the drawers of the dear departed's desk.

The crimes with which Petiot was eventually charged were all committed between February 1942 and March 1944. His technique was always the same. He would suggest to a patient or acquaintance that if they wanted to get out of France and away to the freedom and safety of South America he was in contact with people who could help. His victims were generally Jewish but they included Resisters and even gangsters with names like 'Jo *le Boxeur*' or 'François *le Corse*'. When they fell for the bait he told them to come alone, that same night, with a suitcase containing all their valuables to a rendezvous in central Paris after the curfew. He would then take them back to the deserted *hôtel particulier* and murder them, almost certainly by giving them a cyanide injection on the pretext that they had to be vaccinated for the trip. He would then take the body down to the cellar and dissolve it in quicklime. He would burn whatever was left in the boiler which served the whole building. None of the people he offered to help was ever seen again. None of the friends or family of his victims knew his address in the rue Le Sueur. They had always contacted him fifteen minutes' bicycle ride – and half a world – away in the rue Caumartin.

In the rue Le Sueur there was a sealed triangular room behind a secret door which led directly off the 'consulting room'. It is thought that after giving his victims the injection Dr Petiot would press a hidden button which made the front door bell ring. He would then tell the startled fugitive to hide in the triangular room while he went to see who it was. Instead he would peer into the triangular room through a spy hole and watch the death agony. The perfect murder, sixty-three times.

Petiot was able to plead that he had been a genuine Resister who had only murdered collaborators because in May 1943 he had indeed been arrested and imprisoned by the Gestapo. The Gestapo heard about his network and had apparently been taken in by it, just like his victims. They also thought, at first, that they were dealing with a Resister. It is not known what passed between Petiot and the Gestapo during his eight-month imprisonment in Fresnes. But before he was released, unharmed, in January 1944 he would certainly have met many genuine Resisters and he would have been able to gather the information which allowed him to claim later that he had been working for a Communist Resistance group called 'Fly Tox' which specialized in vaporizing *les collabos*. It eventually turned out that 'Fly Tox' was the codename of a person and not a group, but even today it is unclear whether or not Petiot did, on some occasions, kill people, either on behalf of the Gestapo or on behalf of the Communist Resistance. It is a fact that before he was finally arrested by French military security in October 1944 he had been sheltered by Communist Resisters.

The beginning of the end for Petiot came on 11 March, 1944, over five months before the Germans left Paris. That day in the rue Le Sueur people began to notice a most unpleasant smell. It was caused by the thick black smoke pouring from the boiler chimney of no. 21. At first no one thought much of it. Parisians were eating some strange things by March 1944, the city was under steady attack by RAF bombers and unpleasant smells were part of life. But after twenty-four hours this smell became too much and the police were called. The *hôtel particulier* appeared to be deserted. The police called the fire brigade who broke in and traced the smell to the cellar. One of the firemen staggered back upstairs and reported that the cellar and boiler were packed with truncated human remains. Shortly afterwards a nondescript stranger wheeling a tricycle pushed through the crowd and demanded to be let in saying that he was the owner's brother. He told the *sergent de ville* that the bodies were those of collaborators and that an important Resistance network was put at risk by the discovery. The patriotic policeman believed him at once and gave the stranger ten minutes to remove incriminating files. The persuasive stranger was of course Dr Petiot and it was seven months before he was seen again. He was arrested by French military security while he was himself working for French military security. Disguised in a beard and with false papers he had become 'Captain Valéry of the FFI . . . one of the heroes of the barricades during the Paris uprising.' More to the point, he was one of the officers leading the hunt for Dr Petiot.

At his sixteen-day trial Petiot, well-defended by a famous advocate Maître Floriot (who also defended the Nazi ambassador in Paris, Otto Abetz) thoroughly enjoyed himself. 'Twenty-four corpses have been identified,' said the public prosecutor. 'But you bore me with your twenty-four corpses,' interrupted Petiot. 'I have already told you those were not my corpses . . . The Gestapo released me from Fresnes and found my cellar stuffed with bodies – it's a bit much don't you think?'

When he was handed a hat and a shirt which were supposed to have belonged to one of his victims he examined them with care and pointed out that they were two sizes too big for Dr Braunberger, the man in question. Then he added that since Dr Braunberger had left his home without any money on him he, Petiot, would have had no reason to murder him. Then he threw the shirt over the usher's head, tossed the hat through the air and called out triumphantly, 'So I want to hear no more about this shirt ... or about this hat!' *Le tout Paris* applauded loudly.

But Petiot's most insolent strokes were reserved for his unfortunate judge. 'You earned about 30,000 francs a year?' asked the judge. 'Yes.' 'But you only declared 3,000 francs for tax?' 'Of course, who do you take me for, a lemon? I am a doctor and I am faithful to our professional traditions. It also goes to show that I am a good Frenchman.' The judge, like most of the judges in France, had remained in office during the Vichy regime. Petiot, 'the Resister', referred to this whenever possible. 'Why do you not give us the names of your fellow Resisters?' asked the judge. 'Never!' replied Petiot. 'They are no more guilty than I am. I will never let them be tormented by the scum who took an oath to Pétain.' At this point the judge, beside himself with rage, lifted his hands above his head. 'Don't lift your hands to the skies, M. le Président,' cried Petiot. 'I'll lift my hands to the skies if I want to,' spluttered the judge. 'You'll lift them higher than that before I'm through with you,' Petiot said.

Petiot had most of the best lines but he could never really explain the 49 suitcases, the 5 fur coats, the 26 hats, the 79 dresses, the 57 nightgowns, the 77 gloves, the 22 pairs of shoes, and so on and so on, which he had lodged with an accomplice and which were eventually identified. Nor could he do much in the face of the dignity of Mme Guschinow, widow of Joachim, the Polish furrier and one time patient and friend of Dr Petiot, or the grief of Mme Yvan Dreyfus whose husband had been a Jewish Resister. Petiot's advocate, Maître Floriot, put up a brilliant performance, casting doubt on every single piece of evidence. This method won his client three acquittals, but twenty-four convictions. Twenty-seven murders were just too many even for Maître Floriot.

The one defence Floriot never advanced was insanity. The jury would have been quite happy to believe that, but unfortunately the experts all agreed – Petiot was completely sane. As he himself said during his trial: 'One never knows, Maître, whether one is mad or not. Madness is only a question of comparison!' Petiot knew what he was talking about. He had been committed to a lunatic asylum twice in his life. The first time was in 1918 when he was about to be sent back to the Western Front. The second time was in 1936 when he was accused of shoplifting. On each occasion he was discharged from the asylum, 'completely cured', after a stay of a few weeks. The only serious objection his fellow doctors ever made to his activities was when they accused him of 'advertising' after his arrival in Paris.

It has never been explained why Petiot allowed his boiler to get out of control, so giving himself away. Perhaps when he said that the Gestapo had over-stocked his cellars, he was telling the truth. Perhaps there was a shortage of quicklime in Paris in the spring of 1944. But for the chimney-fire Petiot would probably never have been caught. His story about being a Resister might easily have won him the *Légion d'honneur* instead. One starts by saying, 'Just imagine, he might have become a post-war minister,' and ends by wondering what the secret life of the other ministers was like.

Petiot's execution took place in La Santé prison. The ceremony had to be postponed because the resident guillotine had been damaged during an R A F raid. 'If this goes on much longer, I warn you, I shall die laughing,' said Petiot when they apologized for the delay and explained the reason. On his last morning there was another hitch when one of the junior officials who had been ordered to attend fainted. 'Tell him not to worry,' said Petiot. 'There's still a doctor in the house! Would he like one of my injections?' And the dreadful laugh rang out for the last time.

Maître Floriot, who had become fond of his client, was standing by and he appeared upset. 'Courage, Maître,' said Petiot. 'It only lasts a moment.' And once again he was right.

November, 1990

＝＝＝＝

LOVE YOU TO DEATH

On 1 December, 1988, a French examining magistrate, seven lawyers and assorted policemen dressed up in rubber boots and plastic aprons, spent five hours in a tiny kitchen in the city of Nancy, cutting up lumps of raw meat on the bone, with a chainsaw. They were trying to reconstruct a crime that may never have been committed: the murder of Bernard Hettier, a middle-aged factory foreman, by his former mistress, a widow called Simone Weber. It is a suspected crime which combines some of the standard attributes of French provincial life: anonymous telephone calls, inquisitive neighbours and a prim exterior.

Bernard Hettier was a handyman and he loved the company of women. His life was an example of how someone with no particular talent, twice-divorced, nondescript appearance, no money, no family, no prospects and the misfortune to work in a factory in provincial France in the last quarter of the twentieth century, could still have a very good time. Unfortunately M. Hettier has stopped having a good time. Neither his three children, nor his two sisters nor any of his five other mistresses have seen him since 22 June, 1985. According to the police he was drugged, shot in the back of the neck, and dismembered with the aid of a chainsaw by Simone Weber. Mme Weber, aged fifty-seven, then packed the bits and pieces of her one-time man into seventeen black plastic dustbin bags and drove off from her three-room apartment at 158, avenue de Strasbourg into the night. The head is still missing, as are the four limbs. A torso was recovered from the River Marne near Poincy but Judge Thiel, the examining magistrate, was unable to prove that this was the greater part of M. Hettier.

So, the discreet career of Bernard Hettier has apparently come to an end. He was known as someone who would always help you out. Mowing the lawn, changing a washer, mending the hoover, Bernard was delighted to pop round. He worked in a chemical factory on the night shift which meant that he was available during the day, when the lady of the house was usually alone and in need of a hand. Bernard was very charming as well as being a skilful mechanic. He knew when life was about to become complicated and it was time to move on. He tried to remain on good terms with his old friends, he even went on mending their machinery, and then one day in October 1981 he met Simone Weber . . .

Any woman who has ever refused to change an electric plug or fish a spider out of the bath, can draw inspiration from Simone Weber. Here is someone who should have been a classic case of the helpless female. Middle-aged, abandoned, widowed, unlucky in love, she then lost two of her five children. Her daughter, aged sixteen, drank two litres of Theralene (a soporific) and was recorded as a suspected suicide. Her son, one of twins, shot himself in unexplained circumstances while doing his military service in Germany.

Simone might have been content to overfeed her dachshund and develop a dependency on Valium. She could have retrieved her self-respect by misdirecting strangers, or short-changing tourists or even going in for a little mild shoplifting. Instead she pulled herself together and turned to an ingenious life of crime. To look at her today, short, stout, slightly lost amid the tall policemen who accompany her on every outing she takes from the prison in Nancy where she has been living since October 1985, she could be on the verge of a self-righteous old age, button-up boots, a furry bowler hat and free bus pass to the fore. There is a large community of such old ladies in Nancy, but Simone Weber will never qualify for it.

For instead of collapsing, Mme Weber went decorously berserk. She became a major social menace. Starting with her refusal to accept the explanation of her daughter's death, she sued a nurse at the hospital in Nancy for manslaughter. Then she turned to revolutionary politics. This was during the late 70s so she became a Maoist. Simone Weber attended the meetings of 'Truth and Justice', a group of Nancy militants, and told her new comrades that her daughter had been imprisoned and killed by a hospital nurse.

But she was not just a one-issue revolutionary. She was preparing for the big day. She obtained three containers of nitro-glycerine, a detonator, two rifles, ammunition and two silencers. She became a forger of identity documents. Had she lived fifty years earlier she might have made a formidable recruit for the French Resistance. She has a real talent for the life of deceit which was one of the Resisters' most important survival techniques. She learnt to pick pockets; she took to buying second-hand cars, camouflaging them as better models and reselling them for a profit.

She adopted several false identities. She claimed to be a philosophy teacher, a couturier, a nurse, a company director. She was known as 'Monique', 'Sophie' or 'Françoise'. In the hope of contacting her two dead children she went to 'black masses' held by spiritualists. Losing touch with her living children, she spent more time with her sister Madeleine, who was also a strange one.

Simone and Madeleine were brought up by their father in a suburb of Nancy after their mother abandoned them. They have led curiously similar lives. They married brothers, both were widowed, both had little dogs (Simone a dachshund, Madeleine a poodle). Both continued to live in Nancy and search for Mr Right. Madeleine preferred Catholicism to Marx. Her apartment on the avenue de Strasbourg is still full of devotional objects. On the wall there is a reproduction of the Mona Lisa. Madeleine's place was always very tidy. Simone's, in the rue de Cronstadt, was a pit and the pictures on her walls are always of the dead, her mother, her two husbands, her two children and Bernard Hettier.

Simone has had a sad life, but if people felt sorry for her it wasn't a feeling she returned. The obvious place for a widow living in Nancy to look for Mr Right is in *les petites annonces* of *L'Est Républicain*. These have a certain brutal honesty. 'Company director, 33, earning £25,000 a year ready to open up a world pillowed with tenderness to a woman of 48 with a good figure.' Simone had a good figure before she was exposed to three years of prison food. She herself might have placed this one. 'Former businesswoman, aged 45, sporting, great sense of humour, will enrapture a captivating gentleman; willing to compromise.'

With similar promises Simone attracted the attention of a stubborn old soldier, Marcel Fixard, aged seventy-nine, living in Strasbourg, and discovered quite quickly that he had a little nest egg. She decided to marry him but thought it better not to let him know. So in April 1980 she went to the town hall in Strasbourg with another old man, who was on day release from a nearby asylum and who stood in for Fixard. Fifteen minutes later, unknown to himself, Fixard had a new wife. Then Simone drew up a will in which her loving husband disinherited his family and left her all his money. Then she forged his signature with the help of tracing paper. Six weeks after his wedding M. Fixard, who had been in good health, suddenly died. And his widow, despite the protests of his two nephews in far away Bordeaux, became quite rich.

Just over a year later, in October 1981, Simone's lawnmower broke down. She had inherited a lawn and rose trees with old Fixard's house in the village of Rosières to the great scandal of the villagers. She was selling Wanda beauty products when she bumped into Bernard Hettier in Nancy town centre. They had met once before. She was a friend of one of his former girlfriends. Once he had fixed the lawnmower, Bernard helped her to move house. As Mme Weber was to put it later, 'We lived the life of a couple for two years.'

At fifty-five, Bernard Hettier considered himself a shrewd judge of character and he was confident that he had met cuddly, rather solitary, women like Mme Weber before. He didn't know about her hidden talents. He didn't know that the spare pressure-cooker in the kitchen at the rue de Cronstadt was full of official stamps stolen from the town hall; that the television remote control had been dismantled and reassembled around her false identity card. He never went through people's drawers, or he might have found the pad of prescription forms taken from a doctor's desk, blank air tickets, model wills, false car registration plates, bugging devices, a collection of men's watches and assorted jewellery. In all the time they spent together Bernard apparently noticed only one odd thing about her. She slept with a pistol under her pillow. And when after eighteen months, in June 1983, he found a new friend, he warned his family to keep away from Simone. By then she had added a photostat of Bernard's identity card and his cheque book to her collection and popped them into a box of chocolates.

Louise, the new girlfriend, who lived in the north of Nancy not far from Bernard's little-used flat, had just taken a cure for alcoholism. Simone found out and decided she was not going to be replaced by a 'sot'. For the first time Bernard's legendary powers of disengagement proved inadequate. He would come home and find Simone inside his flat, which was odd because he had never given her a key. So he changed the locks anyway and went to bed and woke in the night to see her face peering in through the first floor bedroom window: she had installed herself on a ladder. She telephoned him incessantly. Driving around Nancy in his (blue) Renault 9 Bernard would glance in his rear-view mirror. All too often there was her (white) Renault 9, with the eager face behind the steering wheel. At the traffic lights it was, 'Coo-coo! Bernard. Could you drop by? I think the sink's blocked again!' Sometimes, when she got tired of following him round Nancy, she would pay a female neighbour to do it for her. If he managed to shake her off by fast driving she would punish him later by unplugging his car battery. At times he found her peering through the window of his car, checking up on the mileage. His neighbours used to note the hours she sat in her car outside his flat, waiting for him to come home. This went on for two years. Bernard's family say that during this period she twice drugged his coffee.

The avenue de Strasbourg is not as grand as it sounds. It is a wide street but most of the houses are broken up into multiple-occupation. No. 158 is an unusually narrow building. Madeleine's apartment occupies the first floor, two windows squashed together in a crumbling façade, the shutters now permanently closed. The shutters of the ground-floor apartment also seem to be closed until one notices as one gets closer that the right-hand one is raised about eight inches. Behind the shutter – dazzling white net curtains. One almost expects to see the snout of a telescope emerge. This is the home of an elderly couple, Marie and Nicolas Haag, who are the chief witnesses for the prosecution. In their old age the Haags have become devotees of a popular national pastime, spying on one's neighbours. They say that on the evening of 22 June they saw a middle-aged man climb the worn steps to the first-floor flat with Mme Weber and that he never came out again. Two days later Mme Weber came to their door to ask if they knew how to fix the blades on to an electric carving knife. And early on the following morning they watched her carry the seventeen black plastic dustbin bags down to her car.

Today the Haags are still on guard. One has the distinct feeling, as one walks down the wide parade of the avenue de Strasbourg towards no. 158, that one is under observation. Before there were just the neighbours to survey, the comings and goings at no. 158, MM Gout, Bensacki and Meyer, to say nothing of Simone and Madeleine. But now the Haags also watch for journalists. On the front door post, the name beside the bell for the first-floor flat has been chiselled out. There is no reply to the other bells.

In the Café Bar a little further up the street they are more interested in the football results and the darts board than in the interminable case of Simone Weber. A tramp comes in out of the rain and is given *un petit rouge* and a bag of food. He tries to take the food discreetly but slips on his way to the door. 'You don't have the right to take the chair as well,' says the patron. The tramp is not embarrassed, he is not even very wet although it is sheeting down outside. Musing about the Weber case Madame, behind the bar, said, 'How do you think she got her family to help her? She must have paid them a bit.' Madame is thinking of the telephone calls apparently from Bernard Hettier after his disappearance, actually made by Simone Weber's cousin. The café is a place for people who have nothing to do. They can pass the time away and forget their problems. '*Sont contents, les garçons . . .*' says the fat lady who has spent all afternoon watching the darts players. Her husband leans an impressive paunch on the counter and chuckles away wheezily when the landlady calls him 'a punctured tyre'. In here, among the neighbours, the mere details of Simone Weber's love life are startling enough; the possibility of a chainsaw massacre as well seems a bit far-fetched. But there is a shop opposite the café which hires out chainsaws. They are laid out in the window in neat rows. For £20 a week you can have the basic model. For £30 you can have a Stihl Rollomatic ('Not to be missed!'). The display may have given Madame Weber an idea. She actually hired hers from a shop in the suburbs and later reported it stolen and forfeited the deposit. The shopkeeper says it was the first time in twenty years that he had supplied a chainsaw to a woman.

The kitchen of no. 158 is a narrow corridor with plastic tiles on the walls and a strip of lino on the floor. If you lean out of the front window of the flat you can just see the convent of the Poor Clares to the right and to the left the roofs of the Central Hospital where Simone's daughter died. In the kitchen the fridge, gas heater and three-ring cooker are in impeccable condition. In fact the whole kitchen is in a suspiciously clean state. The fact that there are no stains of any kind in the kitchen is considered to be a major point against Mme Weber. Someone has been at work with the Eau de Javel – scrub, scrub, scrub!

The third major character in this story is also the new man in Simone's life: tall, thoughtful, black-bearded, he has spent 180 hours talking to her and has made a 7,000 page record of their conversations. She has known him for three years. It is a steady relationship. He is called Gilbert Thiel and he is an examining magistrate. Before that he was a tax inspector. Judge Thiel checks everything. When he found a bloodstain on the sofa Simone told him that 'Poupette', her sister's poodle, had probably been in season. The judge found the blood was human not animal, group AB or A. Bernard was group A. Before he even met Simone, Gilbert Thiel tapped her telephone. She spent hours talking to Madeleine, who now has a flat in Cannes. They talked about 'a new school for Bernadette'. Judge Thiel realized they were talking in code. Madeleine was arrested and proved less stubborn than Simone. She said that 'Bernadette' was the name they had given to Bernard's car which disappeared shortly after he did. The 'new school' was a new garage. Madeleine told the judge where he could find the car in Cannes. The missing chainsaw was in the boot. So far the judge has charged Simone with two murders, theft, illegal possession of explosives and possession of false car registration plates. Madeleine has been charged as an accomplice and released on bail.

You can believe all this, or not. After over 200 hours of questioning Mme Weber still denies everything. She says she is still very fond of Bernard and that he is probably in Majorca. She ridicules the theory of the chainsaw, far too noisy she says, and it would have spattered blood everywhere. According to her lawyers, the official reconstruction of the crime in the tiny kitchen on 1 December tended to support her objections. Other observers say that Mme Weber followed the action with close attention and became very critical when Judge Thiel proposed using white veal meat. 'She wanted red meat, freshly-killed and full of blood.' As for the chainsaw found in the car boot, she says she just wanted a chainsaw. Bernard might have found it useful. And there is at least one man who does believe her.

Joseph Tournel, formerly leader of 'Truth and Justice', a 60s Maoist, now an ex-miner with a 75 per cent disability pension living in Bethune, is convinced of Mme Weber's innocence. He has come out of retirement to fight one last battle, and has formed a Committee of Support for his former comrade. 'I firmly believe that she did not commit the crime,' he says. 'And anyway it is inhuman to lock her up for so long without a trial. She has been in preventive detention for longer than anyone else in France. This is against the European Convention on Human Rights.'

But M. Tournel has not been allowed to visit Simone and in France an examining magistrate can keep a suspect in prison for as long as it takes him to gather his evidence. Meanwhile Mme Weber has hired and fired twenty lawyers in the last three years. She is capricious, and in a case as well-publicized as hers the lawyers do not always expect a fee. So far sixteen demands for her release have been turned down. The fact that it is taking so long to prepare a case against her is, perhaps, the strongest argument in her favour. But if she did not do it, what has happened to Bernard?

There remains the possibility, until his body is found, that he is alive, not in Majorca perhaps but somewhere a little further away. Looked at from his point of view his life had become impossible. He couldn't leave Nancy because he had to work, and even if he did find a job elsewhere in France she had enough money to follow him. The solution lay in having That Woman locked up while he got away. All he had to do was tell her to hire a chainsaw, leave a bloodstain on her sofa, and make sure he entered the flat when the Haags were on the look-out and that he left it without being seen. Then he disappeared. The suitcase fished out of the Marne was an unexpected bonus.

So let's imagine him sitting on a terrace overlooking the beach sipping a rum and coke. He's grown a beard, he's probably running an electrical repair business and ever since he learnt the Portuguese for 'dishwasher', 'lawnmower' and 'fuse box' he's had a little Brazilian friend. Perhaps he sometimes remembers driving round Nancy, and recalls all the times he looked in his rear-view mirror, and reflects that the quickest way from the rue de Cronstadt to the avenue de Strasbourg is past the city prison.*

December, 1988

* Simone Weber, still protesting her innocence, was sentenced to twenty years' imprisonment in March 1991 for the unpremeditated murder of her lover, Bernard Hettier – whose body was never found. Mme Weber was also ordered to pay 100,000 francs to the family of Bernard Hettier in compensation. The court agreed to give her back her typewriter so that she could write her memoirs.

7. THE PCF

The playwright Eugene Ionesco was recently invited to a reception at the French ministry of culture in honour of Vaclav Havel, also a playwright and now of course the president of Czechoslovakia. The sight of his fellow guests was enough to make Ionesco explode with rage.

'They were all there,' he wrote later in *Le Figaro*, 'former Stalinists, former Communists, former Maoists, former and current Castroists . . . the massed bands of the extreme-left . . . delighted to welcome the new "left-wing" president of Czechoslovakia.'

The cause of Ionesco's rage was the fact that some years ago his wife had smuggled the manuscript of a play by Havel out of Prague and passed it to 'one of the fiercest left-wing publishers' in Paris, who had refused either to publish the piece or produce it on the grounds that Havel was 'a reactionary'. And, looking round the reception, Ionesco realized that Havel was being fêted by the very same people who had condemned his work when he was being persecuted, that no representatives of the French centre or right had been invited, and that none of those in charge of the reception had realized the absurdity of this. One might have expected this veteran of the Theatre of the Absurd to have relished the situation; in fact Ionesco was overcome by the indignity.

Ionesco remembered how often since the Second World War the left had been warned about the true nature of Communism, by Raymond Aron, by André Gide, by Arthur Koestler, by André Breton and by himself. And how in return he, and those who agreed with him, were insulted for their pains.

'We were accused of being contemptible fascists, of being cowards and scum. And yet we were right. And now "They" have realized that we were right. And there "they" sit – all of them. Some of them really believed in Marxist ideals, some of them believed in nothing at all and were just happy to play with millions of people's lives. But all of them were warned. Have they yet realized what they did?'

Ionesco's tirade rose to an impassioned climax. Recalling the days when to insult a French intellectual you merely had to call him 'right-wing', he wrote, 'It is frequently said that the French are the most intelligent people in the world. The truth is that in the theatre and the world of letters they are the most shortsighted and the most foolish ... They gather together at the ministry of culture, the ministry of the left, scratching each other's backs as though nothing had happened. But what a pity it is that for so long they deceived France and the French people led by the greatest liar of them all, Jean-Paul Sartre, who I accuse of having perverted all the intelligence and literature of France!'

Since France has been the chosen home of the Romanian-born Ionesco for the past fifty years, and has honoured him with membership of the Académie Française, his final remarks may seem a little intemperate. But in his portrayal of the ministerial gatherings of the official Left, the master of the absurd has conjured up a wonderful image of gracelessness and intellectual confusion in the European city which the Left has always regarded as its spiritual home.

May, 1990

———

There is a savage little argument going on about the reinstatement of 'the Renault 10', a group of union officials who were sacked by the management of the car firm in 1986 for criminal misconduct committed on the premises and during working hours. Backing the Renault 10 is the Communist Party which has been fighting one of its classic, industrial campaigns in which few holds are barred. So far, the party is losing.

Georges Marchais, the Communist leader, is not pleased about this, and the question of whether or not the Renault 10 should be allowed back into the factory, having been disputed in almost every court in the land, now threatens the tranquillity of this week's joyful occasion.

The Renault factory, or 'the Régie' as it is sometimes called, is in Billancourt on the western outskirts of the city and is one of the sights of Paris. For a start, it is enormous. It runs along both banks of the Seine for what seems to be a couple of miles, and at one point it expands on to a large island in the river. The entire island has been roofed over and is now joined by a private bridge to the rest of the kingdom of Renault. Even today one can see what a pleasant place, on a bend in the river, the Ile Seguin must once have been. Today it is surrounded by barbed wire, covered with corrugated iron, guarded by dogs and devoted to one of the most insane occupations of the twentieth century, the mass production of motor cars.

Within this hideous perimeter have been fought many of the greatest engagements of French industrial history and physical violence has played a prominent part in this sector of the economic struggle. In these clashes, workers have been killed by the police or by the company's security guards. In November 1986, Georges Besse, then head of Renault, was shot dead in the street by Action Directe terrorists in the name of one such dead Renault worker. M. Besse had previously carried out a 'rationalization' programme at Renault which caused heavy redundancies.

The troubles now known as the case of the Renault 10 started in August 1986 when those dismissed under the Besse programme included a number of Communist union officials. It was at that time that the 'criminal misconduct' took place. Over a period of several days a number of workers wearing masks and carrying iron bars and led by union delegates, roamed around the Régie Renault spreading alarm and despondency. Doors were smashed down, filing cabinets pillaged, desks forced open, documents taken and members of the personnel department beaten up. Two managers were dragged out of their office and led as prisoners in a procession on to the Renault bridge over the River Seine. The letters 'SS' were painted on their jackets, then they were kicked and punched and told that they would be dropped over the edge of the high bridge into the river.

Eventually six CGT union officials were identified by the management as the ringleaders and were fired, with the agreement of the independent labour inspectorate. One of them was M. Marchais's son-in-law. The masked men were eventually convicted of causing bodily harm and theft, and were fined between £100 and £300. Most of them were also members of the Communist Party. The

Party thereupon singled out ten cases and started a campaign to get them reinstated. Raymond Lévy, the new head of Renault, has made it clear that if any of the ten are reinstated, he will resign.

Over the last three years the Renault 10, supported by CGT militants, have regularly forced their way into the factory to take up their posts. Once inside there is no work for them so they retire to union offices and meditate. Other workers have said that the only time they ever see any of the ten is on television.

The CGT won several early court decisions, but on the question of reinstatement it has now lost in both the Court of Appeal and in the *Conseil Constitutionnel*, whose authority is supreme. So that seems to be the end of the legal road for the Renault 10. Needless to say, it is not the end of the struggle as far as M. Marchais is concerned.

On Monday one of the ten said that in order to get satisfaction they 'would now be taking the necessary steps in the context of the Bicentenary festivities. It would not be possible to commemorate the Revolution without some real live *sans culottes*,' he added. 'We intend to get as close to the Elyseé Palace as possible.' Even with 30,000 policemen on duty in Paris this is no idle threat. And if M. Marchais can arrange for anything to mar President Mitterrand's big week, he will consider it three years well spent.

July, 1989

The agony of 'the last Stalinist party in Europe', the PCF (*Parti Communiste Français*), is being followed with close attention. In the last five years, successive waves of party intellectuals have been caught on the metaphorical barbed wire surrounding the party's headquarters in the Place du Colonel-Fabien as they attempted to renew or reconstruct the PCF. In every case the central committee, led by the general-secretary, Georges Marchais, has prevailed, and the reformers have been driven out into the political and spiritual wilderness that awaits those who step out of line. There are 144 members of the French party's central committee, and even last week only fourteen of them could be found to challenge M. Marchais's leadership.

The issue was whether the PCF had adequately condemned the

KGB's attempted coup against Mikhail Gorbachev. Whereas the rest of France was under the impression that the PCF had hedged its bets for as long as possible, the 128 faithful members of the central committee agreed with M. Marchais that it had in fact opposed the *coup d'Etat* and that everyone else in France, except for those speaking in bad faith, agreed that this had been the case. Charles Fiterman, Philippe Herzog and Anicet le Pors, the most distinguished dissidents on the central committee, can now take their leave – a lifetime of dedicated Communism apparently gone up in smoke.

Under M. Marchais the PCF will remain loyal to Moscow without Moscow, and to Stalin without Stalin. Its members are considerably more Catholic than the Pope, an appropriate comparison since loyal French Communists have started to compare themselves to religious believers and to take comfort in the idea that 'religions do not die'.

Among the last of the faithful is Jeannette Thorez, widow of Maurice Thorez, who was general-secretary of the PCF from 1930 to 1964. Describing herself as a former admirer of Stalin, she says she no longer believes in the dictatorship of the proletariat, in a monolithic Communist Party or in a Communist state, but she still believes in the principles of Marxism-Leninism and says that 'although Communism has suffered a terrible blow it is not dead'. Among those who disagree with her is the sociologist Edgar Morin, who in a recent interview celebrated the death of Communism. 'Dogmatic Marxism,' he said, 'with its religion of earthly salvation and the messianic role of the working classes has died with it,' and 'scientific socialism has been shown to be as scientifically bogus as the racial theories of the Nazis.'

The debate is not merely an historical one in France because although the PCF is a shadow of its former self its electoral alliance with the Socialist Party forms an essential part of the present government's majority, and Socialist leaders are worried about the effect of the collapse on their future. So the former defence minister, Jean-Pierre Chevènement, paid tribute last week to 'the unchallenged importance of the PCF's contribution to French history' and said the party's collapse would mean it would now be necessary 'to re-found the French Left'. And the foreign minister, Roland Dumas, added that 'anti-communists should never forget that the heyday of anti-communism was the Nazi Occupation' and repeated another old PCF battle cry, 'In those days to be a Communist meant you had the right to be shot one hour earlier than everyone else.' These curious tributes are explained by the Socialist realization that without two million Communist votes they will never win the next presidential elections. Too many disaffected Communist voters have turned to the extreme-right *Front National* in the past for the Socialists to feel any complacency.

The Russian counter-revolution may have altered the map of the world, but the street maps of France will also have to be changed. In 1945, when the PCF was the biggest French political party, with 159 deputies in the National Assembly, it had sufficient influence to make its mark in almost every town in the country. In Paris, Karl Marx, the Kremlin, Stalingrad and Leningrad are all commemorated, and there are streets named after Stalingrad or Leningrad in Lyon, Marseille, Grenoble, Toulouse, Toulon, Rennes, Le Havre and many other cities in France. A reader has now written to *Le Figaro* suggesting that the Place Stalingrad in Paris should be renamed the 'Place de Katyn' to commemorate the massacre of Polish army officers carried out by the Soviet Army but blamed on the Nazis for forty years. And numerous municipal pressure groups are clamouring for their local memorials to the power of the PCF to revert to their previous names.

None of the streets in EuroDisneyland are likely to be named after the battle of Stalingrad, and more's the pity. The PCF is the only party so far to condemn the employment qualifications imposed by the Walt Disney Company on the 9,500 French people now being hired for the opening on 12 April. All applicants have to take a psychological test, no one will be employed who has a visible tattoo, a beard or a moustache, no jewellery may be worn by employees except for one ring on each hand, and female employees may wear only minimal make-up. Some of these provisions are almost certainly illegal in France, although it is arguable that EuroDisneyland is not in any meaningful sense 'in' France.

The ban on beards means that no male Muslim fundamentalists can work in EuroDisneyland. France contains large numbers of Muslim fundamentalists. Are they prepared to fulfil the squeaky-clean criteria of *les Disneys*? Since 125,000 applicants are expected to apply for the 9,500 posts *les Disneys* are not too worried.

September, 1991

8. IN THE MIDI

===

Political history as romance, a neglected form, was revived in France this week by the appearance of *L'Idiot International*, an occasional publication once edited by Sartre. The latest issue described a recent visit to Marseille by the Parisian intellectual and self-publicist Jean-Edern Hallier and tells of the evening he spent with Bernard Tapie, the self-made millionaire and self-publicist just elected to the National Assembly by the voters of Marseille's sixth constituency.

M. Hallier is still best remembered for his misadventures in 1982, when he was reportedly kidnapped just before he published a book. The unshaven author eventually turned up, but the police could not trace his captors and there was a widespread impression that the kidnapping may have been a publicity stunt. Since then M. Hallier has played the intellectual clown, and it was in this role that he went to Marseille last month to hold an 'anti-Bernard Tapie' press conference, shortly before the vote in the by-election M. Tapie was to win. The conference, held in the Hôtel Concorde Prado, M. Tapie's campaign headquarters, was a great success. M. Hallier, generously fuelled with iced vodka, described the takeover king and chairman of the Marseille Olympique football club as 'a vampire with a facelift', 'a second Stavisky', 'a carpet (*tapis*) on which I intend to wipe my feet', and much else.

That evening, according to *L'Idiot International*, while M. Hallier lay in his underpants on his bed on the sixth floor of the Hôtel Concorde Prado chanting 'I am the greatest,' drinking vodka and watching Kirk Douglas's appearance on Bernard Pivot's weekly books programme, M. Tapie came to call. He was not alone: he had five men in leather jackets with him, carrying large revolvers.

Before taking the story any further one should say that Marseille not only lost a renowned mayor in 1986 with the death of Gaston

Defferre, but it has since lost a renowned 'parallel mayor' – Zampa, head of the local *milieu* who passed on to the great casino in the sky. Zampa has been replaced by 'Francis *le Belge*', described to M. Hallier by a local restaurateur in tones of profound respect, as 'a really nasty piece of work'.

What passed in the hotel room that evening between M. Hallier and the human dobermanns accompanying M. Tapie is vividly narrated in *L'Idiot International* by a friend of M. Hallier's, identified only as 'Sydney'. The television was still showing Kirk Douglas, though the book programme was over and Douglas was by then wearing a cowboy hat and in black and white. 'We're going to kill you,' barked the dobermanns. 'You won't live till morning.' 'I'm not afraid of you,' replied M. Hallier. 'Oh no?' The two largest thugs seized him by the hair, threw him on the bed, punched him in the face and put a gun to his head. Meanwhile Sydney was knocked down and recorded a kaleidoscope of impressions: a pistol barrel in his mouth, the image of Kirk Douglas surrounded by Red Indians, M. Hallier on the bed, and a glass of Coca Cola spilling over the carpet, the cigarette butts and M. Hallier's trousers, long since removed to reveal his attractive red knickers.

By this time M. Hallier, according to Sydney, was shouting 'Kill me if you like, but my work will survive! It is immortal.' Now and again M. Tapie would pat one of the dobermanns on the shoulder and say the whole thing was outside his control, that these men worked for 'Francis *le Belge*' and that he was merely a marionette. Sydney gave himself one or two good lines. As the gangster spat in his face and said: 'Now I've seen you I'll know you next time. I know where you live!' Sydney said: 'OK. You've seen me, I've seen you, he's seen me and so have a lot of other people including the chief rabbi of France, Monsieur Sitruk, who's expecting me at the synagogue tomorrow morning.' At that point M. Tapie began to look a bit thoughtful, the dobermanns left the room and the three men started to negotiate.

If life in Marseille is not like that, then in the view of Parisians it should be. There are touches of a recognizable Tapie in the fable. He does say things like 'he's going to remember me' – of a political opponent. And he does hit people. Last year he hit a referee after a football match. He has also hit journalists. Afterwards he buys them a drink and tries to purchase any films of the incident. His arrival on the Marseille political scene has confused everyone. Originally imported into the city by Gaston Defferre to revive the fortunes of Olympique Marseille, he became a local hero as the club improved, and decided to try his luck in politics by standing for the National Assembly – not for the right but as a Mitterrandist candidate supported by the local Socialist Party. In Paris the rather pious team who surround the prime minister, Michel Rocard, have no idea what to do with him. In Marseille his arrival is seen as a distraction from the serious business of settling political scores, which can date back generations. Meanwhile, as Marseille and M. Tapie decide what to do next, two determined self-publicists have put on a memorable show.

March, 1989

In Marseille life goes on much as usual and the area around the criminal court has been barricaded off for the trial of a man whose life has been dedicated to tobacco. As a little orphan in Naples, Michele Zaza made his living by selling single packets of cigarettes at the *autostrada* tolls. But he was born with brains. He became European representative of Philip Morris and is now described as one of the godfathers of the Neapolitan *Camorra*. Today he is accused of cigarette smuggling.

According to the prosecution, his method was to purchase Lucky Strikes in Amsterdam by the containerload, drive them across Belgium and France without paying the tax, bribe a French customs officer to remove the customs seals and sell them in Italy or Spain. The allegedly bent *douanier*, Monsieur Defendini, cost only 50,000 francs (£5,000) a lorryload, while Zaza's profits in unpaid taxes are thought to have been more than £25 million. This enabled him to run a Rolls-Royce and a BMW and to purchase a villa in Beverly Hills – which he let to the French Consulate. The rent paid for the education of his three daughters in a French convent school, as he is quick to point out.

M. Zaza is being tried with thirty-four members of his organization. He appears in court in a wheelchair suffering from the traditional heart condition and has been treated with enormous respect by everyone except the judge, Mme Annette Durand, who told him that if he did not stop interrupting he would be removed, adding, 'We are not in Italy now.' He faces a possible long term in Les Baumettes, the city jail, where a suite is being prepared for him.

July, 1991

＝＝

Anyone who first comes to Ajaccio cannot help noticing the number of healthy, energetic males who spend the whole day doing nothing. These men wear dark-coloured sports shirts, blue jeans, polished black loafers, no socks, dark glasses. They generally carry a packet of cigarettes but rarely smoke. They pass the time sitting outside a friend's café greeting the drivers in the passing cars. They have a curious habit of talking to each other while staring the other way.

If one of them makes a joke he generally laughs alone; the others look slightly pained and sometimes take up a new position a few yards further from the disturbance. The dark sports-shirts are changed several times a day and are always crisp. You get the feeling that these men benefit from a considerable female support structure behind the strong shabby doors which cut off their domestic lives from the street.

They watch girls but without expressing any reaction. In any case there are a lot of girls at this time of year in the streets of Ajaccio, frequently dressed in bathing costumes. This life of the café and the pavement and the slow cruise round the block takes place in the midst of the usual bustle of a tourist season. It is unnoticed by the visitors who are buying post cards, booking coach tours or eating ice-cream.

The women who iron the dark-coloured tee-shirts do not wear bathing costumes. They dress rather modestly and walk in pairs – keeping an eye on each other. Every two or three minutes, every twenty or thirty yards, another close friend passes by. All the women are delighted, even though they saw each other yesterday and will see each other again tomorrow. They have fine eyes, straight backs, slim wrists, and dark hair. If they have to deal with the holidaymakers they smile a lot – with their teeth.

Corsica is notorious for its poverty but these Corsicans seem to have escaped from that curse. Their cars tend to be fast, but not flashy. Occasionally the strain of all the street-watching becomes too much and one or other of the watchers will collapse into a chair in front of a small cake and a Fanta orange. They are sober. It is not easy to know what these stony-faced, non-committal people are thinking. It is not easy to know what they do when they are not sitting outside the café drinking each other's free drinks. But there were 524 unexplained bomb explosions in Corsica in 1986. And in the first three months of this year the rate tripled.

Corsica has one of the strangest separatist and terrorist movements in Europe. It is so mixed up with gangsterism that many people believe it is run by the *milieu* as a means of dominating the island's economy. The last seven years have seen an unchecked growth of banditry and terrorism on the island, mainly directed against teachers and civil servants from other parts of France, or against the 17,000 *pied-noirs* who settled in Corsica after fleeing from Algeria in 1962, or more recently against the police.

The aim of the violence is to drive the 'continentals', that is the people from other parts of France, off the island. The chief methods used are threatening notes, demands for protection money, arson and bombings of property. The police are shot.

If this is political nationalism then it is hard to see why racketeering and protection money should be so common. But if it is gangsterism, it is hard to see why non-Corsican teachers and civil servants should be the target. The attacks are carried out in the name of the FLNC, 'the Corsican National Liberation Front', a body which was once a political group. The violence is deplored by the great majority of the Corsican people, but the same people tend to see and hear nothing and say that it is the government's job, not theirs, to deal with crime.

Last January the government decided to try again. The three senior police officers on the island were replaced in the course of one week. One of those leaving was asked why he had been moved. 'Let's just say that three men who have been here for some time are being replaced by three men who have not been here before,' he said. The administration of Corsica is thought to have been infiltrated by separatists. After a time the 'continentals' get worn out by the instructions which are overlooked, the files which are lost or the tip-offs which are given.

At the time the FLNC showed their contempt for this reshuffle by letting off their biggest bomb so far. It completely destroyed the five storey ferro-concrete tax office in Bastia. Shortly afterwards the police scored a coup. They raided a flat in Ajaccio, seized the armoury of weapons and explosives and found enough documents to destroy the FLNC command in south-western Corsica. Twenty men were arrested, and eleven have since been charged.

The surprise lay in the fact that the people who had been carrying out the FLNC's ferocious bombing campaign around Ajaccio were neither known criminals nor known separatists. They included a bee-keeper, a restaurateur, a *charcutier* and an estate agent. They were not members of any of the powerful Corsican clans. They were apparently respectable members of the bourgeoisie.

The sort of people who would have been anxious for their children to do well at school, the stalwarts of the 'parent-teacher association', were the people who had been sending anonymous notes telling the teacher to 'leave Corsica or be burnt out'.

August, 1987

In 1982 Graham Greene published a pamphlet, *J'Accuse*, that opened with the words: 'Let me issue a warning to anyone who is tempted to settle for a peaceful life on what is called the Côte d'Azur. Avoid the region of Nice, which is the preserve of some of the most criminal organizations in the south of France.' Greene accused local police officers, magistrates and lawyers of encouraging criminals and guaranteeing them immunity. 'I have deliberately given this pamphlet the sub-title *The Dark Side of Nice*,' he wrote. 'For of course Nice has its sunny side also, but I can leave it to the Mayor of Nice, Monsieur Jacques Médecin, to talk about that.'

M. Médecin, who is facing charges of misusing £1.3 million of public money, has taken refuge in Uruguay after resigning on Sunday. Yet he still finds supporters in unexpected quarters. The former prime minister, Jacques Chirac, said that he was 'sad' to hear of M. Médecin's resignation. And Alain Juppé, general-secretary of the Gaullist RPR, said that he had been 'an outstanding mayor'.

The former mayor's defenders point to what they consider to be an essential fact; *le Midi est pourri*. Viewed from Paris, the politics of Nice appear rather overripe, not to say rotten. Nice only became part of France in 1860. Before that, it followed the customs of its Sardinian-descended population, a little kingdom regulated by the ancient traditions of the Camorra. The sophisticated view is that Nice today may be the fifth largest city in France, but the exchange of personal favours and absolute loyalty to *le patron* still rules.

Under the *système Médecin* you were either for the mayor or against him. M. Médecin was proud of his system, which gave him 51 out of 69 seats on the city council at the last municipal election. He said he had modelled it on the Communist Party's methods of running a city. In his twenty-five years as mayor, M. Médecin allied himself at various times with the Communists, Socialists, Gaullists, the Jewish community and the extreme-right National Front. It was all the same to him.

Life in Nice, if you had no influence with the mayor, was not always sunny. Mr Greene told the story of a girl who was unlucky enough to marry a gangster and who was then beaten up, tricked out of the custody of her son and threatened with death, while the police and lawyers looked on. There was another story last year of a property developer who had tricked an elderly woman into leaving her home and then knocked it down, which suggested that little has changed.

There also was a rumour about an American woman, Claudette Pezenas-Berke, who blew the whistle on a number of M. Médecin's business deals in the United States. She was found dead beside her swimming pool in 1989 and her husband believes she was murdered.

Jacques Médecin's father, Jean, who ruled Nice for thirty-five years without ever getting into a pickle, had a saying: 'You can't run Nice without the gangsters. But you never give them a lift in your car.' Perhaps M. Médecin's fatal mistake was to forget these wise words.

When he was younger he was said to be connected with several of the most celebrated members of the *milieu*. There was Urbain Giaume, one of the 'French Connection' heroin smugglers, Albert Spaggiari, who pulled off 'the bank robbery of the century', and Simon Gavet, a Mafia fellow-traveller.

There was also the Corsican businessman Jean-Dominique Fratoni, a founder of the Victoria Sporting Club in London in 1964 and later the owner of the Casino Ruhl in Nice. In the 1977 Nice casino war, the daughter of the owner of the rival casino, the Palais de la Mediterranée, disappeared after selling her shares to M. Fratoni, who has been on the run since 1980. He was last heard of in Paraguay in 1987. In the same year, the Casino Ruhl was reopened by a company in which both M. Médecin and a former business partner of M. Fratoni's held shares.

Any other French politician who had resigned in a hurry while travelling between Japan and South America, whose suitcases had been opened at the airport and found to contain £60,000 of currency, who left behind him charges of misappropriating £1.3 million of public money, and who said that he was in no hurry to return to France to answer the charges against him, might be thought to be finished.

But M. Médecin does not accept that. In a full-page interview in yesterday's *Le Figaro*, given from 'a fairy-tale hotel' in Punta del Este, Uruguay, he continued to play the same old tune on his mandolin. 'I am being persecuted by the Socialists. They want my skin at any cost because my father and I have kept them from power in our region for forty-four years.' When the tune is over he has an encore: 'Any attack on me is an attack on Nice,' which is immensely popular with his electorate.

Yesterday M. Médecin even had a plausible defence to the charge that he had been trying to smuggle currency out of France. 'I would have to be dead thick to put my own name on an envelope containing money,' he said. He added that the envelope had been planted on his courier by the police and that it was one of his own staff 'in an excess of zeal' who had originally warned the airport police that the mayor's luggage would be going through the airport. According to M. Médecin, a sub-department of the ministry of the interior has been set up to hunt him down. What did he think of Honoré Bailet, his deputy mayor and for the time being his successor, who had said that it was 'time to clean up the city'.

'Honoré has many qualities, but they do not include either physical or moral courage ... He talks of cleaning up the city. They will have to spend a lot more time sweeping in front of his door than in front of mine.' M. Médecin's American wife, Ilene, who left the country before he did, also went down fighting. The first lady of Nice was heard shouting to the press: 'I'm an American! It's not my country! It's not my business!'

This week in Nice, M. Bailet is said to have had a noisy meeting with Michel Falicon, head of the Médecin supporters' group, during which a chair was thrown across the mayor's parlour. The prefect, the representative in Nice of the central government, has said that even M. Médecin's letter of resignation was improperly made out.

The satirical newspaper *Le Canard Enchaîné* is in a state of shock. It once published a picture of the agenda at a Chirac cabinet meeting that included the heading 'Médecin's tax problems'. Now after only 211 articles in twenty years, the newspaper can hardly believe that M. Médecin has thrown in the towel.

September, 1990

9. THE POLITICS OF THE BAZAAR

━━━

This is a story in which the hostages did not want to come home, their 'captors' held no prisoners, and the western government which succeeded in releasing a 'mother-of-four' from Arab custody gave her a red-carpet reception followed by a six-month prison sentence.

It is the story of a family of hostages who when taken prisoner were fugitives from their own government, and who were lodged in a comfortable villa where they got on so well with their captors that they started a second family. It is a story of a government which held a group of French citizens illegally and was warmly congratulated by the president of France for its 'humanitarian action' in releasing them. It is the story of a family which came to blows while waiting at the airport to give its long-lost members a rapturous welcome home. And it is a story of a band of Palestinians who had not taken any hostages but who were prepared to say they had done so in order to put pressure on a western government which had no connection with the hostages in question. The consequence was that when the time came, they could not think of any demands to make in return for releasing the hostages they were not actually holding.

Finally, it is the story of a Palestinian given a life sentence for terrorism who was told by his jailers that his comrades in the Middle East were demanding his freedom. He had to tell his jailers that the 'comrades' in question belonged to a different group of Palestinians who had previously been trying to kill him. Asked if he would be prepared to change groups so that he could be liberated in exchange for the hostages, he unexpectedly agreed. None the less, he is still in prison.

On 8 November, 1987, a Palestinian splinter group, the Fatah Revolutionary Council, claimed that two weeks earlier the converted fishing boat *Silco*, flying Israeli and Belgian flags, had been captured off the coast of Gaza by a Palestinian gunboat and that all those on board, suspected Israeli spies, had been taken prisoner and were being held in south Lebanon. Some months later there was a second communiqué stating that on Christmas Day, 1987, one of the hostages, Jacqueline Valente, a French mother of two, had given birth to her third child provisionally named 'Sophie-Liberté'. Later another baby, a boy, was said to have been born.

In due course, on 27 December 1988, Jacqueline's two older children, Marie-Laure and Virginie, were released into the custody of the president of the Franco–Arab Friendship Association. And on the evening of 10 April this year, Jacqueline Valente was greeted at Villacoublay military airport outside Paris by a junior French government minister after spending more than three years as a hostage in the Middle East. With her were Sophie-Liberté and the child's Belgian father Fernand Houtekins. The other four members of the *Silco*'s crew remained in captivity. Six weeks after her red-carpet reception Jacqueline Valente stood in the district criminal court in Toulon to be given a six-month prison sentence for abducting her own children. Today, out of the confusion surrounding her liberation, the truth has begun to emerge.

Jacqueline Valente is a hippy with the striking looks of a gypsy. She has high cheekbones, dark eyes and very straight hair. In December, 1980, while she was working as a washer-up in a café in Toulon, Jacqueline married Pascal Betille at Ollioule near Toulon. In the next two years she had two daughters called Marie-Laure and Virginie. In 1982, a few days after the christening of the two little girls, Jacqueline Valente left her husband and went with the children to live with a Belgian cook called Fernand Houtekins in a 'cabin' or 'shack' (depending on whose lawyers were describing it) outside Toulon. There followed a series of reconciliations and partings until the day in 1983 when divorce proceedings were started. During the legal battle the father, Pascal, won custody of his two daughters mainly on the grounds that they should not be taken out of a house to live in a shack.

Jacqueline was allowed to have the children with her for the first month of the summer holidays in July 1985. She was supposed to return them to their father on 5 August but failed to do so. Pascal started a search and discovered that she had set sail with Houtekins from a port in Finistère in a converted sardine fishing boat called the *Silco*. Also on board were Fernand's brother Emmanuel Houtekins, his wife Godelieve and their two teenage children, Laurent and Valérie. No one knew where the *Silco* was bound for, but there had been talk of starting a new life in Australia.

Pascal tried everything he could think of to discover where his daughters had gone. Both children suffered from an eye disorder, strabismus, and had been receiving monthly treatment. Since Jacqueline Valente had become a fugitive from justice the French government joined in the search, without results. For a year Pascal had no news of his children. In France the legal calendar continued to run its course. In 1985 Jacqueline Valente was sentenced in her absence to one year's imprisonment for abducting her children.

Eventually, in July 1986, the *Silco* was reported to have been taking on stores at Syracuse in south-eastern Sicily. Witnesses said that the crew were talking of cruising along the north African coast and then passing through the Suez Canal. By the time this news reached France the boat had set sail and vanished once again.

Another year passed. Then came the radio news bulletin in November 1987 from Fatah-RC. For Pascal, the father of two children abducted after a custody case, it was an unpleasant shock. What was worse was that for six months the French government refused to recognize that Pascal's children had been taken hostage. For this there were two reasons.

The first was that in November 1987 the French Gaullist government led by Jacques Chirac was in the middle of a marathon secret negotiation to liberate a number of French citizens who had been taken hostage by various armed groups in the Lebanon. M. Chirac was a candidate in the following year's presidential elections and he saw their release as a possible election issue. The hostages included television journalists and diplomats. Their names and the number of days they had been held was given out nightly on the television news but the names of the crew of the *Silco* were never among them. It seems that the negotiations were complicated enough without adding anyone else to the list.

The second reason was that the crew of the *Silco* were supposed to be held in south Lebanon by Palestinians but the French government suspected that they were not in south Lebanon at all and that they had not been captured by Palestinians. The French had received a Spanish secret service report which suggested that the *Silco* had not been captured off the coast of Lebanon in November 1987, but 1,200 miles to the west, somewhere between Malta and Libya and over a year earlier.

With the release of three well-known names just before voting in the French presidential election in 1988 the French government stated that 'no more French hostages remained in the Middle East'. But not even this won the election for M. Chirac and in 1988 Valente's sister and brother-in-law, Anne-Marie and André Metral, started a publicity campaign so that Jacqueline and her family should be recognized by the new Socialist government as hostages and efforts made to gain their release. M. Metral is a municipal dustcart driver in Lyon earning about £9,500 a year. He had no contacts in the press and the television stations refused to print his sister-in-law's photograph. For some time he got nowhere. Eventually the Metrals decided to go on hunger-strike. Their postman lent them a caravan which they parked in the centre of Lyon. These tactics had some success. President Mitterrand said that his Socialist government would take up the cause of the 'forgotten hostages'. On 27 December 1988 the two little girls Marie-Laure and Virginie were released not in Lebanon but in Tripoli after 'the intervention' of Colonel Gadaffi. They came home not to the Metrals but to Pascal, the father they had not seen for three and a half years.

With the fugitive children safely home, the French government once again lost interest in the case. It knew by now that the family were living in reasonably good conditions as 'guests' of the Libyans. André Metral has since said that they were abandoned because they were not television personalities or foreign ministry officials but 'social zeros whose life was not worth a ransom'. On the point of giving up hope, the Metrals instead started a second hunger-strike. It received little publicity until the day when Mme Metral was summoned to the Quai d'Orsay to be given news of a letter received from her sister. This behaviour, to a woman who was on her sixteenth day of hunger-strike, seemed so callous that it was reported in the newspapers and the official was obliged to travel to Lyon instead. The 'social zeros' were back in the news and the government resumed secret negotiations.

When the liberation came in April this year it was marked by even more than the usual confusion. Once again the first announcement, on 4 April, was made in Tripoli. Brother Gadaffi, guide of the Libyan revolution, appealed to all Islamic countries to release all political hostages in honour of Ramadan. He mentioned in particular the crew of the *Silco*. The following day, in Beirut, Fatah-RC announced that it was disposed to respond to Brother Gaddafi's call. Twenty-four hours later it said that it would only release Jacqueline Valente, her daughter and Fernand Houtekins. Her fourth child, the little boy, was said to have died.

The main surprise however came on 10 April in Beirut when the press first met the released hostages. Reporters, pursuing the 'human interest angle', remembered that Sophie-Liberté had been born on Christmas Day 1987 and were expecting to see a child of fifteen months. But to the experienced eye she seemed rather large for her age. Her mother admitted that she would in fact be four years old on 25 May. Since she had been 'born in captivity' the story of the Fatah gunboat operating off the coast of Gaza in November 1987 was now obviously untrue. Then Fernand Houtekins referred to his 'fatigue after a long journey'. The fatigue was genuine. He was so tired that he had forgotten he was supposed to have made a fifty-mile car trip from South Lebanon. In fact the family had just been flown from Libya to Damascus and had then been driven to Beirut via south Lebanon. They had not been held by Fatah-RC at all but by Colonel Gadaffi.

What had actually happened was that in the late summer of 1986 while the *Silco* was cruising between Malta and Libya it had been routinely stopped and searched by a Libyan patrol boat. Most of the crew spoke Flemish, which the Libyans had never heard before. When they found that one of the adults had a passport with an Israeli stamp in it they became suspicious. The *Silco* was accordingly towed into Tripoli. In 1986 Colonel Gaddafi was still brooding over the American bombing which had taken place that April. He was also considering the damage done by a European Community trade embargo. In these circumstances he apparently decided to hold the *Silco*'s crew until they came in handy. Since he had no legal reason to hold them, and since 'Libya does not take hostages', he instructed Fatah-RC, who are beholden to him, to concoct the official story. This they did, overlooking the important detail of Sophie-Liberté's age.

In the course of the weeks following their release the official story of the hostages of the *Silco* fell to pieces. None of the three hostages were suffering from the usual symptoms of such an ordeal. The conditions under which they had been kept became known. After an overnight check-up in a Paris hospital they vanished, officially to Belgium, actually to the country house of Philippe Rondot of the DST (the secret service) where they were given a debriefing and instructed not to talk to the press. Since the remaining members of the Houtekins family were still in Libya this was a routine precaution. But there was another reason for the official secrecy. By now the French government was as anxious as the Libyans to obscure what had really happened.

At the time of the release President Mitterrand had expressed his personal thanks to Colonel Gadaffi for 'the major role he had played in securing the release of the hostages', and had mentioned 'the suffering they had endured with so much courage'. This message provoked British and American apoplexy. Since it was actually Colonel Gadaffi who had held them and since they had been lodged in some comfort in a large villa and had been on excellent terms with their guards President Mitterrand's message looked a bit excessive even to the French. Furthermore it had been revealed that early in March the French government, in defiance of the EC embargo, had returned three elderly Mirage jets which had been impounded in 1986 to Colonel Gadaffi. The French argued that since the Libyans had 500 combat aircraft and only 200 trained pilots, the Mirages were neither here nor there, and were certainly nothing to do with the return of the hostages. But the trouble with this argument was that it made people ask what the real price had, in that case, been. All in all the French preferred to have the whole business forgotten as soon as possible.

And perhaps there was no real price. The trouble with the hostages of the *Silco* was that from everyone's point of view they were valueless. They were not so much 'social zeros' as 'political zeros'. Gadaffi could never admit that he had taken them and could not therefore bargain very hard over their release. Fatah-RC had a more serious problem. The crew of the *Silco* were French and Belgian and the only two members of Fatah-RC held in Europe are in prison in Switzerland. At one point the Palestinians did demand the release of these two prisoners but they were told that the Swiss, though European, were not the same as Belgians and would not be prepared to swap their prisoners for Belgian hostages.

It was then that Fatah-RC, under orders to stay in the game, demanded the release of the only Palestinian in Belgian custody, even though he was not a member of their group. The Belgians first encouraged this bargain but later after public protests, rejected it.

As for the French, who officially 'do not bargain for hostages', they could not be seen to be bargaining with Fatah-RC, who did not hold the hostages, but could be seen to be talking to Colonel Gadaffi – who did. It was a situation to test the resourcefulness of even the Quai d'Orsay. Naturally they were not enthusiastic about a high-profile liberation since they knew that when Jacqueline Valente came home she would have to face trial. There may well have been a moment in Beirut when Jacqueline Valente wondered whether she could manage to get on a plane for Australia rather than Paris. Perhaps her new minders dissuaded her by mentioning that her two older girls were waiting for her in France. If so, they lied. Although her prison sentence has subsequently been suspended, she has only been allowed to see Marie-Laure and Virginie occasionally since her return.

The moral of the story is that a woman should always be involved in planning these elaborate international charades. For a woman would surely have noticed the problem of Sophie-Liberté's size.

October, 1990

———

Those who think that the British government does not do enough to help British hostages in Lebanon may be interested to know how differently such matters are ordered in France.

Both the British and French governments say they refuse to negotiate over hostages. In practice, the present British government has apparently kept to this rule, whereas the French government not only negotiates over hostages, but takes 'counter-hostages'. Evidence given in a libel action which started in the High Court in Paris yesterday has confirmed that one of the reasons why the Chirac government was able to persuade the Iranians to free two French hostages in December 1987 was that it had itself taken an Iranian diplomat hostage. This has never been admitted, either then or since, but it has become increasingly clear that in the summer of 1987 that was what the policy of Jacques Chirac's Gaullist government amounted to.

In June 1987 five French hostages were held in Lebanon by Shia militants loyal to Ayatollah Khomeini. Two French ministries were trying to obtain their release, the ministry of the interior and the Quai d'Orsay or foreign ministry. At the same time the minister of the interior, Charles Pasqua, was trying to arrest those who had been responsible for the 1986 Paris bombings in which thirteen people died and 255 were injured. Seeing an opportunity to make some progress in both matters, M. Pasqua put it about that Wahid Gordji, a well-connected interpreter at the Iranian embassy in Paris, was wanted for questioning over the bombings. Gordji was on good terms with diplomats at the Quai d'Orsay, who did not believe in the authenticity of M. Pasqua's allegations and who tipped him off. Accordingly, Gordji refused to appear before the examining magistrate who was investigating the bombings, Judge Gilles Boulouque, and took refuge in his embassy instead. The French police surrounded the building and laid siege to it.

Meanwhile, the ministry of the interior leaked certain details of the 'case' against Gordji to the press, which obligingly published them. After all, if you can't trust the information services of a democratic government about investigations into terrorist murders, when can you trust them? Perhaps never. Many of the details leaked about Gordji by the ministry of the interior subsequently turned out to have been invented.

The siege of the Iranian embassy lasted six months. At one point the Iranians took a further hostage in the person of a French diplomat in Tehran. But on 29 November it was the French government which came out on top. Gordji was allowed to leave France and the French diplomat and two of the original French hostages were returned to France. For form's sake, Gordji called in at the office of Judge Boulouque on his way to the airport. At the end of the brief meeting, the judge said that Gordji had no case to answer after all.

Judge Boulouque is now suing two French newspapers, *Le Monde* and *Libération*, for their reports of what was at the time an astonishing *dénouement* to the six-month embassy siege. *Le Monde's* cartoonist, Plantu, in a famous drawing, showed the anti-terrorist judge questioning Gordji. 'Aisle seat or window seat, smoking or non-smoking?' he was saying. Later the paper's reporter wrote that the judge had 'bent to the wishes of the ministry of the interior, even though he was an independent man'. And *Libération* wrote that the jet which carried Gordji to Tehran was already warming up its engines while the interpreter was still with Judge Boulouque, a coincidence which turned the latter 'into a sort of ticket collector'. The judge now claims that these comments were defamatory.*

November, 1989

---

* Gilles Boulouque lost these libel actions. He subsequently committed suicide.

10. DR MITTERRAND'S MONSTER

The starting pistol has not yet been fired but that does not bother Jean-Marie Le Pen. The leader of the *Front National*, the first candidate to declare himself in the presidential race, is tearing into his second circuit, waving delightedly to the empty stadium and looking forward to being recalled for the official start.

On Sunday, perhaps sensing that a television interview was dragging a little, he made an ambiguous comment about the existence of the Nazi gas chambers. The result is that he has been in the newspapers ever since.

In fact if one reads the text of M. Le Pen's remarks they are not quite as sinister as some might wish them to be. M. Le Pen said: 'I do *not* say that the gas chambers did not exist.' That sentence is not the stuff of which headlines are made. But he went on, 'I was not able to see them for myself. I have not made a special study of the question. But I think it is just a detail in the history of the Second World War.'

One could hear the sighs of relief from sub-editors around the world – 'Gas chambers? A mere detail' – which was indeed the headline chosen by the sub-editors of *Le Monde* for the following day's edition. The story was not originally given much prominence by *Le Monde*, in fact it started with M. Le Pen's answers to a quite different set of questions, but it grew and grew, achieving its maximum importance, at the time of writing, with a double-page spread in *Libération*, a journal of the Left.

In musing about the existence of the gas chambers M. Le Pen was acknowledging the work of the 'revisionist historians', led in France by Robert Faurisson, a literature lecturer at the University of Lyon. This previously obscure school of pamphleteers who question the existence of a 'Final Solution', have received an exceptional amount of publicity this summer in France due to the trial of Klaus Barbie, the wartime commander of the Lyon Gestapo, for 'crimes against humanity'.

The revisionists' pamphlets have always found favour with the members of the National Front, and their work is associated with an extreme right-wing tendency to exalt the military achievements of the Third Reich and rehabilitate Nazism. But the most difficult question they have raised is nothing to do with the Nazis, it is what to do about the revisionists. The world is divided into those who think that their theories should be examined and then rejected (a boring process in popular terms since it involves scholarship), and those who think the more exciting thought that their theories should be treated like plague bacilli, and locked away for centuries.

M. Le Pen was adroit enough to try to turn the tables on his interviewer by touching on this disagreement when he was pressed on the subject of the gas chambers. 'Do you want me to say that it is a revealed truth which the whole world must believe as if it were a moral obligation?', he said. 'I merely say that these are matters which historians debate . . . I am a partisan of freedom of thought and I am opposed to any form of thought-control.'

This is a more conventional electoral tack, Le Pen as defender of freedom of expression. His protest continued: 'I am Jean-Marie Le Pen, I write and I speak. I should be judged on the opinions which I express.' And no sooner were the words out of his mouth than 'hoopla' his prayers were answered. For it is on the opinions which he has expressed, in private, that France has been able to judge him this week, thanks to an unscrupulous Canadian journalist who infiltrated herself on to M. Le Pen's triumphant tour of the beaches last August.

M. Le Pen, in private, as a nationalist: 'Advertising and the cinema try to present an image of a cosmopolitan France, small, brown and curly . . .'

'Like Michel Boujenah?' prompted the disguised journalist.

'Exactly! A Tunisian Jew. You've noticed it too? But that's a false image, that's not France.'

Le Pen on the subject of racialism: 'If Harlem Desir (the chairman of SOS-Racism) gets a good press, if he is raising funds, it's because he's half-Jewish.'

On the defence of France: 'If I had the choice I would rather be invaded by the Germans than by the Arabs. At least they had

Goethe, Schiller. The Arabs have never made anything memorable; just a few decorated windows.'

This is the voice of the last man at the bar before the café closes, the genuine voice of the intolerant, unsuccessful Right, the voice of the enduring constituency which a talented populist leader can count on to carry him forward into obscurity. The last time this point of view was widely expressed in France, the country *was* invaded by the Germans. At least M. Le Pen has that much sense of history.

September, 1987

In his wildest dreams, and we have it on the authority of his former doctor that these have been pretty wild, Jean-Marie Le Pen might have been surprised by the events of the last two weeks. A slip of the tongue on television, a glimpse of the fellow not-so-well-met, has been turned into the sort of international publicity which minority party leaders never get. And the leader of the French National Front hasn't had to lift a finger.

Le Pen has received the full treatment; demonstrations outside the National Assembly, a court case, demands that he lose his parliamentary immunity, massive coverage for his party rally, demands that he be sent to Coventry, a packed press conference hanging on his every word and forbidden to ask questions, demands that he be barred from the presidential elections. And at the end of it all, he was back on to one and a half hours of peak-time television for a programme which topped the ratings that night and gained a 65 per cent 'satisfaction' figure.

When people ask Le Pen if he uses a political publicity firm he says that 'politics is not like selling soap', but if he had been selling soap in the last two weeks he could have founded another Unilever.

In their frantic efforts to say that Le Pen must not be allowed to matter, his opponents have made him matter more than ever. The essential thing about Le Pen is not that he himself is anti-Semitic as his opponents have been striving to prove, but that he uses racism to gain votes. There is a wave of anti-immigrant feeling in France which is mainly directed against the Arabs, not the Jews. Le Pen rides this wave like an expert surfer. The more people who stand on the beach to watch him, the better he does. From his position he can't tell whether they are cheering or yelling abuse, and he doesn't care.

One rather selective opinion poll, taken at the height of last week's excitement, claims that he lost a fifth of his supporters following his statement that the gas chambers were 'a detail in the history of the Second World War'. But when the polls open, few of those who are attracted to Le Pen because he is opposed to Arab immigration will care what he thinks about the Nazi gas chambers. And no one who is still concerned about the Nazis would have been likely to vote for Le Pen in the first place. When today's issues return to dominate the debate, the row about the gas chambers will be forgotten but Le Pen will be much better known.

At fifty-nine, after over thirty years in politics, seventeen of them in the *Front National*, the party which he helped to found, M. Le Pen has never been so successful. The party's first policy was opposition to immigration and its popularity has grown as immigration has continued. The Front's share of the national vote now ranges between 10 and 13 per cent, but in strongholds like Marseille and Nice it receives more than 20 per cent.

As a rough rule of thumb, in urban constituencies where immigrants represent more than 7 per cent of the population, the National Front gets twice as high a percentage of the vote as there are immigrants. This is an equation that enrages M. Le Pen's opponents; but he has a phrase for such people – he calls them *bourgeois imbeciles*.

The man at the centre of this tumult is the son of a self-employed Breton fisherman who was drowned during the last war when his boat hit a German mine. This death caused the name 'Le Pen' to be placed on the war memorial of the little village of La Trinité-sur-Mer among those '*Morts pour la France*'. Le Pen himself claims to have joined the Resistance, but since he was only sixteen in 1944 when the Occupation ended his claim has been treated with some surprise.

His name is not listed in any of the Resistance records and when he is pressed on the point he says that he hid some guns that his father had been storing illegally. The curator of the local Resistance museum in his part of Brittany is not impressed with these credentials, saying that thousands of people did as much as that.

It seems that in both cases the truth may have been improved. Le Pen's father might well have died fighting for France, if he had ever been called upon to do so. Jean-Marie might well have fought with the Resistance, if the Occupation had lasted longer. On the other hand he might have joined the *Milice*, the French Gestapo, like hundreds of other wartime teenagers hoping to fire a gun. In a curious way the distant events of his youth still seem to dominate his life. The options which he lays before his countrymen today are as simple as the choices in a wartime comic strip, Le Pen being the horny-handed hero with a heart of gold.

After the war the would-be Resister took a law degree at the influential Ecole de Sciences Politiques in Paris and then proved his courage as a paratroop officer in Indo-China. Next he went to Algeria with General Massu. Massu is the legendary paratroop commander who justified the use of torture by electrical shocks when his men were faced with the FLN's 'blind terrorism'. Le Pen has since defended Massu's doctrine and he is frequently accused of having himself been a torturer in Algeria.

When *Le Monde* published this allegation, Le Pen sued for libel, denying that he had ever been a torturer. *Le Monde* defended itself by arguing that it could not be libellous to accuse someone of committing an act which he considered to be defensible, but Le Pen eventually won the case. Now the more cautious of his critics are content to describe Le Pen's service record in Algeria as 'electrifying'.

Today Jean-Marie Le Pen still sometimes gives the impression that he would be happiest at an old comrades' reunion, drinking beer and singing military songs. His 'love of military music' once led him to publish the Songs of the Waffen SS, many of which are of course in French. He has since defended this move as 'educational'. Certainly his record publishing business has been a success and has made him a millionaire. Today he has his own *château* and he can well afford to employ an expert chef, from the French West Indies – further evidence, in his opinion, that he is not a racist.

The fastidious opponents of Le Pen who sneer at him for 'the hideousness of his soul' overlook the fact that they are faced with a shrewd politician with a talent for demagoguery who has learnt his politics the hard way. He started his canvassing in the street markets of Paris as a Poujadist deputy in 1955, then built his own party from the wreck of the Algérie Française movement.

When the Communists look pleased with themselves for pointing out that he is a millionaire, Le Pen roars with laughter because it is precisely to those working-class voters who dream of winning millions that he tries to appeal. The National Front started with an imbalance of highly-educated supporters who were useful for publicity. Le Pen is now going for the far more numerous, under-educated *petits blancs*, a class which was formerly only found in the French colonies but which he would argue can now be found in France – thanks to immigration.

To win their support he has pitched his arguments at an even more vulgar level than previously. He wants the National Front to replace the Communist Party as 'the people's tribune', and thanks to his governing idea of opposition to immigration he has had some success. Add to that patriotism, the death penalty, a strong army, lower taxes and locking up homosexual AIDS patients, and you have virtually the complete manifesto. The slogans are '*Les Français à l'Elysée*', and 'Frenchmen first'.

His wife, Pierrette, with whom he is going through an acrimonious divorce, and who will say virtually anything about him, claims that she has learnt to shoot because she has been receiving kidnap threats. She also says that her husband's character changed when he received a large inheritance. She is referring to a story which at one time threatened to involve Le Pen in a serious scandal, but which he survived with his habitual gusto.

Last year one of his oldest friends Dr Jean-Maurice Demarquet, once his medical adviser who had served with him in the paratroops, said that Le Pen had done nothing to stop a young friend called Lambert, who was also Demarquet's patient, from drinking himself to death in 1976. Lambert was the heir to a cement fortune and after his death Le Pen was found to be the beneficiary of his will. In the legal battle that followed Dr Demarquet's accusation the doctor said that Le Pen suffered from 'Kraepelin's paranoia', a condition characterized by megalomania, authoritarianism, tyrannical behaviour and contempt for other people. Le Pen sued Dr Demarquet for breach of professional confidence (towards young Lambert), and won yet again.

When he announced his candidacy for the presidency last April, Le Pen chose to do it in La Trinité-sur-Mer, surrounded by the people who gave his party 52 per cent of the vote at the last election. He ended his unusually quiet speech with the words 'God will help us!' He makes quite a lot of the fact that he is a practising Catholic, but when he went to Lourdes in the middle of this summer's campaigning tour he was abused by a priest for profaning the Grotto. Typically Le Pen enjoyed the last word. 'I am here to talk to God, not to his intermediaries,' he said.

September, 1987

Jean-Marie Le Pen, leader of the *Front National* has been driven out of the French West Indies by hostile crowds. And he is not pleased.

On Sunday M. Le Pen and a party of forty extreme right-wing supporters and Euro-MPs boarded an Air France jumbo jet for a one week working visit to Martinique. Even before they had taken off the staff of the Hôtel Méridien in Martinique, hearing who was coming to stay, had gone on strike. By the time the jumbo was ready to land at Fort-de-France a crowd of 350 angry demonstrators had overwhelmed the gendarmes and were milling around on the runway.

The jumbo circled five times while M. Le Pen hurled down imprecations from the sky, then it set off for Guadeloupe. By this time the 439 holidaymakers on board had invaded the Club Class and started to protest.

The cry 'Le Pen – Out' was heard. His bodyguards were called to help the stewards. On landing at Raizet in Guadeloupe, M. Le Pen's party was asked to leave the plane so that the holidaymakers could return to Martinique. M. Le Pen refused. Outside a thousand more demonstrators were waiting.

Four hours of uproar ensued. A police inspector was called. No one could leave the plane. Pregnant women started to protest. Holidaymakers started to film the scene. M. Le Pen was in his element. 'It's a point of principle,' he shouted. 'The government sends the troops to Chad and can't even keep order at home. Here I am on Republican territory and I am being kicked in the bum. And I can tell you I'm not going to lower my pants. The government must face up to its responsibilities.'

A *sous-préfet* was called to remonstrate with the enflamed presidential candidate. M. Le Pen then produced one of his classic Freudian analogies. 'And supposing the demonstrators were shouting, "Give us the five Jews on that plane," would you surrender them?' he asked.

'If you were real men you would go and shout at the demonstrators,' said a holidaymaker. 'Shut up or I'll smack you in the kisser,' replied one of the travelling politicians. After four hours M. Le Pen had won. The almost empty plane returned to Paris with the National Front party singing their patriotic songs and leaving behind passengers in Guadeloupe and baggage in Martinique; the end of another triumphant election tour for M. Le Pen.

December, 1987

=====

Jean-Marie Le Pen, the candidate for the *Front National*, is currently expected to pull in between 8 and 10 per cent of the vote in the first round of the presidential election. President Mitterrand is expected to win 37 per cent, Raymond Barre 22 per cent, Jacques Chirac 21 per cent, and André Lajoinie (Communist Party) 6 per cent. The figures are important because they illustrate that if M. Le Pen did not exist, and if M. Barre and M. Chirac would decide which of them should lead the Right in France, the election could be decided in the first round with an overall majority, and victory, for the Right. That is why President Mitterrand 'invented' Jean-Marie Le Pen in 1983, by introducing proportional representation, and by allowing him maximum exposure on electoral television programmes.

M. Le Pen's support has slightly declined over the last year but he continues to fascinate his fellow-countrymen. When he appeared on television last week for a one and a half hour interview, he scored one of the highest viewing figures ever recorded by a politician on that sort of programme. Last week, as so often, the chief interest lay in whether or not his hostile questioners would be able to persuade him to 'climb out of his pram'. In the event they failed and he remained reasonably calm throughout. But there is a dramatic tension about his public appearances as he struggles to master the violent impulses which have driven him throughout his life.

In terms of personal violence M. Le Pen has a record which stretches back to his schooldays. His father, a Breton fisherman, died when his boat hit a German mine in 1942, an event which seems to have left his fourteen-year-old son muddled, embittered and truculent. He was frequently in trouble with the Jesuits of Vannes, in south Brittany, who had the task of educating him. They must have been puzzled by this turbulent child who was also a brilliant pupil.

In Paris, reading law, Le Pen became the president of the 'Corpo', the law students' union, a distinction which he shared with the then president of the Republic, Vincent Auriol. He passed into 'Sciences-Po' and might well have continued on to one of the élite *grandes écoles* but at that point his 'Mr Hyde' personality took over, and it has been dominant ever since.

Having a few drinks and punching people in the face became one of the burly young man's regular occupations. His favourite opponents were 'les Cocos' (the Communists), but if there were no philosophical disagreements to pursue there was always the bouncer in a nightclub, or the waiter in a café. In 1951, aged twenty-three, he was even arrested, drunk, at the altar rails of the church of Notre Dame in Aix-les-Bains, where he had been abusing the elderly parish priest. 'A derisory incident', is how he describes this event today.

In 1958, while heckling a political opponent in Paris he was told to leave the hall. Instead he climbed on to the platform and attacked the candidate. The stewards threw him out and during a violent struggle he was kicked so hard that he lost the sight in his right eye, which later had to be removed. In 1965, aged thirty-seven, he was fined £2,000 by the Tribunal de Paris after a fight in another bar. After that his wife, Pierrette, took to shouting 'Jean-Marie, 20,000 francs, 20,000 francs ...' if he looked like punching a fellow motorist who had got the better of him at the traffic lights. She says that this trick worked.

Now aged fifty-nine, he confines his violence to words. He has polished up his original technique. 'M. Mendès-France, you must be aware that you look as repulsive patriotically as you do physically,' he once said to France's former prime minister in the National Assembly. Today he is suspected by his opponents of using a private language to conceal racial references. His idea of reassuring people, on this point is to say: 'If Fabius hears me say Jewish (*judaïque*) when I say AIDS-sufferer (*sidaïque*), he should buy an ear trumpet.' Like Mendès-France, Laurent Fabius, the former Socialist prime minister, is Jewish.

For most of his life M. Le Pen has chosen to remain an outsider.

Now he wants to come in and no one will open the door. His life has been dogged by failure. During the Indo-China war he volunteered for the Foreign Legion's first parachute battalion, but he reached Saigon after the fall of Dien Bien Phu and saw no action. Volunteering again for the Algerian war he was diverted to the Suez Canal, where his unit arrived too late once more and he was put to work burying Egyptian bodies. Then it was on to Algiers where he took part in the usual business of round-ups and interrogations. He defends France's use of torture in Algeria, but denies that he ever took part in it himself.

Demanding the last word on this subject he says, 'Everyone in Algiers wants to be able to say that they were tortured by Le Pen, just like half the population of Lyon claims to have been tortured by Barbie.' As a means of getting the last word, this observation is highly effective, since his audience is left speechless while they try to imagine what he must have been saying in private during the Barbie trial.

In common with François Mitterrand, Jean-Marie Le Pen has little to offer the electorate, except himself. He would 'send the immigrants home and save the country 100 billion francs' (£10 billion). He would restore the death penalty; he would decimate the ranks of social service workers – 'they are well known to have an absentee rate of 40 per cent; he would give employment priority to native-born French citizens. He offers a series of pugnacious slogans that guarantee his failure on the national level. People vote for him if immigration is the only issue they care about, or if they are prepared to vote for a symbol.

He is still an outsider, still being used to bury the bodies – as François Mitterrand hopes – of Candidate Chirac and Candidate Barre.

February, 1988

For his last big campaign rally in the south of France, Jean-Marie Le Pen hired Marseille football stadium and filled it. They warmed up with a French catalogue of horrors. There was the president of the regional committee of 'Christian Solidarity' who talked of Arab immigration as 'the genocide of France'. There was the man who had stabbed an Arab criminal to death twenty years ago, and been 'persecuted ever since by the left-wing press'; he wanted to restore the death penalty. There was the regional president of the association of ex-political prisoners who had been sentenced for sedition at the time of Algérie Française and who spoke of immigration as 'the destabilization of Europe'.

We had got as far as Gratieux Lamperti, former national French boxing champion, who had nearly had his throat cut by a different Arab, when the band struck up the 'Chorus of the Hebrew Slaves' from Verdi's *Nabucco* and from the depths of the dressing room rose the Demon King. He strode on to the empty pitch, a man alone but for his 30,000 adoring followers. It was the best bit of theatre in the presidential campaign.

As Jean-Marie Le Pen reached the centre-spot he turned to embrace each side of the stadium in turn with a goalscorer's double-wave. The noise was tumultuous. Not even the Pope had thought of that. Then as Jean-Marie ascended the podium the 'Chorus of the Hebrew Slaves' reached another crescendo, but was almost drowned by the stamping feet and hysterical chants of 'LE PEN LE PEN LE . . .'

'*Françaises, Français* . . .' he started, 'we are a wave which came from the sea . . .' the young woman seated beside me, wearing a neat blue suit, silk scarf, black stockings and high heels, had achieved lift-off. 'Jean-Marie,' she shrieked, 'President.' She waved her flag pole around like a pike staff, and jumped up and down as though on springs, the light of unreason burning in her black button eyes. Not even her mother could calm her down. Her lips were already flecked and we were due for two more hours of this.

'We are going to win,' he said. 'We are going to win,' she shrieked. 'Who are the competition?' he asked. 'The men of Power. But the men of Power today are losers. They are the men who have presided over France's decadence, the growth of immigration, unemployment, illiteracy and DRUGS. We are at the end of the twentieth century,' he said, 'and we can't have everything. We can't have six million immigrants and six million civil servants.

'Ninety per cent of the children in some of the schools in my part of Paris are immigrants. Mitterrand visited one school where they spoke seventeen languages. How can our little French children be taught in that Tower of Babel? They will be condemned to illiteracy, and in the twenty-first century that means a lifetime's unemployment ... As President Bongo of Gabon said to me, "Gabon is for the Gabonnais", and I say to you, "France is for the French".' The stamping and cheering broke out again.

'Mitterrand to the Gulag,' shrieked the young lady in the blue suit, so missing the raucous voice bellowing, 'Togolese doctors trained in France should go home to look after the people of Togo, not work in Normandy. And I am giving you the opinion of their own governments.'

M. Le Pen uses the rolling eighteenth-century phrases of the soap-box orator – 'the supreme magistrate whose power is delegated by the people of the Republic' – but his soap box has grown to fantastic proportions. Yesterday it was an open air stage 40 yards wide, across which he strode, one hand in his pocket, the other stabbing the air around his horns. He was clearly having the time of his life, and so was everyone else.

'France has 80,000 illegal immigrants a year,' he said, 'and that's not counting the ones who are coming in container lorries. In twenty years, as Boumedienne of Algeria has said, France will be an Islamic republic. Well, I want to save France from that!' She was on her feet again, and 30,000 others with her. 'LE PEN LE PEN LE PEN ...' She was not keen about this Islamic suggestion. Further along our row one of the guard dogs started to bark. It is thought that M. Le Pen may take 25 per cent of the Marseille vote in the first round of the presidential election on 24 April.

April, 1988

Watching Jean-Marie Le Pen at his rally in Paris on 1 May, it was hard not to laugh. He looked like a rich Walter Mitty who was living out all his most exaggerated fantasies. Once again he strutted before cheering crowds while the loudspeakers played the 'Slaves' Chorus' from *Nabucco*.

After an hour of the same tune, he switched to the theme from the last movement of Beethoven's 'Ninth Symphony'. Then thousands of sun-tanned women stood on chairs screaming 'Jean-Marie! Jean-Marie!' After a while he got bored with that too, but how could he improve on it? Costumes! A woman in a suit of armour on a white horse! Let's pretend she's Joan of Arc!

Next some pretty children holding bouquets of flowers. They shower him with petals. Charming. Now, what about a real Youth Movement? And yes, here they come, in uniform, led by a strapping blonde leading a large dog on a chain. She was there, in the flesh, in the rue de Rivoli on 1 May. One of them barked out an order and all the children saluted Mr Mitty. 'Look! There are some fine heads among them,' he was heard to say.

But it is insensitive to laugh at M. Le Pen, because at his rallies you can also see some of the darker pages of recent French history return to life. Many of his supporters are essentially harmless. There are the Christian Brothers of the Lebanon who seem to be suggesting a new crusade, and who talk of 'the genocide of the 1.5 million Lebanese Christians'. There are Tridentine Catholics who provide a chaplain to bless the banners of the National Front and who sing Mass in Latin knowing that M. Le Pen is about to give a speech in which he will blame all France's ills on many of its poorest inhabitants.

Then there is an ingenious organization called AGRIF, the General Alliance against Racism and for the French Christian Identity. 'The only racism which is not opposed today is anti-French racism,' they say. 'The only religion which one can mock openly is Christianity.' AGRIF is supported by the writer Henri Coston, a veteran of the 1930s Popular Front and the author of an absorbing book called *The Return of the 200 Families*, which traces many weird and wonderful links between the Rothschilds and Josef Stalin. Then there are groups of people anxious to defend Catholic schools, and others trying to popularize the pilgrimage from Paris to Chartres.

But mixed in among these relative innocents are the modern partisans of the ideas of Action Française. This movement was founded by Charles Maurras, who became the leading intellectual of the wartime collaboration. After the Liberation, Maurras was tried in the Palais de Justice in Lyon. Peering shortsightedly from the dock as he received his life sentence he was heard to hiss: 'It is the revenge of Dreyfus!'

The great heroine of Action Française was Joan of Arc. M. Le Pen's publicity department does not quite have the nerve to cite

Maurras, but they do mention, among Joan of Arc's great admirers, Voltaire, Malraux and . . . Brasillach. By the last they must mean Robert Brasillach, editor of the wartime fink paper *Je Suis Partout*, who paid the price for his collaboration before the firing squad at Fresnes in 1945. Brasillach was never captured. He gave himself up when he heard that his mother had been arrested, and he is said to have died bravely, wearing – according to the historian Richard Cobb – an elegant red scarf, and probably shouting '*Vive la France!*' Well, he too lived again on the rue de Rivoli on 1 May.

May, 1988

11. AN OUTBREAK OF
REVOLUTIONARY MADNESS

The celebrations of the Bicentenary of the French Revolution are beginning to warm up, thanks to the French Royalists. Last Saturday several Royalist movements combined, most unusually, in an organization called 'Anti-89' and held ceremonies to mark the 196th anniversary of the execution of Louis XVI. A wreath was laid in the Place de la Concorde where Louis XVI was guillotined and on Sunday masses were said in several parts of Paris for the repose of the king's soul. For the Royalists Louis XVI is an uncanonized saint who died for his devout beliefs although the Vatican has not yet been persuaded that matters were so simple. The issue might have been resolved long ago if right-wing French Catholics did not insist on mixing politics with their religion. So, on Sunday, the Abbé Aulagnier, a follower of Monsignor Lefebvre, condemned the Revolution as 'the negation of God and the triumph of rationalism and a humanitarian society'. He was followed by a speaker who said that the Revolution marked 'the birth of cosmopolitanism and the introduction of the right of foreigners to treat France as their own property'.

In Paris on the same day a group of ardent Republicans were singing the 'Hymn to the Guillotine' and listening to a speech also on the Place de la Concorde by the writer Jean-Edern Hallier who said that the 'most beautiful pages in the history of France were written in blood by the pikes of the Revolution'. Given these fierce historical disagreements, a living re-enactment of the whole business seems distinctly possible.

January, 1989

This year the nation described by de Tocqueville as 'the most brilliant and the most dangerous in Europe' has invited the whole world to celebrate its history. More than 600 functions have been arranged in eighty countries. The French government has organized a succession of major international conferences in Paris this year. On 14 July the Group of Seven will be meeting here and in the autumn there will be the European summit during which France will assume the presidency of the European Community. The French are rightly confident that the world is intrigued by the Bicentenary. But what do they themselves make of their Revolution, two hundred years on?

If the French still have the Revolution in their bones, they do not necessarily have it in their brains. A third of those questioned among 16,000 people in a recent opinion poll were unable to mention a single important Revolutionary event. Of the rest, 37 per cent recalled the Fall of the Bastille, 16 per cent the Declaration of the Rights of Man, and 16 per cent the execution of Louis XVI. Only 4 per cent mentioned the Guillotine or the Terror. Again, 33 per cent were unable to recall a single important social change introduced by the Revolution. The only notable Revolutionaries cited by more than 12 per cent of the sample were Robespierre and Danton, and more than 50 per cent of those questioned could not even name them. Asked which French leaders in the last two hundred years had continued the ideals of the Revolution, 30 per cent answered 'General de Gaulle', a tribute which might have surprised him. All this should be set in the context of another opinion poll, taken a year ago, which found that 17 per cent of the French people were in favour of the return of the Monarchy. French Royalists seem to be more numerous than British Republicans, even if they are less respectable.

In a recent article in *Le Monde*, Jean-Denis Bredin, author of a highly praised history of the Revolution, examined what the three Republican ideals mean to France today. His conclusions were bleak. 'Liberty,' he wrote, 'has never been our natural element . . . We prefer security to liberty' – and he gave as an example the way in which people charged with crime in France and awaiting trial are treated as pariahs on whom any public shame can be heaped, 'although the law pretends to regard them as innocent'.

'Our true passion,' wrote Bredin, 'which stems from our history, is a hatred of inequality . . .' The Revolution, 'was intended to establish equality of taxes, equality before the courts and free access for everyone to the machinery of government . . . In fact it took nearly another hundred years for the French to win equality of political rights and even under the Third Republic women were not accorded the vote until 1945 . . . And what of the inequalities of knowledge and opportunity today? We know well that our schools are no longer able to correct them . . . We celebrate the abolition of the nobility's privileges with great pride, but the registers of the *grandes écoles* demonstrate our talent for reinventing what we have destroyed.'

As for Fraternity – symbolized originally by the wild cry, 'Be my brother or I kill thee!' – Bredin contrasted it with the exclusion practised by an insecure society and reflected on the frequent solitude of modern old age. He concluded his gloomy analysis by describing contemporary French politics which are steeped 'in distrust and rejection' as 'a political system which holds the French people in even greater contempt than the French feel for it'.

February, 1989

=====

A guillotine was sold yesterday by the Paris auction house of Drouot for 270,000 francs (£25,000). The machine was made of oak, stood 13 feet 10 inches high, and was fitted with leather straps, a blade with bevelled edge and a neck-hole lined with metal. It went to a German collector.

June, 1989

=====

As part of the security operation for the Bicentenary celebrations, the army has requested permission to move anti-aircraft guns into Paris. The generals want to position their guns on the Pont de Tolbiac in central Paris, from where they would have a clear field of fire down river as far as the Ile St Louis. It has been agreed that an unspecified number of 20mm ack-ack guns will be trained into the skies in order to ensure the security of the thirty-seven heads of state who are coming to the party. The great unanswered question is, will the gunners be given any ammunition? It is one thing to put up a reassuring display of force but if an enemy plane is brought down in flames on to central Paris there may be trouble.

Among those who will not be present are the crowned heads of Europe. President Mitterrand has been mocked for refusing to invite any kings or queens to the celebrations but he is a man with a sense of history. He will certainly know that the balcony of the Admiralty in the Place de la Concorde, and the balconies of the neighbouring Hôtel Crillon from which the thirty-seven heads of state will view the parades of 14 July, were built before 1793. In other words the execution of Louis Capet, 'alias Louis XVI', took place beneath those balconies. No living kings and queens have been invited to stand on the same balconies to celebrate the events which led up to that spectacle.

The guillotine may become the topic of the month in Paris. There has been a return of 'guillotine mania'. The memoirs of France's last public executioner have just been published, and in them he admits that he did not like executing women. 'The guillotine,' he explains, 'is a thing between men'. People are asking what did it feel like, was it just a tickle on the back of the neck as Dr Guillotine claimed? And if so how quickly did it kill you? It was said at the time that when Charlotte Corday was executed, the carpenter who had erected the scaffold snatched up her head and slapped it. The crowd noted with approval that Charlotte blushed, then looked him straight in the eye and glared at him. It was also popularly believed that when the head of an executed priest was thrown into the same sack as the head of a disgraced Revolutionary, the priest immediately bit his former enemy savagely.

The job of executioner was a dangerous one since the crowd who came to applaud could easily turn nasty if the victim was not dispatched at once. Sanson, the hereditary public executioner of the day, was delighted by the guillotine since before that his work had consisted of spreadeagling his victims on a cartwheel, lashing them down, breaking their limbs one by one and then plunging a knife into their chests. Now all he had to do was stand back and pull the cord. The only time he showed any emotion was when his little son, who was beside him on the scaffold, fell off while Sanson was holding up a victim's head and was killed by the fall. The crowd then saw the unexpected sight of Sanson bursting into tears.

Since Sanson had been the state executioner for the *ancien régime* he was used to earning a decent living. With the arrival of the Revolution his earnings fell, even though his work increased. He made up the difference by selling the heads of his victims to Marie Grosholtz who had just started a waxwork collection. She was better known in later life in London as 'Madame Tussaud'.

The descendants of the *ancien régime* have been protesting against the Bicentenary by inserting memorial notices in *Le Figaro* for their executed ancestors. It is of course considered rather chic to have an ancestor who was guillotined. Now, for the first time, it is possible to consult the official record of more than 17,500 names which was previously buried in the archives and only available to scholars. The list shows that most of those who died were workers. They included 4,900 peasants, 5,250 workers and 3,500 tradesmen. The result is that these ancestors are not quite as chic as they used to be. By one calculation as many as 11 million Frenchmen are now descended from the victims of the Terror.

One of those who escaped the guillotine was an aristocrat called M. de St-Cyr, and it would be nice to think that the story of how he did so was true. Dragged before a Revolutionary tribunal he was asked his name. 'De Saint-Cyr,' he replied. 'Nobility has been abolished,' said the president. 'Well then, Saint-Cyr,' he said. 'The time of the saints is passed,' said the president. 'All right then, Cyr,' said the aristocrat. 'We no longer use the word "Sire" since the execution of the king,' said his tormentor. At this point, the aristocrat lost his temper. 'Since I have no name I must be an abstraction and since there is no law allowing you to try an abstraction I must be acquitted,' he shouted. The judge then said, 'Citizen Abstraction, you are acquitted but you had better choose a good Republican name in the future if you wish to escape suspicion.'

3 July, 1989

The campaigns of *détente* can be more hazardous than those of the Cold War, as President and Mrs Gorbachev learned on the first day of their visit to France in the Place de la Bastille yesterday. The visit was supposed to have been Mr Gorbachev's pilgrimage to one of the holy places of world Revolution. It turned into a twenty-minute fist-fight conducted backwards and forwards across the great square between the professionally-trained bodyguards of France and the USSR on one side and the far more numerous squad of the world's press photographers on the other. Somewhere in the middle of the boiling scrum of communicators were the president of the Soviet Union and Raisa, Roland Dumas, the French foreign minister, and Eduard Shevardnadze, his Soviet counterpart.

To those following the engagement at close quarters it was clear that the Gorbachevs were having an unpleasant time. But to the crowd, held back round the edge of the square it must have looked like the prehistoric ancestor of a game of rugby. They cheered enthusiastically as bodyguards sent each other flying, photographers struck out with aluminium ladders, and a beautiful policewoman received a sharp blow in the face from one of her colleagues.

Each time the Soviet leader drew nearer to the crowd for an official moment of informality, the fighting grew fiercer, reaching a climax by the bus shelter at the top of the rue St Antoine. 'Gorby, Gorby' chanted the crowd. 'I love you,' bellowed an elderly man wearing a blue and white bobble cap. 'Stand still, stand still,' chanted the photographers. Mr Gorbachev looked appalled, M. Dumas looked furious. Only Mr Shevardnadze seemed to find the whole business genuinely funny, but then nobody was trying to take his photograph. After he had spent ten minutes battling across the square Mr Gorbachev asked M. Dumas a question. 'Where is the Bastille?' he said. The foreign minister pointed in the direction of the Banque de France. Four feet away from them a police motor-cyclist was driving slowly over the leg of a prostrate television cameraman.

On two occasions Mr Gorbachev managed to break through and touch real people. The first group were the strategically placed young Communists holding a welcome banner in Russian. The second group, chosen at random, turned out to be American tourists. Romaine Sheets, fourteen, from Manhattan, who happened to be passing the Bastille, suddenly found herself face to face with the second most powerful man in the world. 'He shook my hand but he didn't really say anything,' she later told an insistent mob of reporters. What did she think of Mr Gorbachev? This was a tricky one for Romaine, who had clearly been brought up to speak the truth but who didn't want to start the Third World War right in the middle of her visit to Paris. Finally she settled for, 'I don't really know. I just hope we have better relations with the Soviets.' Phew.

Earlier in the day at Orly airport, President Mitterrand had welcomed President Gorbachev saying, 'The French welcome you with joy and a great sense of hope. Everyone in France is interested in you and your actions.' He added, 'This meeting will allow us to cover many of the questions which affect world peace.' The two leaders then climbed into an armoured Peugeot limousine and joined a motorcade of thirty vehicles which sped them into central Paris. On his last visit in 1985 the Soviet leader had used a vast black Zil, specially imported from Moscow, but it broke down.

4 July, 1989

An ominous calm has descended over Paris in the last few days. Insomniacs and parents of small children awake at 6 a.m. cannot hear any traffic noise at all. All over the city people give the impression that they do not quite believe this can be happening to them. Yesterday (Monday) a shopkeeper in the 5th *arrondissement* said that he did not expect to be able to make any deliveries for four days this week. 'You must understand the situation we are in,' he said. 'Last week one head of state, "Gorby", was at the Sorbonne for two hours and they closed this district down completely for the whole morning. This week we have thirty-seven more of them coming. I will do my best but count on nothing. I expect the whole city to be paralysed from Wednesday onwards.'

Rumours have started to sweep up and down the boulevards. There will be elephants in the grand parade down the Champs-Elysées on Friday night. They will be accompanied by men carrying shotguns loaded with tranquillizing darts. Military cranes will be standing by in case two anaesthetized elephants block the avenue. The Métro system will be closed by a strike on Friday night. The letter post is already disrupted by unofficial strikes in certain districts.

The original Revolutionary spirit is reviving. On Saturday the mayor of Paris, former prime minister Jacques Chirac, attended a

Franco-American friendship ceremony. He was pelted with baby-feeding bottles by angry mothers who were protesting because the city's *crèches* have been on strike. Then the police guarding President Mitterrand's private residence in rue de Bièvre were overwhelmed by a Communist-led demonstration demanding that workers who had smashed up part of the Renault factory should be reinstated. M. Mitterrand was made even angrier by the pop concert in the Place de la Bastille attended by 200,000 people protesting against 'the rich man's summit' which is due to start on Friday. The last time so many left-wingers gathered together it was to celebrate his re-election last year. He intended this week to be a celebration of Socialism and the Rights of Man. Now it is being criticized as much on the left as it is on the right.

One hears a noise like a distant vacuum cleaner coming from the sky. There is an airship circling overhead. This is manned by police spooks who are operating the latest surveillance equipment. The airship is in the air for twenty-three hours a day and is there to protect the visiting heads of state. It is the first military airship to fly over Paris since the Zeppelin. It was made in Britain. Summit conferences are wonderful things.

10 July, 1989

With impeccable timing Margaret Thatcher told French television viewers last night that the French Revolution was a highly dubious event. Asked on the 8 p.m. news programme if the Revolution had a universal message for today's world, she replied, 'Forgive me for saying so but, no. It heralded the Reign of Terror. And then came Napoleon who tried to take Europe by force.' Asked if human rights were not a French invention she said, 'Good heavens, no. We had the Magna Carta in 1215.'

None of this will have comforted Parisians who, with three days to go to Bastille Day, continue to abandon the city, fleeing from the security precautions surrounding the Group of Seven conference. Many coach operators are reported to have cancelled their tours. Rumours continue to circulate. One paper claims that every hotel is already full. But *Le Monde* says that occupancy is running at only 50 per cent in many districts.

At the eleventh hour a 'monarch' has been invited to the celebrations. Some weeks ago President Mitterrand ruled that it would be 'inappropriate' to invite any crowned heads to the party. But everybody underestimated the determination of Mobutu Sese Seko, the despotic 'emperor' of Zaire. When his hints were overlooked Mobutu came on a private visit to Paris. His presence has now been noted and in order to avoid a diplomatic incident he too has been issued with his invitation to honour the Rights of Man.

Because of the ban on crowned heads the list of thirty-seven official guests reads strangely. The greatest number, thirteen, come from Africa. Asia is sending five, Latin America three, but among the European democracies which will not be represented at this celebration of the birth of democracy are the five Scandinavian countries, Switzerland, Austria, Spain, Holland and Belgium.

Meanwhile President Mitterrand has become so sensitive to criticism about 'the rich man's summit' that he has issued a clarification concerning the food to be served to the various heads of government. Everyone is relieved to hear that the Third World leaders will be served just as rich a menu as the leaders of the seven richest nations.

11 July, 1989

=====

With two days to go to Bastille Day the last of thousands of Parisians to flee the capital met the first cortèges escorting the arriving heads of state. The motorway around Paris ground to a halt yesterday afternoon and motorists started to sunbathe on the central reservation.

As television stations showed film of ferocious bodyguards drilling bullet-holes in the heads of human dummies, one reporter succeeded in circling the heavily-guarded Elysée Palace, the official residence of President Mitterrand, with a rifle concealed in his knapsack. Another reporter entered the tent where police bodyguards were queueing for their identity cards, and found bored policemen, tired of waiting, secretly attaching paper clips to the backs of each other's jackets.

The characteristic noise of the city centre is the thunder of low-flying security helicopters. This will not be assisting the work of

900 historians summoned from all over the world, to take part in a symposium at the Sorbonne University on 'The Real Meaning of the French Revolution'. The symposium started last week but since it was opened by President Mitterrand it has been completely forgotten, and may indeed have ended without anyone noticing.

More experienced self-publicists are prospering. Monsignor Gaillot, the rebellious bishop of Evreux, has had a good week. Last Saturday he marched arm in arm with Trotskyists to a pop concert held in favour of the Third World. Yesterday, noting the French hierarchy's reservations about the benefits of the Revolution, he issued a statement claiming that 'the Revolution was the most important event since Jesus Christ'. Meanwhile Cardinal Glemp of Poland was carrying out a two-day visit to the Vendée, the most Royalist and Catholic area of France where up to 300,000 men, women and children were massacred by the Revolutionary army.

As M. Mitterrand prepared to greet his official guests he revealed that he was bored by the growing volume of criticism of this week's celebrations. 'I won't be running in any more elections,' he said. 'So from now on I only have to agree with myself.'

12 July, 1989

This week's official celebrations of the Bicentenary of the French Revolution opened yesterday in Paris with a solemn reading from the Declaration of Human Rights in front of the Palais de Chaillot. It was an intimate moment shared by thirty-seven of the world's leaders and '200 human rights professionals'. No one else had been invited. The guests were protected from any contact with the people of Paris by a human wall of bodyguards, men who are both 'psychologically stable' and prepared to die for a total stranger during working hours only.

To the well-amplified humming of a heavenly choir, actors and actresses, including Jane Birkin, read aloud from the works of Mirabeau, Condorcet and Sieyès. As the performers tripped on and off the stage they were accompanied by a selection of small children from around the world.

In the evening came the second official event, the opening of the new opera house at the Bastille. The thirty-seven heads of state were once more present, accompanied this time by a rather larger number of notables who had been instructed to wait inside the auditorium for two hours on one of the hottest evenings of the year, 'for security reasons'. The short concert which followed included Berlioz's 'Te Deum'. This is thought to be the first and only mention of God during the bicentenary celebrations of an event which was supposed to have abolished him. Among those performing – magnificently – were Barbara Hendricks, Teresa Berganza and Placido Domingo.

Following the concert President Mitterrand, who is known for his simple tastes, invited the thirty-seven heads of state to a light banquet at a little railway terminus which has been converted into a museum, the Musée d'Orsay. This was the fourth banquet of the week. Following yesterday's banquet, at the Elysée Palace, the president and his guests strolled onto the Elysée lawn to find that an *ad hoc* troupe of 1,789 children, who had been flown to Paris from many lands, were waiting to sing them one song entitled 'Black and White'. Following the song the children were flown home again.

And so ended another perfect presidential day. Meanwhile in other parts of the city Parisians began to enjoy the traditional street balls and concerts which were the first celebrations in which they have been allowed to take part. Watched by 6,200 members of the world's press corps, who had been specially accredited for the occasion, the dancers were able to forget what must be the most quarrelsome build-up to Bastille Day since 1945. Final skirmishes included the article in *Le Parisien* which complained that Mrs Thatcher was impossible. 'You lay out a new Field of the Cloth of Gold for her, and all she does is spit in the soup'. The writer concluded that ' "*la Dame de Fer*" is fit to be guillotined'.

The Bicentenary remained a source of Franco-French discord to the last. Philippe de Villiers, an opposition representative of the Royalist Vendée, wrote to President Mitterrand asking him to remove the name of a Napoleonic General Turreau from the Arc de Triomphe, since the man had been responsible for the 1793 punitive campaign in which one-quarter of the Vendéens were killed. Meanwhile leaders of the opposition, including Valéry Giscard d'Estaing, Jacques Chirac and Raymond Barre, let it be known that they had all refused invitations to tomorrow's highpoint of the week, the evening procession down the Champs-Elysées. No doubt the 1.5 million spectators who do turn up will miss them sadly.

13 July, 1989

━━━

It was the best of parades, it was the worst of parades . . . It was certainly the most highly-publicized of parades but for the man who thought it up, Jean-Paul Goude, only one question mattered as the big day drew near. Would it rain?

The rest of France was asking a different question. Whether they were for or against the show what the French wanted to know was, 'Who is this man Goude?' And M. Goude was not providing many answers. Asked at a press conference how he should be described, Goude replied, 'As a very sensitive boy.' He is in fact a very sensitive backroom boy who has discovered that he has a natural talent for the spotlight, and he seized his chance with both hands. Until Jack Lang, the minister of culture, gave him this parade, 6,000 dancers and £10 million to spend, Goude was unknown outside the hothouse world of publicity and advertising.

Realizing this might be a problem he suggested that they should call the event '*Bleu, Blanc, Goude*', a pun on the French national colours of '*bleu, blanc, rouge*'. Even Jack Lang thought this was a bit strong and Goude was tactfully directed instead towards the idea of *La Marseillaise*. But his first choice served its purpose; from then on the whole of France knew that someone previously unknown was energetically trying to draw attention to himself, and the French like that.

Explaining the basic theme of his extravaganza Jean-Paul Goude said, 'It will have an African rhythm, there will be Africans in it wherever possible. That is because I am against the purity of races. I am against the very idea of purity.' So this was a homage to *La Marseillaise* which opened with flag-bearers and drums, but the drummers were dressed up as a camp version of coalface workers. The drummers actually refused to wear their costumes at first, thinking they would look ridiculous. Goude himself had to be photographed in costume before they would agree.

When it came to the British contingent, the bands of eight of the proudest cavalry and line regiments in the British army, there was no question of messing about with their uniforms. Instead Goude had the mischievous notion of making them march through an artificial rainstorm. Which explains how the Royal Scots Dragoon Guards with their drum horse, Ramillies (note the name), and the Queen's Hussars carrying colours won at Waterloo, came to find themselves marching down the Champs-Elysées behind fire engines whose crews were drenching them in water. Behind them came other typical British sights, two elephants, Highland reelers and groups of Indian ritual dancers. It was a British Tourist Board nightmare come true.

And then there were the Russians on a moving ice rink, and the butchered Chinese students, and Jessye Norman on stilts singing *La Marseillaise*, and whatever else you thought about it you had to agree on one thing at least, there was no damn purity about it at all.

14 July, 1989

12. LA DAME DE FER

=====

'It was a very good summit,' said Margaret Thatcher at her final press conference, after four days of being booed and hissed all over central Paris. It may indeed have been an excellent summit, but Paris has not been a public relations triumph for '*la Dame de Fer*'.

A large part of the French public remains intrigued by Mrs Thatcher who is exactly their idea of the traditional British nanny. But the fact remains that having been cast as the black sheep of the Bicentenary, Mrs Thatcher did very little to make a better impression. 'Mrs Thatcher attacks the Revolution', 'Mrs Thatcher objects to being kept waiting by the protocol', even 'Mrs Thatcher is made to sit with a lot of African leaders who don't speak English'. For the French headline writers it has been one tease after another. They were joined by the television commentators. When the camera showed Mrs Thatcher watching the Bastille Day pageant through binoculars, one of them said, 'She's inspecting the British dancers, probably looking for anyone who is claiming unemployment benefit.'

When Mrs Thatcher told the French that the Revolution was symbolized by the Terror and that anyway the British had acquired human rights much earlier, M. Mitterrand generously agreed that the British had 'showed the way' but pointed out that it was the French declaration which the world remembered. A graceful compromise? Not at all. Yesterday morning Mrs Thatcher presented the French president with a copy of *A Tale of Two Cities*, summarized in the French press as 'a novel by Dickens which contrasts the terror which reigned in France during the Revolution and the tranquillity of life in England'. This is her bossy side which the French love to point out.

If Mrs Thatcher's relations with M. Mitterrand are said to remain cordial, despite fundamental political differences, the same certainly cannot be said of her relations with Michel Rocard, the French prime minister. M. Rocard has in the past been lectured by Mrs Thatcher on the warlike record of Continental Europe, and he did not enjoy the experience.

It was M. Rocard who chose to attack her on British television, the night after she arrived in France, for the 'social cruelty' of her policies which might 'damage British democracy'. When Bernard Ingham, the prime minister's press spokesman, was asked about this he replied, 'I don't think Mrs Thatcher is even aware of what M. Rocard said, and I certainly haven't bothered to tell her.' Mr Ingham then said that he 'just happened to have on him' the OECD analysis of comparative unemployment rates in Britain and France and that these were not to the French advantage. The figures he produced showed that since 1987 the British rate had fallen from 10.2 to 6.6 per cent, whereas the French rate had only fallen from 10.5 to 10 per cent.

What Mr Ingham did not mention was that in 1987 the French prime minister was not M. Rocard, it was his right-wing opponent, M. Chirac. No doubt if Mrs Thatcher was asked to take responsibility for Mr Callaghan's unemployment rates, Mr Ingham would be the first to object. Still Chirac, Rocard, what's the difference, they're all Frogs.

But this gritty, 'Bah goom, British is best' approach may not be the right one in Paris. M. Mitterrand is the current president of the European Community, and there are serious Anglo-French differences on monetary union and the proposed 'social charter'. The French president is a visionary in a hurry to do everything possible to unite east and west Europe. Mrs Thatcher is a practical politician who is unmoved by that vision. Behind this week's pleasantries M. Rocard and M. Mitterrand have accomplished the useful purpose of making her look even more isolated and less persuasive.

July, 1989

———

The second volume of memoirs by Valéry Giscard d'Estaing, president of the Republic until 1981 (*Le Pouvoir et La Vie: Vol. II*), has just been published to widespread praise. In it, Giscard reveals the shattering effect that his defeat in the 1981 presidential elections had on his self-confidence (a similar experience has since been suffered by Margaret Thatcher). For a long time he was unable to read a political news story or watch the television news in case his name was mentioned, and he compares his condition, which lasted for several years, to a type of adult 'autism'. Giscard has now recovered and is revealing some skill as a storyteller, and also a genuine eccentricity. It seems that his habitual air of deep detachment is not entirely assumed. He ends his book with a little story about Mrs Thatcher.

In 1980, at the Venice Summit, he recalls that 'Madame Thatcher' invited him to breakfast in her suite at the Cipriani Hotel. On arriving, Giscard noted with interest that she was staying in the same suite that he and his wife had occupied some years before. He found himself sitting down at the same table, gazing out of the window at the same view and being served the same breakfast as on his last visit, except that on that occasion he had been wearing pyjamas and opposite him had been not Mrs Thatcher but Anne-Aymone de Brantes, his beautiful wife. Through the communicating door Giscard could see the corner of the bed in which he had slept, now, of course, occupied by Mrs Thatcher.

Thrown into a reverie by this unexpected situation, Giscard decided to share the curious experience with his hostess. She was in the middle of an analysis of Franco-German relations. Giscard interrupted her. '"How amusing," she replied . . . and I saw at once that her response was merely polite and that she was quite uninterested by my memories.'

Allowing Mrs Thatcher to continue talking, Giscard sipped his capuccino (she was drinking tea) and decided 'to penetrate her mental process and gain an understanding of her inhibitions. I realized her immense pride in running the United Kingdom and I realized that she looked on other countries with a deep condescension, apparent not in her courteous manner but in her occasionally brusque and categorical judgements . . . I divined the fundamental trait in her character: for her, her interlocutor had no dialectical existence. She was prepared to meet him only on condition that he accepted her point of view in its totality. If he expressed even a slight reservation she would fight him until he gave in.'

Giscard counted it a notable victory for Gallic civilization when on his way out he succeeded in making her walk through the door in front of him.

May, 1991

So it's goodbye to the first British prime minister since Pitt to be booed in the streets of Paris. Goodbye to the press conferences at which Bernard Ingham, holed up in the British embassy's press room in the Faubourg St Honoré, refought the battle of Agincourt or hissed complaints about French cheese.

On Tuesday night we had the last unforgettable sight of Mrs Thatcher in Paris arriving late for the ballet in the Palace of Versailles and proceeding to rearrange the seating in the second row while President Mitterrand waited patiently in the aisle to get past her. He was only able to reach his seat after Cardinal Casaroli, representing the Holy See, had been moved along in the direction of Chancellor Kohl and replaced by the Spanish prime minister, Felipe Gonzales. Europe is going to have to arrange its own seating in future with no help from Mrs Thatcher. It will not be the same.

Mrs Thatcher will not be surprised to know that her resignation was the most important political story of the week here as well, overshadowing the problems of the Rocard government and thrown into relief by the thirty-four nation CSCE meeting on the future shape of Europe. She must be the first British prime minister forced to resign because she displeased too many foreign voters. It has been a big story because people identify Mrs Thatcher with isolationism and dependence on the United States and they think that these tendencies will be less important now. In other words they think that what happens in Britain can matter in France. There was never much evidence that Mrs Thatcher and her advisers thought that the converse could be true.

When she arrived in Paris last week, reporters were immediately assured by her press secretary, Mr Ingham, that Mrs Thatcher welcomed the CSCE conference as the culmination of the process of disarmament started at Helsinki. But for everyone else who attended the CSCE conference it was not just an end but a beginning, the first chance to discuss the shape of the new Europe. They always knew in Paris that Mrs Thatcher was not anti-European, but they also knew that her Europe was a loose community of sovereign nations protected by NATO, dominated by the United States and made prosperous by free trade alone. There was no question of a more intimate relationship with an Iron Lady. The most telling reaction to her departure was prime minister Michel Rocard's refusal to make any comment, not even the usual polite noises, because he said he preferred to discuss the future of Antarctica.

Watching the leaders of Europe watching the ballet at Versailles was an instructive experience. Michel Rocard arrived with a boxer's victory salute to the photographers after winning his vote of confidence and had to be told to sit down by his wife. To his left Vaclav Havel sat between Ion Iliescu, the Romanian leader and Raisa Gorbachev. Mr Havel's private meeting with Mr Gorbachev had just been cancelled because he had described the Warsaw Pact as 'washed up'. But this did not stop him from chatting to both the Gorbachevs while Iliescu looked on in the background, smiling uneasily. Gorbachev wore a poker face, his eyes following the swirling leaps of the principal dancer, Patrick Dupond, his mind elsewhere. His is not the first empire to dissolve while its leader sat listening to music in the Palace of Versailles.

Then there was Gianni De Michelis, the playboy Italian foreign minister, falling asleep during the '*Napoli – pas de six*' written and presented in Italy's honour: and Charles Haughey with his quick, confiding wink and his eternal air of a man who's got a horse. Their host, President Mitterrand, had the immobile features and wax complexion of a Venetian doge, only his eyes alert, surrounded by his court and his family. And directly behind him Mrs Thatcher, straight back, head forward, at work as usual, Watching The Ballet.

Mrs Thatcher's courage in putting herself in this public situation half an hour after her defeat in the first ballot was admired. One Greek observer said it was impossible to imagine a French leader putting himself through the equivalent ordeal in London. But Europe requires subtlety as well as courage. This week in France we have had the story of Philippe de Villiers's tax investigation. M. de Villiers is a Gaullist deputy in the National Assembly. He has been one of the few to insist that a police report into the misuse of Socialist election funds should be acted on, not buried. Recently he learnt that his own political funds, which have already been investigated twice and found to be clean, were to be investigated a third time. M. de Villiers said he had no objection to the investigation but that it was being mounted in an attempt to shut him up.

Last week in the National Assembly the budget minister Michel Charasse met him in the corridor and said, 'Since you are pouring shit all over us, we will do the same to you.' M. Charasse has threatened to do this before. Shortly after his appointment he was grilled on television and once the programme was over he threatened his interviewers with a tax investigation. He seems to look on tax investigations as a political weapon. This is a French political problem, like the misuse of election funds which occurs because the Fifth Republic has never developed a satisfactory method of distributing election funds. The story illustrates the weakness of French political institutions and Mrs Thatcher has been right to argue that Britain could provide Europe with a useful model in this area. Unfortunately, in the European political chorus, she was always singing in the wrong key.

November, 1990

13. HAND IN HAND

There is a famous picture of François Mitterrand and Helmut Kohl walking together hand in hand. It is a rather comical picture and also a rather touching one. It was taken during a Franco-German ceremony at Verdun, and the handholding was apparently spontaneous. Mr Kohl is known to be an impulsive person and may be given to such gestures. M. Mitterrand is a colder fish but he remains French and one can assume a certain *savoir faire* in these emotional areas. The picture quickly became a symbol of the mutual trust and warmth between France and Germany, Now one looks at it again and notes how the bulky German chancellor towers above the French president.

In less than two months the 'special relationship' between France and Germany seems to have collapsed, to be replaced by memories of the previous relationship between the two countries. According to the opinion polls, the French people are solidly in favour of the reunification of Germany – this week's figure is 74 per cent. But their enthusiasm is not entirely shared by the politicians, military strategists and academics who debate the matter on behalf of the nation.

Part of the confusion may be a result of the speed of events in Europe. Only last July the 'European question' was about 1992 and President Mitterrand's dream of a 'federal European Community'. Then the Hungarian and Czech frontiers were opened, the Berlin Wall fell, and an evil Empire disintegrated during the course of a summer vacation. Now that bright prospect has itself been overshadowed by ghosts supposedly laid to rest in 1945. The brilliant new chapter in European history seems, in France at least, suddenly to be closed.

The public discussion on German reunification has turned into a discussion on the dangers this poses for France. The fears of another 'greater Germany' have revived a political vocabulary, and some political alliances, which seemed long buried. Among the fiercest critics of French 'inertia' on this issue are the right wing of the Gaullist Party and the Communist Party. The Communists were last in alliance with the Gaullists during the Occupation.

The PCF's political bureau recently issued a declaration on the 'serious dangers for the future of France' posed by German reunification. 'Millions of French people are worried by it . . . the tragic experience of the recent past is deeply engraved in the memory of our people . . . and the arrogance of Chancellor Kohl increases steadily . . .' The Communist statement then criticized, in neo-Gaullist terms, 'the policy of submission and national decline followed by successive French governments', and urged that France 'can and should reoccupy the leading place which she should never have abandoned in Europe and in the world'.

This clarion call was echoed by Michel Debré, de Gaulle's longest serving prime minister, in an article in *Le Figaro* headed, 'From a European Germany to a German Europe'. M. Debré compared Mr Kohl's plans for immediate reunification with Hitler's annexation of Austria, 'in the name of the German nation fifty years ago', and argued that if reunification was the wish of the German people it should only come about under certain conditions agreed by France, Britain, the United States and the USSR. He suggested that Germany was once more 'dreaming its old dreams of world power', noted 'the energy, ability, frugality and discipline of the German people' and concluded that these could only lead once again 'to the abuses which Germany commits in every domain as soon as it has the chance to do so'. For M. Debré, Germany has a tendency to confuse German will with German rights, and he warned against another Munich.

To further the historical parallel the one French political group which is unhesitatingly in favour of German reunification is the extreme-right *Front National*. Its leader, Jean-Marie Le Pen, can claim some foresight in this matter since he spent four days in Munich last autumn, celebrating his party's close links with the extreme-right Republican Party – led by Franz Schönhuber who is a former member of the *Waffen SS* – and calling for German reunification, one month before the fall of the Berlin Wall.

The gloomy traditional wisdom of French statesmen is being

quoted on all sides. When President Pompidou was asked, off the record, in 1970, how he proposed to counterbalance German influence he said: 'By relying on the United States, the Soviets and Britain while cultivating the best possible relations with Germany. Though that's not something I can ever say in public.' President de Gaulle put it more bluntly when he was asked by Dr Kissinger in 1969 how he proposed to prevent Germany dominating Europe. 'By war,' he is said to have replied.

The prospect of a greater Germany has alarmed French military planners who have begun to discuss – again in private – the possibility of a united Germany electing a neutralist Social-Democrat government next December, then leaving NATO and then, before the year 2000, acquiring its own nuclear weapons. It is said that Mr Gorbachev, despite his insistence on a neutral united Germany, would secretly prefer a greater Germany in NATO and under its control than banging around like a loose cannon between the Atlantic and the Urals. It is said that M. Mitterrand, who has always claimed to be in favour of a united Germany, secretly asked Mr Gorbachev in Kiev last December to oppose reunification.

There are several alternative French versions of the 'German disaster scenario'. One is of a united Germany full of underprivileged East Germans providing a cheap labour source for the fat cats of West Germany who thereby become even fatter. This leads to a resurgence of the extreme leftism which is already flourishing in West Germany, to a counterbalancing extreme nationalism, also well-established, and to a replay of the political instability of the 1930s.

What all French analysts assume is that an unstable Germany would destabilize Europe and that a united Germany will dominate central Europe and west Europe with ease. For France, this is a bitter pill to swallow. It is the end of the Gaullist dream of a European Community dominated by a Franco-German alliance in which France alone enjoys the advantage of an independent nuclear deterrent.

French depression has even reached the stage where they are comparing Mrs Thatcher to Winston Churchill. The French appreciate that, unlike French politicians, she can voice her reservations on this subject '*sans complexes*'. And that she never needed to be photographed walking hand in hand with Chancellor Kohl.

March, 1990

All week the nuclear bombers have been thundering low over Paris. This happens every year in the rehearsals before the military parade on 14 July. Today the Mirages and Rafales will make one last pass down the Champs-Elysées and then they will be gone for another twelve months. France must be one of the last democracies to behave in this way, with tanks and missile carriers rolling down the broadest boulevard in the capital city past the president of the Republic in an annual display of power.

The first such procession in Paris was in 1919. It was a celebration of victory over Germany in the Great War. Today's Bastille Day procession is not a Gallic Trooping the Colour. It is about killing enemy soldiers and civilians in the modern manner. It is an echo of the country's historic fear of invasion and has a lot to do with events of fifty years ago. There was no military procession down the Champs-Elysées on 14 July 1940. A small detachment of Free French was inspected by General de Gaulle in London, but in France the troops had surrendered.

July 1939 had been a different matter. War had not been declared but was widely expected, and the generals put on a magnificent show. It was the finest display ever seen and designed to reassure people. 'Don't worry about being invaded,' the generals were saying, 'look what impressive means we have to defend you.'

The Bastille Day procession of 1939 can now be seen as one of the darkest jokes of the twentieth century: 30,000 men and 350 tanks and armoured cars paraded down the Champs-Elysées. In addition there were 3,500 horsemen and, as though the French cavalry uniforms were not gorgeous enough, there were detachments from all five British Guards regiments in bearskins and scarlet tunics. And overhead the reassuring presence of the RAF.

For the real thing, which started two months later, the RAF eventually had to be withdrawn and the Guards changed into khaki, but the French kept their horses. Dragoons were among the first units ordered into Belgium as the Panzer regiments broke through the 'impenetrable' Ardennes forest. Superannuated in 1914, the Dragoons were remounted and sent back into action in 1940, this time to face even faster tanks, even more powerful machine guns, and of course the Stuka dive-bombers – whose sirens had a dramatic effect on men, let alone horses. This month virtually all the French newspapers and magazines have been running series recalling the disaster, to the extent that one sometimes has the impression that it is current. The Swiss historian Philippe Burrin recently said that the growing French obsession with the Nazi era was 'astonishing' and that at a time when Europe was trying to establish a new unity this obsession with events of the past 'threatened to become an important historical event in its own right'.

Perhaps it is this obsession that explains why there has been no suggestion that the annual Bastille Day ceremony should be dropped, even though such military parades are beginning to look as old-fashioned in the new, uniting Europe as the views of Nicholas Ridley. Today's parade is intended to convey the same reassuring message as that of 1939. The difference is that fifty years ago everyone knew where the attack would come from. But where is it supposed to come from in 1990? Peking? Tokyo?

Mr Ridley has faced predictable criticism in France. An editorial in *Le Monde* said: 'It is possible to be born an aristocrat without ever becoming a gentleman.' But not everyone disagrees with him on the dangers of a powerful Germany. Among his critics was the editor of *Le Figaro*, Franz-Olivier Giesbert, who described the remarks as 'foolish' and 'primitive' anti-Germanism. You won't get anything as crude as that in *Le Figaro*. What you get is rational and polished anti-Germanism. Here are some other remarks made by M. Giesbert in the same article in which he chided Mr Ridley:

'Helmut Kohl, puffed up with his own success, exudes power. You must never underestimate your enemies and still less your partners ... Helmut Kohl has imposed German unity against the wishes of his European partners, against the advice of his own experts, even against the will of the Bundesbank ... He has conned both Mikhail Gorbachev and François Mitterrand, neither of whom wanted to see the return of a greater Germany ... An historic figure is formed by the meeting of a man and an idea. Helmut Kohl seems to have become the historic European figure of the last quarter of the twentieth century. But in achieving that status he has shrunk France ... It is a sign of the times that it was not the French president who met Mr Gorbachev to lay plans for a new Europe after the Group of Seven meeting in Houston, but the German chancellor. Does this not recall the Treaties of Rapallo in 1922 and Berlin in 1926 when Berlin and Moscow first moved towards agreement on how to deal with Western Europe? And then there was the Nazi–Soviet pact, which arranged the division of Poland . . . It is now M. Mitterrand who stands in Mr Kohl's shadow rather than the reverse . . . But it is not France's fault if Germany is once more 'Germany' – powerful, arrogant and full of itself . . . So if Mr Kohl says that he wants a European Germany, not a German Europe, we must take him at his word . . . It is the only solution.'

No doubt a German reader would find M. Giesbert's comments less offensive than Nicholas Ridley's, but they are hardly more trusting or friendly. It helps if you can express yourself without using words such as 'Adolf Hitler', for underneath the abuse there is a real debate. Mr Ridley talks about 'the balance of power' and apparently regards the Continent of Europe as an area of warring tribes where Britain's role is to keep the peace by making sure no nation becomes too powerful. M. Giesbert expresses an equally traditional French view, that Europe is divided into eastern and western sectors and that the western sector ends on the Rhine in sight of the battlements of Strasbourg.

The third view – the dominant one, held by George Bush, François Mitterrand and Jacques Delors – is that Germany must be forced to be friendly by being sewn into a united Europe, like Gulliver, by thousands of threads. The threads will be labelled European Monetary System, devolved sovereignty, European Parliament and so on.

Meanwhile it is acceptable for the rest of us to express our feelings by pissing in Gulliver's boots, like M. Giesbert, but inadvisable to indulge in crude abuse.

July, 1990

14. BORN TO FACE
A FIRING SQUAD

Whether or not he was the greatest Frenchman of the century remains a political question in France. By one of those strange coincidences, May 1990 is the tenth anniversary of the death of both Jean-Paul Sartre and Charles de Gaulle, and there has been no shortage of reminders of that fact. In comparing the two men it is striking that de Gaulle – who frequently said, 'We are not here to laugh' (*'On n'est pas là pour rigoler'*) – none the less made many more jokes than Sartre. There are few photographs of either man smiling but life with the general was considerably more *rigolo* than it was with the sage.

There are so many de Gaulle stories that people have stopped trying to distinguish the genuine ones from the imitations. Perhaps it hardly matters, since both real and false stories bring the same extraordinary character to life. When he gave his famous televised press conferences he was brilliantly imitated by a comedian called Henri Tisot. Although nobody ever dared mention Tisot to him he once said, before parting the red velvet curtains and stepping on to the rostrum, 'I must try to match up to the national parrot.'

His wartime dispute with his rival General Giraud brought out his sarcasm. Once, bored by yet another recital by Giraud of how he had escaped from a German prison camp, he said, 'Now why don't you tell us how you were taken prisoner.' Later Giraud, who was irritated by the cries of *'Vive de Gaulle'* that accompanied their public appearances when they were joint presidents of the National Liberation Committee in Algeria in 1943, suggested that something should be done to discourage such demonstrations since they tended to divide the French army. 'Yes,' said de Gaulle, 'I suppose we could always issue an order telling people to shout, "*Vive* the co-president with limited responsibility and shared command of the National Liberation Committee".'

His home life with '*Tante Yvonne*' has probably provided most of the apocryphal stories, but some still insist that he really did once say to her after a televised recording of one of his most famous speeches, 'Please Yvonne, do stop looking at me as though I were the Messiah.' 'But Charles, you really were very, very good.' 'Oh not more ecstasy,' he is supposed to have groaned. 'With you it's always ecstasy.'

In a way it was unnecessary for de Gaulle to make jokes since his mere appearance was enough to put people into a good humour for the rest of the day. But it helped that the president of the Republic loathed talking on the telephone. When asked about this he said, 'Why should I be summoned by a bell as though I were a drum-major's horse?' He loved animals and once refused to eat home-produced chickens from his estate at Colombey-les-deux-Eglises preferring steak, on the grounds that, 'One does not eat animals one has been introduced to.'

There is a famous picture of de Gaulle standing on the steps of the Elysée Palace with Harold Wilson and George Brown, taken after an official lunch in 1967. Wilson and de Gaulle appear to be smiling thinly but Brown, then the foreign secretary, is clearly enjoying himself hugely. During the lunch at which his behaviour had become increasingly exuberant, Brown had at one point put his arm affectionately round de Gaulle's shoulders – to the horror of the French officials present, as the president of the Republic was well known to detest any form of physical contact. But to their surprise de Gaulle's only comment after the departure of his guests was, '*Je le trouve fort sympathique, ce George Brown.*'

De Gaulle was a unique mixture of modesty and arrogance. Both characteristics are shown in a true story from the day when he landed at Cherbourg on 20 August 1944, to be greeted by an ecstatic crowd. Above the noise of drums, military salutes and wild cheering could be heard the hysterical voice of a woman shouting '*Vive le maréchal! Vive le maréchal!*' Well aware that equally excited crowds had been greeting the public appearances of Marshal Pétain only a few weeks before, General de Gaulle turned to his aide-de-camp and said, 'Another one who doesn't read the newspapers.'

Although the Gaullist period sometimes seems to have ended much longer than twenty years ago his shadow still looms over the Fifth Republic which he created. For Admiral Philippe de Gaulle, the General's son, his father was the founder of modern France, the man who not only devised the Fifth Republic, but who launched the TGV high-speed train, the Airbus, the Concorde, the nuclear programme, the Mont Blanc tunnel and the new franc, and who raised the school leaving age to sixteen. The admiral confesses that he did not have a very amusing childhood, but then neither had his father ('*On n'est pas là pour rigoler*'). He cannot recall ever seeing his father wearing anything other than a military uniform or a suit and tie. The only time he saw him weep, or at least with tears in his eyes, was when his youngest daughter, who was handicapped, died.

De Gaulle understood the French people very well. After the war, when he lived on little money in retirement in Colombey, he was offered the chance to pay no more income tax. He refused it. 'I don't want to owe the French anything,' he said. 'It's they who have a debt to me.' When he finally retired in 1969 he went on holiday to Ireland because it was very beautiful and also because it was 'a land without money'. 'Supposing I had gone to Switzerland?' he said. 'The French would all have said that I had gone to salt away my hoard.'

As time passes his stature grows, so that now he seems not only one of the greatest Frenchmen but one of the greatest men of the century. And he had one more advantage over Sartre: no fear of death. When he was small, Philippe de Gaulle asked his father how his grandfather had died. 'For a Christian,' replied Charles de Gaulle, 'that question has no importance.'

De Gaulle's destiny was decided in 1940 and it is difficult today to realize the extent of his isolation on 18 June when he woke up in 8 Seamore Grove, London (now Curzon Place), after his unauthorized departure from Bordeaux. He was aged forty-nine, the youngest and newest general in the French army. On the previous day, during the flight across the Channel the little biplane had refuelled in Jersey where de Gaulle had mistaken the tea for English coffee. In London he had been taken to lunch at the RAC, then conducted to Downing Street where he found Churchill dozing in a deckchair on the lawn.

Churchill was disappointed. He had sent General Spears to Bordeaux on a fishing expedition, telling him to bring back as many French leaders as possible before the final collapse of France. He had been hoping for the commander-in-chief, General Weygand, or the former prime minister, Paul Reynaud, at least. Instead he was looking up at an excessively tall and very junior general who spoke good German but no English. This was apparently the most senior officer of the French army who was prepared to leave France in order to continue the fight.

Churchill and de Gaulle knew each other slightly from the previous ten days of joint war cabinet meetings. But Churchill did not know that de Gaulle was by background and inclination an anglophobe. As a child de Gaulle had been brought up 'never to forget Fashoda'. Between the wars he had been influenced by the right-wing Catholic movement Action Française whose leader, Charles Maurras, described Germany as France's 'Enemy No. 1', and England as 'Enemy No. 1b'. Furthermore, De Gaulle was full of indignation about the 'derisory' extent of British military assistance to France since the outbreak of war in September 1939. But he was also full of admiration for Churchill, and it had been his task the day before to read out over the telephone from London the text of Churchill's offer of political union to Paul Reynaud.

Overcoming his disappointment, Churchill promised his support and it was agreed that de Gaulle could make the broadcast which was to become so famous and in which he would defy his own government and launch the idea of Resistance. But first he would have to wait until the position of the new government, led by Marshal Pétain, had been clarified. Later that afternoon, after de Gaulle had left Churchill, the text of Pétain's morning broadcast from Bordeaux, in which he announced that he would be seeking a separate peace with Germany, reached London. This decision to request an armistice was a breach of France's agreement with Britain and the evening papers on 17 June carried the banner headline 'France Surrenders!'

Earlier in the day de Gaulle had sent a telegram to Pétain's new war minister, General Colson. It opened laconically: 'Am in London'. He asked for orders, implied that he was in London at Reynaud's request and noted that he was 'henceforward without authority'. De Gaulle's purpose in sending this telegram is mysterious. It is possible that he did not know at this stage whether or not his family had been able to leave France. But that evening as he was driven from his temporary residence in Seamore Grove to dine with Jean Monnet, the sight of the billboards overcame his discretion and at dinner that night be made a furious attack on 'Pétain's treason'.

So there he was waking on the morning of 18 June confident that he would shortly be on the air. He did not know until much later what a close thing it was. Churchill was 'incommunicado' that morning, writing his own speech for the debate in the House of Commons ('This was their finest hour'). In his absence the war cabinet was chaired by Neville Chamberlain who, with the support of the foreign secretary, Lord Halifax, objected to de Gaulle's broadcast. A general who was *persona non grata* in Bordeaux should not be allowed to broadcast to France until a last attempt had been made to persuade the new French government to put their fleet beyond the German reach. The cabinet eventually decided to ban the broadcast. Churchill, who was by then having another little nap after making his speech, had to be disturbed by General Spears and warned of what had happened. The prime minister immediately arranged for the members of the cabinet to be approached individually and persuaded to change their minds.

Early on the evening of 18 June, after a day spent working on his heavily-amended text, de Gaulle set out for the BBC. He dropped the typist off in Brompton Square and arrived at Broadcasting House where he was led up to studio 4B. He always denied that his speech had been cleared by the Foreign Office but several reliable sources contradict him on this point. He had never made a broadcast before in his life. Asked to say something to give the sound engineer a 'voice level' he helpfully uttered the words '*la France*'. The BBC have always denied that a recording was made of his broadcast. It is not even certain at what hour it first went out, though it was apparently at 6.30 or 10.30 in the evening. In his speech, he blamed the heads of the new French government for being surprised by the German tactics. Those responsible for the defeat had now decided to treat with the enemy. But France was not alone. She still had a vast empire. There was also the British Empire and the industrial wealth of the United States. He ended with the words 'I, General de Gaulle, at present in London, invite the French officers and men who find themselves on British territory with or without their weapons to contact me. Whatever happens the flame of French Resistance must not and will not be extinguished.'

Although this broadcast was to become so famous, very few people actually heard it. On 18 June France was still in a state of turmoil. Columns of refugees in fear of being machine-gunned by German planes were still moving south across the country choking all the main roads, and people had quite a lot to do apart from listen to the BBC. But among those who did hear the speech was the general's mother, who he knew to be seriously ill in a country refuge which his plane had overflown the morning before. The devout version of his legend has her saying, 'Charles always knows what has to be done.' But her daily cleaner claimed that she actually said, 'My God! Does he know what he is doing?'

The broadcast of 18 June was translated and published in next morning's *Times* and it was also reported in an abbreviated form by several French papers in Lyon and Marseille. *Le Progrès de Lyon* which published a report on page two described this unknown figure as 'General de Gaulle, the author of numerous papers on tank warfare'.

The morning after his broadcast, de Gaulle received a reply to his earlier message to General Colson in Bordeaux. It came via the French embassy in London and he was simply asked to 'return without delay'. That evening he made his second broadcast in which he went much further. 'Faced with the liquefaction of a government which has passed into the service of the enemy . . . I, General de Gaulle, conscious that I am speaking in the name of France . . . state that every Frenchman still bearing arms has the absolute duty to continue resistance . . . It would be intolerable if the panic of Bordeaux should spread across the sea to (the empire of) Africa . . . Soldiers of France, wherever you are, step forward!'

The second broadcast was clearly the end of the road for the youngest general in the French army. On 22 June the Bordeaux government cancelled his temporary brigadier's appointment. On 23 June he was invited to apply for his pension. On 28 June he received via the French embassy the order to surrender himself to the prison in Toulouse within five days before facing a court-martial. He replied, 'This communication is completely without interest from my point of view.' His official humiliation continued at this stately pace. In due course he was charged with inciting soldiers to disobedience, sentenced to four years' imprisonment, stripped of his nationality, sentenced to exile, charged with treason, desertion and serving a foreign power, and sentenced to 'death, military disgrace and the confiscation of all his possessions . . .' It was the same disgrace the French general staff had reserved for Captain Dreyfus in 1893.

One can assume that all this was not in truth 'completely without interest' to a soldier whose life had been dedicated to the service of his country. As a young man he had been a cadet at the military college of Saint-Cyr, where his nickname was 'the big asparagus'. Ninety-eight of the cadets in his year – out of 211 – died in the First World War. He himself was bayonetted three times and eventually taken prisoner at Verdun. He subsequently escaped four times, always to be recaptured. After he left school he wrote a poem saying that he hoped to die in action. Perhaps his mother's question is the most interesting. Did he indeed know what he was doing?

What was running through his mind as he gazed, without much enthusiasm, at the photographer from behind the BBC's microphone in studio 4B? He had an instinctive dislike of publicity and complained at one point that 'Churchill is trying to sell me like a cake of soap.' None the less he became a master of the radio broadcast. Officially he never had much difficulty in answering his mother's question. The battle of France was lost. It would be followed by the battle of Britain. The French, too, had to fight on. There were about 35,000 French soldiers and sailors still in Britain, the remnants of those evacuated from Norway and from Dunkirk. Before leaving France, de Gaulle had established that the recently-resigned prime minister, Paul Reynaud, intended to leave for North Africa to continue the fight from there. (Later Reynaud changed his mind.) Officially therefore, de Gaulle was the man sent to lead the fight from England until someone more senior could take over.

On 19 June de Gaulle said, 'If the English win the coming air-battle, and it's possible that they will, there will be no invasion, the situation will stabilize and will subsequently be reversed by the use of the American arsenal. We will then win the war.' But no other French general or politician shared this accurate analysis. De Gaulle's view was all the more original since the mood in France in June 1940 was strongly anti-British. The evacuation of Dunkirk was seen as a betrayal by the French and it was not generally appreciated, and would not then have been known even to de Gaulle, that British army losses during the June campaign against the Panzers' *blitzkrieg* had been at 68 per cent, more than twice as high as French losses. The French government was infected with defeatism and had rejected Churchill's imaginative offer of an Anglo-French political union. Pétain and his ministers were convinced that German victory over Britain was inevitable and that it was now a question of getting on good terms with the victors as soon as possible. De Gaulle was sickened by this attitude. 'I saw treason being committed before my very eyes,' he said, 'and my heart revolted and refused to allow its victory.'

In a sense, of course, de Gaulle already outranked most other army generals since he had been seconded from his armoured division to the French war cabinet as under-secretary for war on 6 June. But this appointment had ended on 16 June with the resignation of Reynaud and from then he was once more a humble temporary brigadier. He acknowledged this in England three times by contacting more senior French generals and offering to serve under their command if they too wanted to fight on. None of them replied.

So with his dutiful offers rejected the second question is, what did other people think he was up to? To some he appeared to be an opportunist, one of those gentlemen *desperadoes* like Churchill who were transformed into statesmen by their ability to get it right. There were rumours that the French commander-in-chief, General Weygand, had been on the point of arresting de Gaulle before his departure. In England, on 16 June, de Gaulle had wildly exceeded his authority by diverting a ship full of American war supplies destined for France to Britain. He had left Bordeaux with 100,000 francs in cash, drawn from Paul Reynaud's '*pot de vin*' or slush-fund. This is significant considering that France had already sent 47 tonnes of Tsarist gold to London for safe-keeping. It seems that de Gaulle always knew that he was likely to be denied access to official funds. Almost the last thing he had done before leaving France was to arrange for his wife and family to receive passports so that they could take the last ship out of Brest. It was more the exit of a political fugitive than a military leader.

De Gaulle was in a way a man born to be shot by a French firing squad. In 1928 he had been asked to ghost a book for Marshal Pétain, formerly his battalion commander at Verdun. When the Marshal failed to give him due credit for his work he, then a major, took one of the most famous soldiers in France to court. He lost the court battle so ten years later he published the book under his own name anyway. In January, 1940, during the phoney war, as a colonel without a command, he circulated a signed tract to eighty national leaders, including the commander-in-chief and the prime minister, in which he denounced the incompetence of the general staff. In May when still only a colonel attached to an armoured division he tried to overturn the commander-in-chief's brand new battle plan with a scheme of his own.

The immediate effect of de Gaulle's speech in London was almost as muted as in France. There was a trickle of visitors to his door on 19 June. A mechanic working for Hispano-Suiza was the first, then a publicity agent, two junior attachés from the French embassy, and the director of the Institut Français. Meanwhile the Foreign Office under Lord Halifax and Sir Alexander Cadogan, responding to pressure from the French embassy, persistently tried to block and censor his speeches. In this situation it did not help that very few members of the French community in London had heard of General de Gaulle. Nor did they flock at once to join the colours. 'London in June 1940,' as one of them later said, 'was not a city where one arrived but a city which one was leaving.' Or as de Gaulle himself said in August, 'the French in London can be divided into two groups. Those who are already in the United States and those who are preparing their departure.' One of those who stayed, Pierre Maillaud, wrote, 'We were a few French people who trailed round the streets of London like broken toys, useless and ashamed spectators of great events . . .'

On 3 July all de Gaulle's problems were made much worse when the Royal Navy attacked the French naval squadron which was trapped in Mers-el-Kebir. Three cruisers were sunk and 1,297 French sailors were drowned. Earlier on the same day Royal Marine boarding parties overpowered and arrested the crews of all the French ships which had taken refuge in Portsmouth and Plymouth. Several days later de Gaulle had to broadcast a reaction to these events. It was perhaps the most difficult speech of his life. He spoke of his 'sadness and anger' when he heard of this 'hateful tragedy' but he also said that since the Pétainist government had refused to place the ships beyond German control it was better that they should have been sunk in this 'fratricidal attack' rather than used one day against England.

However, his own hopes of recruiting supporters from among the French forces stationed in England had suffered a serious blow. All the good work of his speeches was undone. He had managed to recruit some Foreign Legionnaires and '*Chasseurs Alpins*' who had returned from Norway but by the time of Mers-el-Kebir he had won over only 1,994 soldiers and sailors, less than 6 per cent of the available total. By Christmas the Gaullist forces in England had risen to 7,000. Meanwhile 31,000 of the French servicemen remaining in Britain had applied to be repatriated. The Gaullist movement remained a minority French interest until the improvement in Allied fortunes in 1943.

At various times during his career General de Gaulle ordered five other French generals to be tried on capital charges and at various times he himself had played the same role as two of them, Pétain and Salan. In 1940, like General Salan in Algeria, he had raised his own armed force to oppose the government of France when in his view it refused to fight on in defence of the national interest. In 1958, like Marshal Pétain, he was recalled in old age to head an unelected government which brought to an end the existing republic and set up a new constitution. All three men, Pétain, Salan and de Gaulle, were tried for treason, but only the first two were punished. Today it is easy to forget how close he came to suffering the same disgrace.

Years later André Malraux, reading the text of the 18 June broadcast, said to de Gaulle that it hardly reflected the agony of the decision that must have preceded it. '*Mais Malraux,*' he said, '*c'était épouvantable.*' 'It was appalling.'

June, 1990